ACCELERATED LEARNING FOR THE 21ST CENTURY

Also by Colin Rose

ACCELERATED LEARNING

ACCELERATED LEARNING FOR THE 21ST CENTURY

.

The Six-Step Plan to Unlock Your MASTER-mind

COLIN ROSE
and
MALCOLM J. NICHOLL

Delacorte  Press

Published by
Delacorte Press
Bantam Doubleday Dell Publishing Group, Inc.
1540 Broadway
New York, New York 10036

Library of Congress Cataloging in Publication Data

Rose, Colin Penfield.
    Accelerated learning for the 21st century : the six-step plan to unlock your master-mind / by Colin Rose and Malcolm J. Nicholl.
       p.   cm.
    Includes bibliographical references and index.
    ISBN 0-385-31703-4
    1. Learning, Psychology of. 2. Educational acceleration—United States.
3. Memory. 4. Creative thinking. I. Nicholl, Malcolm J. II. Title.
LB1060.R67 1997
370.15'23—dc20   96-34020
                                         CIP

Manufactured in the United States of America
Published simultaneously in Canada

March 1997
10 9 8 7 6 5 4 3 2 1
BVG

To Joanna, Susan, Helen, Alexander and Catherine,
who are my personal 21st Century
Colin Rose

To Maggie and Mom and Dad,
who have all taught me so much
Malcolm J. Nicholl

Contents

ACCELERATED LEARNING FOR THE 21ST CENTURY

Introduction

The empires of the future will be the empires of the mind.
SIR WINSTON CHURCHILL

- The world is changing at an ever-accelerating pace.
- Life, society, and economics are becoming ever more complex.
- The nature of work is radically altering.
- Jobs are disappearing at an unprecedented rate.
- It is an age of uncertainty.
- The past is less and less a guide to the future.

These are the defining characteristics of the final turbulent years of this millennium. These are the challenges that need to be met by parents, educators, businesses, and governments.

Success in the 21st century will primarily depend upon the extent to which we and our children develop the appropriate skills to master each of the interconnected forces of speed, complexity, and uncertainty. It is in our hands.

The speed at which the world is changing demands a matching ability to learn faster. The increasing complexity of the world demands a matching ability to analyze situations logically and solve problems creatively.

Accelerated Learning for the 21st Century gives you the essential core skills of learning fast and thinking creatively. In that sense it is a personal how-to book.

But it is more than that. This book also lays out some key recommendations: how we can, and how we must, significantly improve the way we educate. As a society we urgently need a huge increase in the numbers of people who can be described as highly educated. We are doing a pretty good job of educating a minority. We must extend that trait to the majority.

Whether you have school-age children or not, this subject is of immediate and vital importance to you. It affects you as a taxpayer, as a citizen, and as a member of the workforce.

The worthwhile jobs of the future will either be jobs of the mind or jobs requiring a finely tuned talent—in the worlds of music, art, or sport, for instance. Repetitive, mechanical jobs are either being taken over by computer-controlled machines or exported to overpopulated countries where people are prepared to work for lower wages and where their governments offer incentives to business. There simply won't be any work for inadequately educated people.

Even if you do have a "mind job," it is still your concern. Unless the whole educational standard of our nation is vastly raised, you will suffer higher taxes, lower national economic output, and the costs of social disruption.

Low educational attainment and poor analytical and decision-making skills lead to economic dependency. You will encounter higher taxes in the future because a nation comprising mostly people who can't function in a high-tech world will mean higher unemployment benefits, higher welfare costs, and higher crime-control costs. And even higher health-care costs—because there is a clear correlation between educational status and health. Studies show that people with higher education are generally healthier and live longer.

Looked at positively, the wealth of our nation is the sum of the brains of its people—their creativity and skills. In other words, our best asset is our collective ability to learn fast and adapt thoughtfully to situations we can't predict.

At the moment, though, the focus of schools is on deciding **what** children should learn and **what** they should think.

We will argue that in a time of such rapid change, the first priority is to teach our children **how** to learn and **how** to think.

Only with these two "super skills" can you cope with change and complexity and become economically independent—and employable in the 21st century. Only then have you the core skills for personal happiness, stable relationships, and growth. Your ability to earn is directly proportional to your ability to learn.

So, to the extent that you want to live in a flourishing, safe, optimistic, and creative society, you need to be very concerned indeed with what goes on in our schools. Whether you are a parent of a school-age child or not. It is everyone's concern.

A LIFELONG ADVENTURE

Learning is not just knowing the answers. It's not just acquiring bits and pieces of general knowledge. It can't simply be measured by grades and exam results. It's not just taking on board what other people know.

Learning is a lifelong adventure. It's a never-ending voyage of exploration to create your own personal understanding. And it crucially must involve the ability to continuously analyze and improve upon the way in which you learn. The ability to be conscious of the process of your own learning and thinking. Learning must begin much earlier than the child's first day at school and it must continue well into retirement. We must never stop learning—and implementing what we learn.

What are the implications? We need to make changes—urgently. We need to help all parents create a rich, stimulating, thought-provoking home environment in the preschool years. Studies show that 50 percent of one's potential brain capacity is developed in the first five or six years of life. Doesn't it make sense, therefore, that a concerted effort should be made to turn those early years into a fun—yet powerful—learning and growth experience?

In the primary school years, we need smaller class sizes and the active collaboration of parents with the school to provide their children with interesting, challenging, and relevant projects that stimulate curiosity and thought.

In the early secondary school years, we need to ensure that stu-

> **The marketplace for learning is being redefined dramatically from K–12 to K–80, or lifelong learning, whose major segments are customers, employees, and students, in that order.**
>
> STAN DAVIS AND JIM BOTKIN IN
> *THE MONSTER UNDER THE BED*

dents become capable of learning on their own so they can fully utilize the dazzling opportunities of the new interactive learning aids. Yet they should also be working collaboratively to tackle problems, such as community issues, that engage their interest because they are relevant to their lives. This way students develop their basic skills and simultaneously learn critical creative thinking skills. In other words, we need changes both in *what* is learned and in *how* it is learned.

And what about the adult—even the well-educated, "fully-trained" adult with a wealth of qualifications? His or her skills may be perfectly adequate for 1997—and become woefully inadequate as soon as the year 2000.

Knowledge is doubling every two to three years in almost every occupation—and this means **your** knowledge must double every two or three years just for you to stay even. People who are not aggressively and continuously upgrading their knowledge and skills are not staying in the same place. They are falling behind.

You need to ask yourself, where are you going to be? Imagine if your industry disappeared. What would be your next career move? What skills do you have? What do you need to be excellent at? Are you prepared to deal with accelerating change?

"Change, after all, is only another word for growth, another synonym for learning. We can all do it, and enjoy it, if we want to," says British futurist Professor Charles Handy, former chairman of the Royal society for the Encouragement of Arts, Manufactures, and Commerce (RSA).

Handy tells an excellent personal story to illustrate the pace of change. In the late 1950s he went to work for a world-famous multinational corporation. They projected his career path for him—leading all the way to the chief-executive slot at a company in a country at the other end of the world.

When Handy left the conglomerate some years later, not only did the job they had originally envisioned for him no longer exist, neither did the company he would have run—*nor even the country*. Change, indeed.

But change needs to be valued. Unless your job involves continuous learning (to handle change), taking initiative, using judgment, making good, rational decisions, and inventing creative solutions to problems, it is either going to be badly paid, taken over by technology, or "exported" to another country.

These used to be skills only a few "top managers" needed. Now we all need them to survive. *Everyone* needs to focus quality thought on what he needs to know to perform well at his job, for tomorrow as well as today.

"It used to be that the main difference between people in our society was between those who 'have more' versus those who 'have less.' Today, however, the difference is between those who 'know more' and those who 'know less.'" says Brian Tracy, author of *Maximum Achievement* and one of America's top professional speakers and seminar leaders.

John Sculley, the ex-chairman of Apple Computers, also lays it on the line extremely well: "In the new economy strategic resources no longer come out of the ground. The strategic resources are ideas and information that come out of our minds.

"The result: We have gone from being resource rich in the old economy to resource poor in the new economy almost overnight. Our public education has not successfully made the shift from teaching the memorization of facts to achieving the learning of critical thinking skills."

Time magazine, in a major story headlined "Jobs in an Age of Insecurity," commented, "On no opinion are the experts so unanimous as that the future belongs to the knowledge worker, master of his PC, fiber-optics whatsit, E-mail gizmo, and whatever takes its place . . . a high-tech worker must be ready to go back to school and learn new skills, on his or her own, if any employer will not finance it, at a minimum of every five to ten years."

One of those experts, computer genius Bill Gates, founder of Microsoft Corporation, in his book, *The Road Ahead*, says, "In a changing world, education is the best preparation for being able to adapt. As the economy shifts, people and societies who are appropriately educated will tend to do the best. The premium that society pays for skills is going to climb, so my advice is to get a good formal education and then keep on learning. Acquire new interests and skills *throughout* your life."

And futurist Daniel Burns, author of *TechnoTrends—24 Technologies That Will Revolutionize Our Lives*, emphasizes, "The future belongs to those who are capable of being retrained again and again. Think of it as periodically

> **Education needs to be reinvented.**
>
> **CHARLES HANDY IN**
> **THE AGE OF UNREASON**

upgrading your human assets throughout your career. Let's face it, the corporate jewels are its information and its people, not its buildings and hardware. Humans are infinitely upgradable, but it does require an investment."

That investment, we believe, should be in attaining the vision of lifelong learning through a partnership that involves students, parents, teachers, business executives, and government leaders. A partnership which recognizes that education is a mutual, shared responsibility. A cooperative undertaking to harvest the rich resources of the human mind.

1

The Changing World

All life is an experiment.
OLIVER WENDELL HOLMES

The world *is* shrinking. The global society *is* becoming a reality. As the 21st century approaches, instant communication across all seven continents is a daily commonplace event.

Scientific and technological breakthroughs seem to be reported on a daily basis. The world's data banks are expanding at an unprecedented level. Knowledge—measured by the output of research papers—is doubling every two to three years.

Just consider:

- Today a computer chip can perform electronic operations as fast as 4 billionths of a second. By the year 2000—200 *trillionths*.
- With the press of a button, in a matter of seconds, E-mail is zapped from computer to computer anywhere in the world. A single hair-thin optical fiber can transmit the contents of the *Encyclopaedia Britannica*—all twenty-nine volumes—in less than a second.
- Satellite technology enables instant visual communication from Mongolia to Manhattan, from Laos to London. At times, more than 1 billion people turn on their TVs to watch the same sporting event.
- Today the average American home can receive 39 television channels—a figure that has doubled in a decade. Coming soon: 500 channels.

- Research projects that used to take weeks can take minutes. From the comfort of your own home or office—through the Internet—you have quick and ready access to major libraries, universities, scientific journals, newspapers, magazines, and many other sources.
- More than 50 million people in 160 countries are already on the Net with projections of 200 million devotees by the year 2000.
- Every day 3 million people travel from one part of the globe to another. Today the world's airlines carry 1 billion passengers a year. By the year 2000—2 billion.
- Over the next four years alone the number of newborns will exceed the entire population of planet Earth at the time of Christ. Each year the world's population rises by more than the combined citizenry of France and the UK. All of these new arrivals will need food and ultimately jobs.
- Our grandfathers often held one job for their entire lives. Our parents probably had two or three jobs. Today's school-dropouts face the daunting prospect of three or four career changes during the course of their lifetime—*careers,* not just jobs. It is no longer relevant to ask, "What do you want to be when you grow up?" The question instead should be, "What do you want to do *first?*"

Cellular phones. Car phones. Fax machines. Voice mail. Call-forwarding/call-waiting. E-mail. There's a dizzying menu of communication tools.

Says trend-predictor Faith Popcorn, author of the best-selling book *The Popcorn Report,* "It's as if time itself has become, well, *faster* than it used to be. Immediate is really immediate—there isn't a chance to stop and take a breath.

"The 'speed of technology' brings us the facts of life faster than we can assimilate them. And information technology not only makes information accessible to *us* at all times—it also makes *us* accessible to the information. We are, quite often, literally, 'on the line' much of the time. Nowhere to run to, nowhere to hide. There's just no excuse not to be reached.

"The same advances we love for *giving* us time are so electron-speedy, electron-greedy, they're taking our time *away.* They're contributing to the Acceleration Syndrome that's driving us out of our still-in-human-time minds."

From fast food to fast communication the pace of everyday life has undeniably accelerated. We live in an age when space satellites beam pictures home from Jupiter; when Americans and Russians orbit this planet together at 17,500 mph; when revolutionary scientific and medical discoveries are being made at a breathtaking rate; when the intellectual resources of the world's great libraries are *literally* at our fingertips for ready access.

DISAPPEARING JOBS

Yet we also live in an age when jobs appear to be vanishing at an accelerated pace. Enter almost any boardroom and the talk is typically of plans to produce twice the output with half the workforce.

It's not that these business leaders are unaware of the social consequences. They are coping with an increasingly competitive world and feel the need to automate because their competitors are already substituting software for manpower—at all levels. The implications are so profound for *your* learning—and for education, in general—that we need to take a close look at these issues.

We are all aware that automation is replacing low-skill repetitive jobs. That is hardly news. But the scale and social consequences of that shift are not quite so obvious. Neither is the fact that great swathes of jobs requiring quite high skills are also being eliminated.

In his brilliant book *The End of Work* Jeremy Rifkin provides many specific examples of job eliminations, some of which are summarized below. The analysis should serve both as sober warning and proof positive that the *only* solution to the coming social upheavals is a massive advance in educational standards.

> The year 2000 is operating like a powerful magnet on humanity, reaching down into the 1990s and intensifying the decade. It is amplifying emotions, accelerating change, heightening awareness, and compelling us to reexamine ourselves, our values, and our institutions.
>
> JOHN NAISBITT AND PATRICIA ABURDENE IN *MEGATRENDS*

Which Jobs at Risk? More Than You Think!

Sixty percent of all jobs in industrial countries are fairly simple and repetitive. Automated machinery and sophisticated computers can do most of these tasks. Put into context, in the U.S. alone some 30 million jobs are at risk from the process of computerized automation.

Some facts:

- In the U.S. 1.8 million manufacturing jobs disappeared between 1981 and 1991—yet productivity soared by 35 percent.
- In the world's largest trading block—the European Union—there were some eighteen million people unemployed in 1996. If they stood in one line, it would stretch halfway around the world.
- Only 17 percent of the U.S. workforce is now in blue collar manufacturing and only 2 percent in agriculture.
- Military expenditure (which essentially solved the unemployment problems of the 1930s) has been cut back from 7 percent of the workforce in the eighties to under 5 percent in the nineties. Some 800,000 jobs were lost between 1989 and 1993. A further 1.2 million are projected to be scrapped by the year 2000.
- Each industrial robot is estimated to replace three to four jobs and pay for itself in around twelve months. *The Financial Times* of London forecasts a quadrupling of world robots in the next decade from 600,000 to 2.4 million. If that's true, it could mean the elimination of a further seven million jobs.
- Half of the textile workers in the U.S. and western Europe have been made redundant in just ten years—thanks to the export of their jobs to low-labor-cost countries or computerization. The jobs of 60 percent of mine workers and 50 percent of steelworkers have disappeared in the last twenty years; 30 percent of tire makers in eight years; and in the chemical industry, 25 percent in fifteen years.

Maybe that doesn't sound surprising. Some of these jobs were, after all, in smokestack industries. But how about General Electric, a world leader in electronics? Surely that's a safer industry? However, GE downsized (or "rightsized"—call it what you will) from 400,000 employees in 1981 to 230,000 in 1993—and tripled sales in the process.

The fact that we haven't fully appreciated the scale of the trend is because our mental model of automation is a robot-type machine stamping out parts or spray-painting cars. The truth is far more complex.

The new science of nanotechnology will revolutionize manufacturing within the next twenty-five years.

Essentially nanotechnology is molecular engineering by remote-controlled micromachines. Scientists are developing machines so tiny that they will literally "grow" machinery and products by building them up atom by atom. Such molecule-size machines are almost here now in medicine, where they will travel through the bloodstream and clear away cholesterol deposits from clogged-up arteries.

In manufacturing they will break down waste matter and garbage into its original atoms and reassemble those atoms into new products, machines, and components. Nanotechnology offers an entirely new way to manufacture with huge cost savings and huge labor savings too. And all within a generation.

The Japanese government, for instance, has launched a ten-year program to develop computers to operate like the human brain using "fuzzy" logic, speech recognition, neural networks, optical scanning, and parallel processing. (Though whether we should try to duplicate a human brain when it can be made in nine months with unskilled labor is another matter!)

We could be as little as fifteen years away from a new generation of computers that will recognize your patterns of speech and thought so they can conduct an "empathetic" conversation with you. Certainly, the new generation of computers will also generate holographic images of human faces, so they will *appear* like humans as well as *think* like humans.

> **The American workforce is coming to be the American economy. That is the way you begin to define the American economy—in terms of skills and capacities of the people who are here.**
>
> **ROBERT REICH,**
> **U.S. SECRETARY OF LABOR**

Many supermarket computers already measure sales at the checkout counters and automatically transmit reorders to manufacturers' computers. In the manufacturers' warehouses goods are automatically picked, packed, shipped, and invoiced. Result: fewer people at every level of the operation.

Ah, yes, goes the conventional argument, but we've been through all this before. The sweeping mechanization of the Agricultural Revolution led to the demise of labor-hungry farming practices, and of course that meant a decline in workers. But those workers were redeployed in the new growth Manufacturing Sector. Now that manufacturing work is disappearing, they will surely be employed in the Service Sector.

Hang on a minute. Let's look at the Service Economy.

- Commercial banking and Savings and Loan companies in the U.S. have shed 300,000 people in the last five years—and project to lose another 700,000 jobs before the turn of the century. That's 30 percent of the workforce. Insurance companies are following the same track. "Forty percent of insurance workers to go in the next five years" was a recent headline in *The Times* (London).
- AT&T is replacing 6,000 long distance operators (and 400 management jobs) because of voice-recognition technology. Over a ten-year period, 40 percent of workers have been discarded, while calls increased by 50 percent. The telecommunications business, as a whole, has shed 180,000 jobs in eight years.
- Over 40,000 U.S. postal workers have been made redundant since sight-recognition technology was introduced six years ago.
- The retail trade will be fundamentally changed by the information superhighway. As interactive TV comes of age you'll see movies transmitted down the phone line. This means the elimination of video rental stores and the inevitable closure of the duplicating plants that churned out the videos for those stores. And, of course, via interactive TV you will be able to buy most goods direct from the manufacturer, cutting out the wholesaler and retailer.

But surely doctors, musicians, artists, actors, and others who perform highly specialized functions have safe jobs? Don't be too sure.

- On November 7, 1992, Robodoc, developed by the University of California at Davis, performed the world's first robotic operation on a human. Many hospitals are testing computerized diagnostics.
- Some 50 percent of music on TV commercials is made by individuals working with a synthesizer—instead of a group of musicians.
- It's already possible to digitize the images and movement of long-dead actors and reprogram these millions of images to produce a completely new storyline. And many of the new feature-length cartoons and special effects are computer generated.
- There's even a computer system that can faithfully duplicate the voice of any Top Ten singer and have him or her perform any song you like. You could have "Michael Jackson" singing opera or "Pavarotti" belting out "House of the Rising Sun."

Let's draw a breath. What does all of this mean for us and for our children? Is there an "upside" as well as a "downside" to the vision of a world with more people and fewer jobs? What's the implication for your future as a learner? How should we educate our children in the light of a shrinking job market? Surely this analysis is one sided?

It's true that there is an alternative and highly optimistic vision. One that sees the Information Age as the dawn of inexpensive production and booming productivity, one that sees exponential growth in breakthroughs, and the ability for small companies to globally market products through the Internet—what Microsoft's Bill Gates calls "friction-free marketing." A utopia of great leisure with machines serving us.

Granted jobs are being lost, but they are also being gained. Technology and computers are bringing higher productivity, which means cheaper goods and greater profits. And the chance to export more.

Cheaper goods increase the consumer's purchasing power—at least for those still working. This increased demand will produce new jobs—especially in high-tech industries.

> **The revolution in communications is just beginning.**
>
> **BILL GATES IN *THE ROAD AHEAD***

Unemployment, the argument continues, may be tough on those involved, but eventually competition for jobs reduces wages and employers start to hire again. It's a cycle we've been through three times—the Agricultural Revolution gave way to the Industrial Revolution, then to the Service Sector Revolution, and now it's the Knowledge Revolution. Each time, low-skill jobs were lost, but the new-wave industries always created new jobs.

But this time there are some disturbing differences. This time it is not just the totally unskilled jobs that are going—semiskilled, clerical, and middle-management positions are vanishing too. And the pressure from competition on a global scale means that individual companies won't stop the process.

The trouble this time is the new-wave industries simply don't have the need for the same numbers as before. And the skills that are needed aren't the skills the unemployed possess. You can't retrain a bank clerk into a biochemist overnight.

Worldwide, one third of all able-bodied adults were unemployed in 1996—according to figures from the United Nations. So the upgrading of skills is a worldwide challenge.

We're experiencing a skills shortage simultaneously with high unemployment. Those with work are working longer hours. But they can't offload the pressure because the unemployed can't do what's needed.

And can we realistically expect to export more to countries in the same position?

If the numbers of *structurally* unemployed people were to reach the level privately predicted by many observers, the unemployed (or severely underemployed) in the U.S. and western Europe could reach 20 percent. (In 1996 it was 24 percent in Spain, 16 percent in Ireland, 9 percent in Germany, and 8 percent in France). That 20 percent unemployment would be 60 million people.

> **Virtually the only predictable trend is continuing change.**
>
> LINDA A. TSANTIS, PHD,
> IN *CREATING THE FUTURE*

The result, laying aside for the moment the human toll of stress, misery, and illness that unemployment brings, would be a massive depression, because unemployed people don't have the purchasing power to buy the goods the productivity gains are creating. And higher taxes for unemployment benefits, social security, and health care would reduce the buying power of the *employed*. Result: too many goods competing for too little money.

It's already happening. Over the last twenty years, American blue collar workers have lost 15 percent of their buying power. Yet, in the same period, payments to top management have soared. In 1979 the average CEO made 29 times the income of the average factory worker. By 1992 it was nearly 100 times. The rich have gotten a lot richer; the poor, poorer.

In fact, according to a 1996 United Nations report, the world's 358 billionaires have more assets than the combined incomes of countries representing 45 percent of the planet's population.

This is not "the politics of envy"—it is a statement of fact. Productivity advances have put downward pressure on the incomes of workers while allowing an elite to prosper. Just one percent of Americans now own over 37 percent of all shares and over 50 percent of all private business assets, while some 38 million Americans live in poverty.

Quite apart from any arguments about social justice, the practical outcome will—if changes aren't made—be catastrophic. First, demand will drop if incomes drop among 80 percent of the population. A 20-percent elite of knowledge workers and shareholders simply can't spend enough to mop up the output of the "workerless factories." So the whole trend is self-defeating.

And it is history repeating itself. The Great Depression of 1929, when U.S. unemployment rocketed from one million to 15 million in four years, was triggered by what the famous economist John Maynard Keynes called "technological unemployment." Automation was displacing people faster than innovation was finding them new jobs. Sound familiar?

Don't expect governments to create public work programs to solve the problem. They are overborrowed already. Some 20 percent of U.S. government expenditure is **interest** on debt!

This is the economic cost. The social costs are especially appalling. The potential for social unrest is enormous.

If the trend continues without

> **Business, labor, and government must work together to plug the skills gap and keep America competitive.**
>
> **JOAN C. SZABO IN *NATION'S BUSINESS***

action we can anticipate a huge rise in crime and urban ghettos, while social security budgets and unemployment budgets implode. Already the estimated U.S. cost of providing for the "underclass" is $230 million a year. We can expect stress, domestic breakdown, and a health crisis—all known results of high unemployment.

It is in *no one's* interest to allow the scenario we have sketched to happen.

UNCERTAINTY

The swirling forces of speed of change, increasing complexity, and disappearing jobs have bred widespread insecurity and uncertainty.

You can no longer buy success tomorrow with what you know today. You can no longer rely on your employer to provide a job for life. You can no longer rely on society—the state—to guarantee to provide for you in sickness or during unemployment or in old age. Not because the world is getting less caring, but because the economics don't stack up.

We're faced with complex issues that seem beyond our personal control—pollution, the depletion of resources, the frequency with which science produces products that create ethical dilemmas. And yet most of these problems can only be solved if the majority of people understand and get involved in creating solutions that will need unprecedented levels of cooperation and high levels of analytical and creative thinking.

As Richard Paul, of the Foundation for Critical Thinking, says: "All government is finally made up of the people, and people can only rise to the height of their own ability."

> **There is no security on this earth; there is only opportunity.**
>
> **GENERAL DOUGLAS MACARTHUR**

Just when global and social issues are causing insecurity, the supportive structures of family, traditional values, and religion are crumbling for large numbers of people. The result is a longing for the perceived stability of yesteryear, and we become vulnerable to what Richard Paul calls "satiny voices tempting us astray with slick, simplistic messages that appear to guide us back to the 'tried and true.' "

Hence the cry for "back to basics" in education—by which is usually meant a return to the format of teachers lecturing *at* passive students. Yet this style of teaching is in direct conflict with what we know about motivating, effective learning. "Back to basics" teaching doesn't require students to think for themselves, when that is exactly what they will need to do to deal with the increasing complexity of society.

In spite of the incredible technological advances we live in an age when too much schooling is stuck in the horse-and-buggy days.

The scenario of row after row of deskbound children watching and listening to a teacher lecturing *at* them, is unfortunately all too often as familiar a sight today as it was a hundred years ago. The school curriculum has students bouncing from the sciences to mathematics to geography to social studies, having dates, numbers, and facts relentlessly drummed into them in compartmentalized subjects. All without the students having had the benefit of those two most essential lessons of all—learning how to learn, and learning how to think—while tackling projects that challenge them to bring their minds to bear on complex real problems.

In an age when the only constant is change, in an era when the furious whirlwind pace of change is ever more challenging, traditional teaching falls short of the mark. All over the world public education is in crisis. Often it is the "front-line" teachers who unfairly bear the brunt of demoralizing criticism for inadequate standards. Yet it is the system itself that is fundamentally wrong, and unfortunately, most of the proposed curriculum changes are merely more of what is not working.

SO WHAT CAN WE DO ABOUT IT?

As we have stated, learning *how* to learn needs to take priority over *what* we learn—especially when one can't predict what skills will be needed and what we learn can become so quickly outdated.

Learning how to think logically and creatively is critical if we are to solve complex personal and social problems effectively.

When the world around us is changing so rapidly, it is absolutely vital that we keep pace. This means that getting an education is not something that we do just between the ages of five and twenty-five to pass a few exams, grab a diploma, embark on a career, and then be "set for life."

Some enlightened educators are experimenting with alternative approaches. *Business Week,* in an article entitled "The Learning Revolution," reported, ". . . teachers' lounges and Parent-Teachers Association meetings are abuzz with talk of 'learning modalities'— the different ways different people learn. If a child learns verbally, he'll respond well to traditional teaching, with its lectures and texts. But studies show that many children absorb more when the information is visual or auditory—or both, as with multimedia."

Most education and training, however, still concentrates almost exclusively on the content and not the process. A significant difference between people who are labeled as "poor learners" and those who are labeled "efficient learners" is simply that the latter have worked out some effective strategies for learning.

If these strategies were made explicit (which they rarely are), most people could become perfectly competent learners. And when their teachers and trainers also understand how to present new material in a brain-compatible manner, the results can be startlingly successful.

Learning How to Learn

To master accelerated change requires Accelerated Learning: the ability to absorb and understand new information quickly—and retain that information.

It means—as individual learners—being as open and receptive to learning when we are thirty, forty, and fifty years of age as we were when we were three, four, and five. For teachers, as we will see later in this book, it means making the acquisition of knowledge as much fun for a forty-year-old student as it is for a four-year-old child.

One survey showed that 82 percent of children entering the school system at five or six have a positive self-image of their ability to learn. But that positive rating dramatically drops to an average of 18 percent by the time they are sixteen years old. Consequently, four out of five teenagers and adults start a new learning experience with a feeling of inadequacy.

And that's another reason why learning *how* to learn is so vital—

because when people learn how to learn, their self-esteem and confidence grow. When people learn how to learn they not only cope with new technology and change—they welcome it. When people learn how to learn, they have acquired the basic skills to become self-directed learners and the basic skills to attain personal growth. They have been empowered to change from passive consumers of education to active controllers of their own learning and their own life.

> **The Accelerated Learning method you'll acquire from this book brings out the abilities that lie within each of us. It consists of a six-step blueprint to learn effectively.**
>
> **In essence, it recognizes that each of us has an individual preferred way of learning that suits us best. When you learn the techniques that exactly match your personal learning style, you will be learning in the way that is most natural for you.**
>
> **Because it is natural, it is easier; because it is easier, it is faster. That's why we call it Accelerated Learning.**
>
> **When teachers (or trainers) use the same six-step blueprint, they ensure the learning experience is complete. And when both learner and teacher work in the same six-step sequence, they are able to collaborate fully to ensure learning is enjoyable, effective, and fast.**

That's why *Accelerated Learning for the 21st Century* is for teachers as well as adult learners and parents as well as students. We strongly urge every parent to read those sections where we recommend how Accelerated Learning can transform the classroom. When teachers use games and activities, emotion and music, relaxation, visualization, role play, color, and learning maps, learning becomes a joyful, stress-free event.

Today, the greatest single source of wealth is between your ears. Today, wealth is contained in brainpower, not brutepower.

BRIAN TRACY, AUTHOR OF
MAXIMUM ACHIEVEMENT

> **The most important educational goal is learning to learn.**
>
> LUIS ALBERTO MACHADO, PHD, IN *CREATING THE FUTURE*

Many teachers want to implement these ideas—the system prevents them. What's urgently needed is a revolution in the way we educate. Use this book to light the fires of that revolution.

Our experience tells us that Accelerated Learning is a key tool for business as well. To stay competitive, companies need their whole organization focused on learning faster and thinking better.

Mindpower Replaces Manpower

Accelerated Learning is a distillation of decades of work, drawing upon seminal research—from that of Bulgarian educational psychiatrist Dr. Georgi Lozanov to Harvard educator Dr. Howard Gardner. It draws on the studies of Nobel laureates such as neuroscientist Roger Sperry and neurobiologist Gerald Edelman. And it takes into account the practical experiences of innovative schoolteachers, college lecturers, corporate trainers, and inspired business entrepreneurs who have all caught the vision.

Individuals from all walks of life and a variety of disciplines have risen to the challenge of making sure that the human brain—"the sleeping giant," as it has been called—is awake to the high-pressure momentum of change. What we have done is draw together all that research and create a practical, simple-to-follow plan of action.

Two skills—fast learning and clear thinking are the key 21st-century personal skills. Together they produce self-reliance. Self-reliance is the ability to manage your own learning from an early age; to master the sheer volume of information, to see its true significance, and to know how to use that information to develop creative products and creative answers to problems. These skills need to be taught in every home, every school, and every organization.

AND THERE ARE OTHER SOLUTIONS

We've tried in the foregoing pages to sound a loud alarm. We do live in turbulent and problematic times. But we can rise to the challenge.

The Early Years

Parents are a child's first—and most important—teachers. The first five years of life are the most critical of all. We show how to help parents of preschoolers create a fun, rich, challenging, and thought-provoking home environment where the seeds of creativity and logic are planted.

The School Years

The current school system does a wonderful job of educating a minority to a good standard, but huge advances in the standard of education of the majority need to be made **in the next few years.** Children are leaving school ill equipped for the jobs of the future—the jobs that will require very high standards of analytical thought, creativity, and flexibility. In fact, who really knows exactly what these jobs will be? Some of the jobs today's school dropouts will ultimately end up performing have yet to be invented!

Accelerated Learning for the 21st Century proposes ways of raising the educational standards of everyone—not just the elite minority. And an emphasis on personal growth rather than just material advancement is, we believe, an important solution to the challenges to come.

The focus of schooling must be broadened from the acquisition of knowledge to include the development of wisdom, character, and emotional maturity. Our technical competence as a society is far outstripping our ability to make wise choices. We urgently need to address this mismatch.

We live in an information-rich society, where the accumulated knowledge of mankind is but a few keyboard entries away. Our children need to know how to access that knowledge and use it creatively and wisely. Yet we persist in teaching as if the information revolution hadn't happened.

The Adult Years

Individuals need to develop skills to make themselves truly employable—to become economic independents. Masters of circumstances rather than victims of circumstances. To master change rather than resist it.

We show you how to make an essential mind-shift from seeing yourself as an employee to viewing yourself as self-employed. In fact, you—everyone—are effectively the president of your own personal services corporation and you get paid in direct proportion to the value of your services. Your current "employer" is merely your best client at the moment. That employer legitimately needs you to add value and to focus on continuous improvement.

The Corporate World

Companies need to become "learning organizations." They need to encourage employees at all levels to learn and problem-solve in informal, collaborative teams, and to give them the time and opportunity to learn these skills. Companies will find that it is in their best interest to become personal growth centers as well as profit centers. People are not simply tools for economic success.

Employees need to become involved in establishing the values and aims of the organization for which they work. Large investments in reeducation and training will have to be made and a fair share of it should be borne by companies doing the downsizing.

Both employee and employer will need to accept broader roles.

The answer to disappearing jobs may well be to spread the work by cutting individuals' working hours. There may be a major increase in people's voluntary contribution to local community projects in order to productively utilize increased leisure time.

Such solutions are not the subject of this book. But it is worth bearing in mind that the prospect of a golden age of increased leisure will happen only if the vast majority—not a minority—leave school having reached the high standards of education needed to cope with the new type of work—and the expansion of leisure.

The Answer Is Quality

Whatever the difficulties, we must ask ourselves are they as frightening as the possible alternative—depression and serious social disruption? The enthusiasts for the high-tech future are right. It *does* look bright—if you are among those gainfully employed. But islands of wealth and work satisfaction surrounded by oceans of relative poverty and anger are an unstable combination. As Robert Heilbroner says in *Visions of the Future,* "When you give a window on the world of affluence but no door you invite trouble."

The quality of our lives is a direct outcome of the quality of our learning and our thinking. How to raise the quality of both is what this book is about.

THE LEARNING MAP CONCEPT

Making notes visually makes them more memorable. Notice we've said "making notes" rather than "taking notes." There *is* a difference.

On the following page you'll find the first of a series of Learning Maps. In this book we are using them at the end of each chapter to recap, review—and *remember*—the key elements. In this instance they become Memory Maps.

There is a full explanation of the Learning Map concept in Chapter 6 along with details of how you can—and should—create your own. For now, notice that the core subject is featured in the center of the page with secondary and further information contained on offshoots.

The visual imagery, humor, and dramatic emphasis enable you to store key information "at a glance" rather than memorizing pages and pages of traditional linear notes.

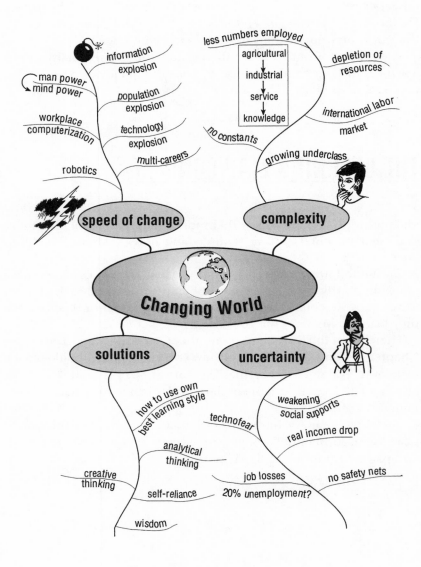

2

The Awesome Brain

We do not know one millionth of one percent about anything.
THOMAS EDISON

It's been called "a sleeping giant," "an enchanted loom," "the most complex piece of machinery in the universe," "the greatest unexplored territory in the world," "a biological supercomputer"—and much more.

Biologists, psychologists, evolutionary scientists, educators, and writers have all competed to produce the definitive description of the human brain, to do justice to the ultimate complex structure.

Regardless of the superlatives, clever analogies, and creative metaphors, *your* brain—along with those of the greatest achievers in history—justifies them all. It is unbelievably more complex and sophisticated than the most high-powered supercomputer.

The brain, in fact, is an equal-opportunity organ. You came into the world with approximately 100 billion brain cells. Give or take a few million, that's something you have in common with the great thinkers, philosophers, scientists, explorers, world leaders, Nobel prize winners—all of the peak performers from all walks of life who have ever lived.

The numbers are staggering. By and large, though, it's not the number of brain cells (neurons) that's important. It's the number of *connections* that are made between those brain cells—and each of those 100 billion neurons can grow up to 20,000 "branches" or dendrites.

Don't bother to do the mathematics. It's a truly mind-boggling number running into trillions. ***What it means*** is what really counts. It tells us that the capacity of the human brain is awesome in the extreme; that the human brain is incredibly more sophisticated than the most "intelligent" computers on the planet. And it reveals the breathtaking potential that none of us ever fully realizes.

As humankind probes the limits of outer space, the greatest unexplored territory of all lies here on Earth—within the confines of our individual brains. *There are more possible connections in the human brain, in fact, than the number of atoms in the entire universe.* That is the way Stanford University professor Robert Ornstein dramatically makes the point.

Our knowledge is advancing at a remarkable rate. More has been learned about the brain in the last ten years than in all previous scientific history. In particular, phenomenal technological advances have empowered scientists to solve some of the mysteries of the mind.

Noninvasive procedures such as magnetic resonance imagery (MRI) and positron-emission tomography (PET) have provided a window on the human brain. The result: scientists can actually "see" a thought occurring, fear erupting, or a long-buried memory enter into an individual's consciousness.

Scientists who use brain imaging technology can now gather in just a few hours the kind of data that used to take twenty years of inferential laboratory work with monkeys and apes. It sounds extraordinary—and it is. Through this breakthrough scientists can distinguish between neuronal groups that are only one millimeter apart—and bear in mind that 30,000 neurons would fit on a pinhead.

At the same time, the cognitive sciences have seen major strides forward with the emergence of theories using biological processes to explain the inner workings of the brain. These theories can finally be put to the test—thanks to brain-imaging technology.

Says University of Oregon education professor Robert Sylwester, "This theoretical work, along with developments in genetics, may spark a Century of Biology, just as Albert Einstein's theories sparked advances in physics that have dominated this century."

One thing is clear: if you want to develop your brain it needs to be exercised—constantly, day after day—in much the same fashion that a physically fit person builds and maintains muscle tone. Research by UC Berkeley's Marian Diamond and others shows that if you don't exercise and maintain your *mental* muscle, it can get just as weak and "flabby" as your biceps or your abdominals.

An appreciation of "inner space"—and the way in which the

brain works—is fundamental to understanding the learning process; why lifelong learning from cradle to grave is so important and how it can be dramatically improved for everyone.

In this chapter we'll explain the significance of:

- Your 3 kinds of brain—reptilian, mammalian, and the thinking brain.
- Your 2 brains—the left-brain and right-brain hemispheres.
- Your 1 brain—the power of "whole-brain" activity.
- Your 8 intelligences—your personal unique mix of abilities.
- Your 4 kinds of brain waves—why they're important and how to make the most of them.

In the next chapter we look into:

- Your 5 kinds of memory—it's more than just "short term" and "long term."
- And you'll discover why your brain is so resilient—and has more in common with the jungle than the computer.

Here, then, is a layman's update on the incredible complexity of the human brain.

UNDERSTANDING THE BRAIN——IT'S AS EASY AS 3-2-1

You have three brains, two brains, and one brain. Confused? It really is as simple as 3-2-1, even though "the brain" is the most complex mass of protoplasm known to exist. Even though pioneering neurophysiologist Sir John Eccles who won the 1963 Nobel Prize for his work on the synapse—the connecting gaps between brain cells—has said that the hair-trigger sensitivity of the brain's intercellular connections suggests "a machine designed to be operated by a ghost."

Look at it this way:

THREE BRAINS IN ONE

As man evolved, the brain went through increasingly complex stages of development leading to what researcher Dr. Paul Mac-Lean, former director of the Laboratory of Brain and Behavior at the United States Institute of Mental Health, has dubbed the "triune brain."

1. The Brain Stem (or Reptilian Brain).

At the base of your skull, emerging from the spinal column, you find the brain element that you share with lower life forms such as lizards, crocodiles, and birds—hence the "reptilian" brain.

This part of the brain controls many basic functions including breathing, heart rate, and instincts such as the fight-or-flight response when danger threatens. The reptilian brain also controls other primitive instincts—your sense of territory, for example, which is why you may feel angry, threatened, or uncomfortable when someone moves too close to you. It also explains that anger is difficult to control because it is often a result either of feeling threatened or of someone trying to take away something you think is yours, i.e., an invasion of your "territory."

2. The Limbic System (or Mammalian Brain).

The central part of the brain wraps around the brain stem like a collar (*limbic* is from the Latin word for border or "collar"—*limbus*). It's the part of the brain similar to that of other mammals.

The key components of the limbic system are the hypothalamus and the amygdala. The limbic system is your emotional controller. It also helps to maintain homeostasis, a stable environment within the body. It controls your hormones, thirst, hunger, your sexuality, your pleasure centers, metabolism, immune function, and an important part of your long-term memory.

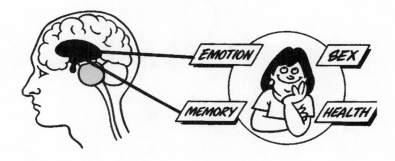

The hypothalamus and amygdala also are important controllers of emotional behavior and goal-seeking behavior. This implies that emotional appeals work better than rational arguments in influencing human behavior. In evolutionary terms the limbic system developed before we "invented" logic.

It is significant that the same part of one's brain that controls emotions also controls health, and equally controls emotions and memory. When something involves strong emotions it is usually very well remembered. You probably vividly recall your first kiss or where you were when President Kennedy was shot. Younger readers may remember what they were doing at the time of the *Challenger* explosion or the Oklahoma City bomb blast.

It also means enjoyment, role playing, collaboration, and games are important elements in learning because they involve positive emotions. We **want** students to say of their learning, "I enjoyed that, I want to do more."

When the brain is in a state of positive emotional arousal, researchers note that opiatelike "pleasure chemicals" called endorphins are released. This, in turn, triggers an increased flow of a powerful neurotransmitter called acetylcholine. This is important because neurotransmitters are the "lubricants" that allow connections to be made between brain cells. In simple terms a brain enjoying itself is functioning more efficiently. So there's a scientific basis for using art, drama, color, emotion, social learning, and even games as educational tools.

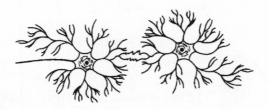

But what about negative emotions? Researchers Mortimer Mishkin and Tim Appenzeller, writing in *Scientific American,* suggest that the limbic system, and especially the thalamus, acts as a sort of switchboard between our senses and our cortex, analyzing incoming information for emotional significance. If you are stressed or fearful, the information may not be fully available to the neocortex. Instead, as author and researcher Lesley Hart puts it, "The human brain is downshifted to the more primitive areas of the brain. We revert to instinctual behavior rather than use rational judgment."

In evolutionary terms it makes sense. If a wild animal is attacking you, you don't want to stop to philosophize. In the modern world such stress and threat may be simply fear of failure. Either way, stress inhibits learning. *My mind went blank* is a commonly used expression among students at exam time.

In *Accelerated Learning* we consciously use relaxation exercises before a learning session and seek to reduce stress and increase energy levels. Luiz Machado de Andrade, a world-class educational researcher from the Uni-

> **The human brain is an enchanted loom where millions of flashing shuttles weave a dissolving pattern, always a meaningful pattern, though never an abiding one, a shifting harmony of subpatterns. It is as if the Milky Way entered upon some cosmic dance.**
>
> **SIR CHARLES SHERRINGTON**

versity of Rio de Janeiro, pointed out as early as 1984 that the limbic system effectively controls the mechanisms for our self-preservation—the most powerful forces within us. When you involve the limbic system in learning and teaching, i.e., *deliberately involve the emotions,* you harness powerful forces that make learning much more effective.

In his book *The Brain of the Brain* he characterizes the limbic system as the central controller of the whole brain, i.e., the primary form of intelligence. He predated the whole emotional intelligence debate by calling for educators to involve emotions in the classroom in order to enable students to use more of their potential.

3. The Neocortex (or Thinking Brain).

Make a fist with one hand. Now wrap your other hand over the top of this fist. If the wrist of your first hand represents the reptilian brain, and the fist is your mammalian brain, the hand wrapped over it represents your thinking brain.

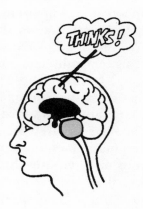

The cortex is only about an eighth of an inch thick and it is folded. If it were spread out it would be about the size of a newspaper page.

This "third" brain is truly extraordinary. This is the seat of intelligence—the part of the brain that makes us most human, that makes humans a unique species.

The neocortex handles seeing, hearing, creating, thinking, talking—in fact, all of the higher intelligences. In the neocortex decisions are made, the world is organized, experiences are stored in memory, speech is produced and comprehended, paintings are seen and appreciated, and music is heard and enjoyed. This brain has all of the capacity you will ever need to learn and remember anything you want.

Of all mammals, human beings have the most enfolded cortex, perhaps because such a large cortex had to fit into a small head to permit passage through a narrow birth canal.

The neocortex itself is divided into specialist parts (lobes) for speech, hearing, vision, and touch. This means we store sensory memories in different places. If we want to create a strong memory we should store the information using all of the senses. When you have heard it, said it, seen it, and done it—you've got it! You'll see how we've used this insight in building our language courses.

In addition, our prefrontal lobes develop substantially in our early teens. These are situated just behind the forehead and are where we exercise judgment, future planning, and higher-order thinking. Because this area is also linked strongly to our limbic system, it is also where we develop compassion, altruism, and a sense of justice. It would imply that it's important to structure part of a young teenager's education so that he or she has a chance to experience the value of contributing to the community. It's at this age that feelings of caring, empathy, and sympathy are most likely to be developed.

Surprisingly, it is true to say that the brain is not primarily designed for thinking. Those attributes we consider most human—language, perception, intelligence—represent only a small fraction of the brain's overall responsibilities to keep us alive and functioning. A major part of your brain ensures that you learn, react, and adapt primarily for survival.

Robert Ornstein and David S. Sobel in *The Healing Brain: A Scientific Reader,* eloquently write about the development of the brain: "We carry our evolution inside us, within the different structures of the brain, structures built in different eras. There are many different brains inside there.

"There is an archaeology as well as an architecture to the brain, because it was built up over millions of years. As in an archaeological dig, there are layers to the brain." Ornstein and Sobel say that the human brain is a compendium of circuits piled atop one another. They are mostly designed to handle immediate survival needs rather than future planning.

And they add, "The brain evolved, as is well known by now, in different levels, each one designed to maintain stability in its organism as animals moved from the sea to land, to the trees, to the savannas of eastern Africa, to Fifth Avenue."

Ornstein, furthermore, says that one of the great mysteries is why the human species is so incredibly advanced relative to our nearest ancestors. "We aren't just a slightly better chimp, and it's difficult, on reflection, to figure out why. This gigantic cortex has given us our adaptability as well as the extra capacity to adapt to the height of the Himalayas, the Sahara Desert, the wilds of Borneo, even to central London."

TWO MINDS BETTER THAN ONE

The human brain—this great bulb of convoluted tissues—can also be considered as being split into two hemispheres, popularly referred to as "left brain" and "right brain."

This division in itself is not a new discovery. The ancient Egyptians knew that the left side of the brain controlled and received sensations from the right side of the body and vice versa.

During the last two decades, however, ground-breaking research has revealed that the two hemispheres perform different functions. Both sides of the brain are connected by an incredibly complex network of 300 million neurons. This network—the corpus callosum—shuttles information backward and forward between the two halves of the brain. But simply put, based on the research of Professor Roger Sperry of the University of California, it is accepted that, in general:

The left brain specializes in what are commonly labeled "academic" aspects of learning—language and mathematical processes, logical thoughts, sequences, and analysis.

The right brain is principally concerned with "creative" activities utilizing rhyme, rhythm, music, visual impressions, color, and pictures. It's our "metaphorical mind" looking for analogies and patterns. Researchers also ascribe to the right brain the ability to deal with certain kinds of conceptual thought—intangible "ideas" such as love, beauty, and loyalty.

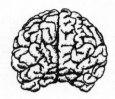

It's important not to exaggerate the difference. Our brain is far too intricate to be categorized so neatly, and anyway the two halves are constantly communicating with each other. Realize, for instance, that when we watch a red ball rolling along a table, our brain processes the color, shape, movement, and location of the ball in four separate areas of the brain to produce a complete appreciation of what is being seen.

Although each hemisphere is dominant in certain activities, they are both involved in almost all thinking. Nevertheless, there is a major lesson to appreciate when it comes to the way in which we process information for learning.

Some people (left brain) prefer a slow step-by-step buildup of information. We call them the "linear" type of learner. Others (right brain) need to see the "big picture"—to have an overview. They are the "global" type of learner.

When we recognize a face, we don't scan it slowly from top to bottom in a linear fashion. Instead we use the right brain's capacity to see patterns very quickly. When we listen to a conversation, the left brain is concentrating on what was said (the content), while the right brain is picking up how it was said (the emotion).

> **One man that has a mind and knows it can always beat ten men who haven't and don't.**
>
> **GEORGE BERNARD SHAW**

When you listen to the words of a song, the left brain will basically be attending to the words; the right brain will be processing the melody. In addition, the emotional/limbic system of your brain will be engaged. In other words, your *whole brain* is actively involved.

It's no accident that when words are combined with music or with pictures, or when words are delivered with emotion, they are easier and faster to learn. Accelerated Learning capitalizes on this fact.

Professor Ornstein found that when the "weaker" side of the brain was stimulated and encouraged to work in cooperation with the stronger side, the net result was a noticeable increase in overall performance.

> **A mind that is stretched to a new idea never returns to its original dimension.**
>
> **OLIVER WENDELL HOLMES**

His findings are particularly significant for those of us educated in the West, where the three *R*'s of reading, 'riting, and 'rithmetic have ruled supreme—all emphasizing left-brain activities.

We need to recognize and take advantage of the human brain's strength. We are generally good at, and enjoy, "global" thinking activities like exploring concepts, finding patterns and connections, predicting, pondering ethical issues, creating analogies, and making intuitive leaps of imagination.

We are less good at (and less motivated by) repetitive work, memorizing isolated facts, spending long periods of time working on our own, and having to compute long series of calculations. That's why the computer has been such a life-changing invention. It far outguns humans in linear processing and calculations. But it needs the creative human mind to design its programs. We should use its power to complement our weaker side and use the time it liberates for us to develop our strengths—our creativity and our emotional capacity.

A SINGULAR ATTRACTION

You are unique. You have one "whole brain," which is the sum of the parts of the mental capacity of your triune brain and the cerebral hemispheres. No one else processes information exactly the same way that you do. Your brain is as individual as your fingerprints.

Virtually everyone, of course, is familiar with the concept of IQ—"intelligence quotient"—and knows that it is a way of measuring one's intelligence. But is it a fair, accurate measure? Are there other forms of intelligence not taken into account when calculating IQ?

There is a more "democratic" approach to estimating intelligence and measuring potential. It's a concept that illuminates even more brightly the full spectrum of human capabilities and represents another way of illustrating the monumental capacity of the human brain.

THE EXTRAORDINARY EIGHT——A NEW VIEW OF INTELLIGENCE

The IQ test as we know it today grew out of the work of French psychologist Alfred Binet, who, in the early years of the 20th century, devised a test to identify children whose learning problems required remedial education.

Lewis Terman at Stanford University standardized it to take population norms into account and the test became known as the Stanford-Binet. Terman later incorporated psychologist William Stern's notion of an intelligence quotient. IQ, as it is universally recognized, is an individual's mental age, as determined by intelligence testing, divided by the person's chronological age—and the ratio multiplied by 100.

Over the years it has become the standard measure of intelligence while provoking fierce, passionate debate among academics, educators, and the lay public.

There is little doubt that IQ tests are reasonably good at assessing and predicting a student's school performance, "but since intelligence is defined operationally as that which intelligence tests test, the test makers are chasing their own tail," declares Michael S. Gazzaniga, director of the Division of Cognitive Neuroscience at Cornell University Medical College.

In other words: intelligence tests measure the ability of people to do well in intelligence tests.

Typically, the IQ test predominantly measures an individual's ability with linguistic and logical-mathematical challenges as well as some visual and spatial tasks.

Enter Harvard professor of education Howard Gardner.

His provocative question: How would the proverbial Martian landing on Earth view the intelligence of the human species?

Would he (it?) demand to know individual IQs? Or would he be interested in those humans performing exceptionally well in particular fields—the chess master, the orchestral conductor, perhaps even the athlete? These accomplished people are undoubtedly considered to be intelligent. Why, then, do our methods of assessing intelligence often fail to identify them? Why is it that people with IQs of 140 end up working for people with IQs of 100?

Gardner came up with his "Theory of Multiple Intelligences," which says, in effect, that IQ should not be measured as an absolute figure in the way that height, weight, and blood pressure are. It's a crucial blunder, he maintains, to assume that IQ is a single fixed entity that can be measured by a pencil-and-paper test.

It's not how smart you are but *how you are smart,* says Gardner.

As human beings we all have a repertoire of skills, he says, for solving different kinds of problems. And he defines intelligence this way: *An Intelligence is an ability to solve a problem or fashion a product that is valued in one or more cultural settings.*

In other words, intelligence can vary by context. If you were stranded with an Aborigine in the middle of the Australian bush without food or water, she would be the intelligent one—because she would know how to survive. Transport her to your office and ask her to use your computer and the position would be reversed.

"Problems" can be anything from creating an end to a story to anticipating a chess move to fixing the brakes on your car. "Products" can range from scientific theories to musical composition to successful political campaigns.

In arriving at his theory Gardner embraced ideas derived from neurobiology, complemented by fields such as psychology, anthropology, philosophy, and history.

Further, he reviewed the extensive evidence from a wide range of disparate sources. He analyzed studies of child prodigies, gifted individuals, brain-damaged patients, idiots savants, normal children, normal adults, experts in different lines of work, and individuals from diverse cultures.

The outcome was his ground-breaking book *Frames of Mind,* in which Gardner convincingly argues for an alternative look at human intellectual competencies and in which he then outlined seven distinct intelligences:

Linguistic Intelligence. The ability to read, write, and communicate with words. Authors, journalists, poets, orators, and comedians are obvious examples of people with linguistic intelligence.

Famous examples: Charles Dickens, Abraham Lincoln, T. S. Eliot, Sir Winston Churchill.

Logical-Mathematical Intelligence. The ability to reason and calculate, to think things through in a logical, systematic manner. These are the kinds of skills highly developed in engineers, scientists, economists, accountants, detectives, and members of the legal profession.

Famous examples: Albert Einstein, John Dewey.

Visual-Spatial Intelligence. The ability to think in pictures, visualize a future result. To imagine things in your mind's eye. Architects, artists, sculptors, sailors, photographers, and strategic planners. You use it when you have a sense of direction, when you navigate or draw.

Famous examples: Picasso, Frank Lloyd Wright, Christopher Columbus.

Musical Intelligence. The ability to make or compose music, to sing well, or understand and appreciate music. To keep rhythm. It's a talent obviously enjoyed by musicians, composers, and recording engineers. But most of us have a basic musical intelligence that can be developed. Think how helpful it is to learn with a jingle or rhyme. (e.g., "Thirty days hath September . . .")

Famous examples: Mozart, Leonard Bernstein, Ray Charles.

Bodily-Kinesthetic Intelligence. The ability to use your body skillfully to solve problems, create products, or present ideas and emotions. An ability obviously displayed for athletic pursuits, artistic pursuits such as dancing and acting, or in building and construction. You can include surgeons in this category, but many people who are physically talented—"good with their hands"—don't recognize that this form of intelligence is of equal value to the others.

Famous examples: Charlie Chaplin, Michael Jordan, Rudolf Nureyev.

Interpersonal (Social) Intelligence. The ability to work effectively with others, to relate to other people and display empathy and understanding, to notice their motivations and goals. This is a vital human intelligence exhibited by good teachers, facilitators, therapists, politicians, religious leaders, and salespeople.

Famous examples: Gandhi, Ronald Reagan, Mother Teresa, Oprah Winfrey.

Intrapersonal Intelligence. The ability for self-analysis and reflection—to be able to quietly contemplate and assess one's accomplishments, to review one's behavior and innermost feelings, to make plans and set goals, to know oneself. Philosophers, counselors, and many peak performers in all fields of endeavor have this form of intelligence.

Famous examples: Freud, Eleanor Roosevelt, Plato.

In 1996 Gardner decided to add an eighth intelligence (naturalist), and in spite of much speculation resisted the temptation to add a ninth—spiritual intelligence.

Naturalist Intelligence. The ability to recognize flora and fauna, to make other consequential distinctions in the natural world, and to use this ability productively—for example in hunting, farming, or biological science. Farmers, botanists, conservationists, biologists, environmentalists, would all display aspects of this intelligence.

Famous examples: Charles Darwin, E. O. Wilson.

Traditionally, academic subjects have been taught in ways that largely involve just two intelligences—linguistic and logical-mathematical.

Now consider what an IQ test basically measures—ability with words and numbers. So students who are naturally strong in linguistic and mathematical intelligences do well on an IQ test. Therefore it's a fairly good predictor of success at school, because the way we teach (lectures) and the materials with which we teach (logically constructed books) depend heavily on these two intelligences. Since teachers are drawn from people who do well at school, it's a self-perpetuating system.

But is an IQ result a good predictor of happiness, of economic success, of success in relationships, of success in life? Not really. In a modern society, of course, linguistic and logical/numerical abilities **are** very important—but there *are* at least six other intelligences. It is when you marshal all of your intelligences that you really begin to use your full brainpower.

But for those students whose strengths lie primarily within the other six intelligences identified by Gardner, learning can be a daunting prospect—because they

> **The human brain is the most complex piece of machinery in the universe.**
>
> **PROFESSOR COLIN BLAKEMORE, UNIVERSITY OF OXFORD**

are not being provided information in a way that they can most easily absorb it.

Accelerated Learning shows all students of all ages how to learn in ways that suit their unique mix of capabilities.

A Balancing Act

Every normal individual possesses varying degrees of each of the intelligences, but the ways in which intelligences combine and blend are as varied as the faces and the personalities of individuals.

Children as young as four and five years old exhibit distinctive profiles of strengths and weaknesses, according to preliminary data secured from one Harvard study.

And as adults some people may have one or two intelligences that are *highly* developed. They may excel in one area and yet be at a complete loss in a different situation. The brilliant mathematician who can solve complex problems but cannot communicate that understanding to others would be a classic example.

Alternatively, an individual may not be particularly gifted in any intelligence; and yet, because of his particular combination or blend of skills, he may be able to fill some niche uniquely well.

But, in general, the better developed the range of your intelligences the more flexible you'll be in meeting a wide range of challenges in life. The aim, especially in education, should be a "rounded" mind.

Gardner himself—recipient of a so-called "genius" grant from the MacArthur Foundation—is a multifaceted Renaissance man with varying strengths in all of the intelligences. An eloquent communicator, prolific writer, physical exercise enthusiast (daily jogger), piano player, college actor—a man of many parts!

No wonder he points out that one intelligence is good but many working in concert is a better mind: "Inasmuch as nearly every cultural role requires several intelligences, it becomes important to consider individuals as a collection of aptitudes rather than as having a singular problem-solving faculty that can be measured directly through pen-

> **The greatest unexplored territory in the world is the space between our ears.**
>
> WILLIAM O'BRIEN, FORMER
> PRESIDENT, HANOVER INSURANCE

cil-and-paper tests. . . . In fact, it may well be that the 'total is greater than the sum of the parts.' "

What about a spiritual intelligence? Gardner says that he has not endorsed such an intelligence but has become interested in understanding better what is meant by "spirituality" and by "spiritual individuals."

He adds: "Whether or not it proves appropriate to add 'spirituality' to the list of intelligences, this human capacity certainly deserves discussion and study in nonfringe psychological circles."

We believe that Howard Gardner's "Theory of Multiple Intelligences" gives us seven different ways to explore any subject, and an eighth to check whether our conclusions are socially and ecologically acceptable.

Gardner disapproves, however (and we concur), with dogmatic attempts to teach *all* concepts or subjects using *all* the intelligences. "Most topics can be powerfully approached in a number of ways. But there is no point in assuming that every topic can be effectively approached in at least seven ways. It is a waste of effort and time to attempt to do this," he says.

In essence, this new way of regarding intelligence tells us that there are "multiple windows leading into the same room"—that subjects can be approached and learned from a number of perspectives. And that when people are able to use their strongest forms of intelligence, they begin to find learning easier and more enjoyable.

It also tells us that "intelligence" is simply a set of abilities and skills. You can develop and improve your intelligence by learning to use your abilities to the full. The Accelerated Learning strategies give you the "tools of the trade" to develop these skills.

MAKING WAVES——FOUR KINDS OF BRAIN WAVES

Your brain transmits information on different "frequencies" in much the same way that radio and TV stations send and receive their signals.

In the brain's case, it generates tiny electrical impulses as thoughts traverse the labyrinth of the mind. Your four kinds of brain "waves"—alpha, beta, delta, theta—can be measured on an electroencephalograph machine (EEG). Electrodes are attached to

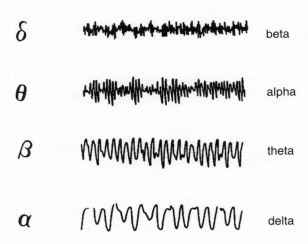

the scalp and the brain waves recorded in cycles per second. And they vary enormously. The brain-wave patterns are very different when you're wide awake and alert as compared to when you're fast asleep.

The four brain waves are:

Beta: the brain wave of your conscious mind. It operates at thirteen to twenty-five cycles per second. You are awake, attentive, alert. Your mind is thinking through and analyzing situations. You're talking and actively involved.

Alpha: the brain-wave pattern that characterizes relaxation and meditation. It operates at eight to twelve cycles per second. In this mode you daydream and let your imagination soar. You're in a state of relaxed alertness.

Theta: the brain wave associated with deep reverie, and the early stages of sleep. It operates at four to seven cycles per second. It's the "twilight zone" when the mind is processing the day's information and when you may have flashes of inspiration.

Delta: the brain-wave pattern displayed when you're in a deep, dreamless sleep. It registers just one half to three cycles per second.

So what's the best brain wave for learning? It depends. You'll need to be in a beta state for taking heavy scientific information "on board," i.e., for the initial effort to understand something. But research shows that the alpha state of *"relaxed* alertness" is very effective for consolidating the information that you've already understood.

In the beta state you're concentrating on tackling the immediate problem at hand or getting through the day's activities. But you're not so open to flashes of intuition. You could say that sometimes we don't see the forest through the trees. In the alpha state—when you're more relaxed—your mind is much more open and receptive.

Alpha seems to let you reach your subconscious, and many researchers have come to the conclusion that you store information most effectively in your long-term memory when you're in a relaxed yet alert state. We have found this particularly true with our foreign-language courses.

When alpha (and, indeed, theta) brain waves become more dominant, logical left-brain activity—which normally acts as a filter or censor to the subconscious—drops its guard. This allows the more intuitive, emotional, and creative depths of the mind to become increasingly influential.

The objective of Accelerated Learning is to:

a. Actively involve the emotional brain—thereby making things more memorable.
b. Synchronize left- and right-brain activity.
c. Mobilize all eight intelligences so that learning is accessible to everyone and the resources of the whole mind are used.
d. Introduce moments of relaxation to allow consolidation to take place. Although understanding something and memorizing it are different, all learning—to be useful—needs to be stored in the memory.

Memory is such a vital part of the learning process that we've devoted most of the next chapter to explaining just how it works.

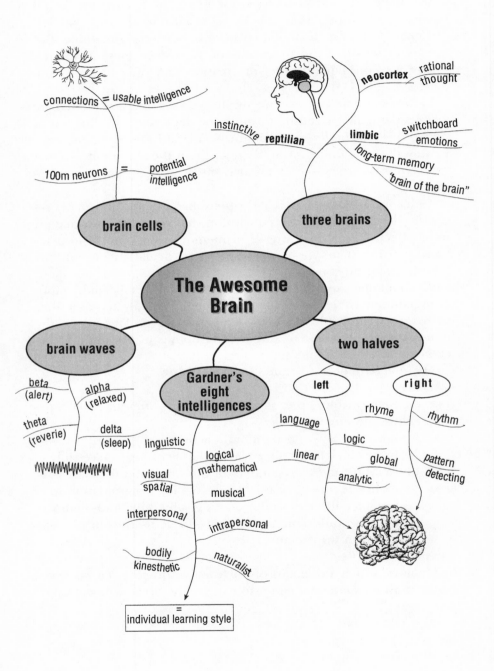

3

Remember, Remember

Memory is the treasury and guardian of all things.
CICERO

"Despite all the noises we scientists make about memory, it is remarkable how little we know," confesses eminent researcher Dr. Arnold Scheibel, director of the University of California, Los Angeles, Brain Research Institute.

Even the simplest act of memory stimulates complex neural networks at several different sites. For instance, the content of an event (what happened) and its meaning (how it felt) are laid down in separate parts of the brain. The names of natural things such as vegetation and wildlife are stored in one part of the brain; the names of man-made items such as cars, furniture, and machinery are retained elsewhere. Nouns also appear to be kept apart from verbs.

However, while aspects of memory are spread throughout the brain, it's believed that one tiny organ has a particularly significant role. That organ—the hippocampus (Greek for "sea horse," whose shape it resembles)—straddles both the right and left hemispheres. At the risk of oversimplification: the hippocampus is an important way station, receiving and sorting information, helping to turn that information into a memory and forwarding it to other parts of the brain. Without the hippocampus we might learn, but we wouldn't remember.

Mark Gluck, PhD, a professor at the Center for Molecular and Behavioral Neuroscience at Rutgers University, New Jersey, agrees that the hippocampus is essential for learning to occur, but points out it's also one of the most volatile, unstable parts of the brain. If the supply of oxygen is reduced, it's one of the first areas of the brain to suffer. "Think of it as a highly maneuverable kayak; it has to immediately capture a whole range of information about an event and needs the ability to go rapidly through many changes," says Gluck. "We think the hippocampus serves as a filter, learning new associations and deciding what is important and what to ignore or compress. That's why it's critical for learning."

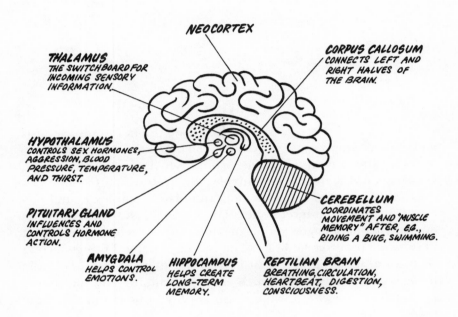

FIVE TYPES OF MEMORY

According to the latest theory there are actually five types of memory.

Neurologist Dr. Murray Grossman, and colleagues at the University of Pennsylvania Medical Center, came up with this model. Remember it by using the acronym W-I-R-E-S and conjure up an image of your brain being wired (more on these two memory techniques later!).

1. **Working.** This is extremely short-term memory—no more than a few seconds long. Situated in the prefrontal cortex, it lets you keep several things in mind at the same time. In conversation, for instance, it enables you to remember the beginning of a sentence until the speaker gets to the end. It also lets you perform several functions at the same time—for example, waving to attract someone's attention while talking to someone else and continuing to open your mail. In many people working memory begins to lose efficiency after the age of forty.

2. **Implicit.** Once you've learned how to do something like riding a bicycle, driving a car, or swimming, it's likely that you'll never forget how to do so. We often call this "muscle memory." Implicit memory does not require awareness, which explains why you can be lost in thought behind the wheel of a car and find—to your surprise—that you've arrived at your destination. Other skills that require automatic recall of a series of motions also don't disappear. Loss of implicit memory (which is stored in the cerebellum) would be a sign of serious mental deterioration.

3. **Remote.** Game-show winners have this kind of memory. It's the lifetime accumulation of data about a wide variety of topics. Remote memory—spread around the cerebral cortex—seems to diminish with age. The decline could be a retrieval problem, however, with the older person having to work harder to sort through an increased accumulation of knowledge.

4. **Episodic.** Created in the hippocampus, this is the memory of specific personal experiences—the food you chose at a restaurant last week, the result of the football game, the plot of the movie you saw, where you parked the car. When important information is presented in an emotionally satisfying form—a story or a conversation or a film—it is usually well remembered.

5. **Semantic.** The memory of words and symbols and what they mean is the kind of memory most likely never to be lost. Even words that you may not have used in years will not fade away. You would continue to remember *reef knot* from Boy Scout days or, for instance, *pogo stick* from other youthful adventures. Corporate trademarks and religious symbols are similarly "unforgettable," as are the basic elements of what dis-

tinguishes a cat from a dog. Semantic memory represents our general knowledge about the working of the world, and is located in the angular gyrus.

LASTING MEMORIES

How do memories become permanent? It's largely dependent on how strongly the information is registered in the first place. That's why it's so important to learn in ways that involve hearing, seeing, saying, and doing and which involve positive emotions such as when we learn collaboratively. All factors that create strong memories.

However, there's new evidence to substantiate the belief that a memory is locked into your brain during sleep or when you're deeply relaxed—the aforementioned theta brain wave state. How do we know? The journal *Science* recently published a study in which electrodes were implanted in the hippocampus of rats. As the rodents explored different parts of a box, the researchers noted which brain cells were activated. When the rats went to sleep the same cells fired again. Researchers have found that when the hippocampus is stimulated with a frequency corresponding to the slow pace of theta waves, memory is enhanced.

In human studies, too, sleep has been shown to boost memory, especially the sleep associated with dreaming—rapid eye movement (REM). *Psychology Today* reported a Canadian project in which students who went to bed after studying all evening retained much more information than their counterparts who crammed throughout the night. And Israeli researchers found that interrupting subjects' REM sleep sixty times in a night completely blocked learning.

> **Your brain is like a sleeping giant.**
>
> TONY BUZAN IN *MAKE THE MOST OF YOUR MIND*

During the day, says psychologist and computer scientist Christopher Evans, the brain is bombarded with sensations, information, and experiences but cannot absorb it all while the brain-computer is still on-line, that is, while it is still receiving information. REM phases occur when the mind moves off-line and processes and fully records the daytime deluge of data in its complex array of memory banks.

During sleep the brain appears to assimilate and file away new information and "make sense of it." According to recent studies we often construct rather bizarre stories while we dream in order for the brain to weave together a whole lot of unrelated new facts, and in doing so make sense of them and file them appropriately.

The fact that dreams (i.e., visual stories) appear to be a natural way to remember things, accounts for the fact that a very good memory device is to make up an easy-to-visualize story in order to remember a series of facts. For example, the ministory *My Very Energetic Mother Just Served Us Nine Pizzas* is a good way to remember the planets in their correct order from the sun—Mercury, Venus, Earth, Mars, Jupiter, Saturn, Uranus, Neptune, and Pluto.

We have used this discovery in our Accelerated Learning language courses. Your new language is learned via a spoken story using lots of pictures and sound effects. Because the language is also embedded in an emotionally involving story—rather than being learned conventionally as a series of unrelated nouns and verbs—it becomes much easier, and certainly more fun, to learn.

These findings, said *Psychology Today,* "give scientific punch" to "faster learning" methods like that of Bulgarian psychiatrist Georgi Lozanov, which "utilizes deep relaxation through diaphragmatic breathing and music, combined with rhythmic bursts of information."

These findings also show why "sleep learning" won't work—the idea that information played to you while you sleep will penetrate your subconscious mind and be remembered. It is an attractive proposition, of course. The lazy man's ideal way to learn. But the fact is that your brain is unavailable for new input during sleep. It is far too busy replaying, registering, and filing away what it learned during the hours you were awake, to be able to absorb new information at the same time.

EMOTION CREATES STRONG MEMORIES

"A memory associated with emotionally charged information gets seared into the brain."

That's the graphic description of writer Jill Neimark, in an excellent article in *Psychology Today,* entitled "It's Magical. It's Malleable. It's . . . Memory."

Scientists are just beginning to understand how emotional memory works and why it is so powerful, says Neimark. Emotional response can be triggered by both positive and negative events. In *any* kind of emotionally arousing experience the brain takes advantage of the fight-or-flight reaction, which floods cells with two powerful stress hormones, adrenaline and noradrenaline.

Says researcher James McGaugh, PhD, of the University of California at Irvine, "We believe that the brain takes advantage of the chemicals released during stress and powerful emotions to regulate the strength of storage of the memory."

These stress hormones stimulate obvious physical reactions—the heart beating faster; muscles tensing. But they also plant extremely vivid images in the brain cells. With good cause: you'll want to know how to react—instantly—the next time an ax-wielding maniac attacks you!

A notable study, conducted by McGaugh and fellow researcher Larry Cahill, clearly indicated how emotion, even ordinary emotion, is associated with improved memory—and learning ability.

Two groups of college students were given a drug that blocks the effects of adrenaline and noradrenaline. Then they were shown twelve slides depicting such scenes as a boy crossing the street with his mother or visiting a man at the hospital. One group was told an ordinary story to correlate with the pictures: boy and mother visit his father, who's a surgeon. The second group heard a dramatic, colorful disaster story: boy hit by car—surgeon attempts to reattach his severed feet.

Two weeks later the study participants were given a surprise memory test. The students who had heard the ordinary "everyday" story had poor recall of the contents of the twelve slides; the group that had heard the dramatic account performed "significantly better" in remembering the slides.

In another test, psychologists asked people to listen to lists of words, including some emotionally charged words such as *breast, corpse,* and *rapist.* The participants remembered the "emotional" words better than the neutral words. Perhaps of greater import, they also remembered better which voice had spoken the word—a clear indication of an increased awareness of associated events.

From the educator's perspective, University of Oregon professor of education Robert Sylwester makes a compelling case for more attention to be paid to the value of emotion in teaching.

He says, "We know emotion is very important to the educative process because it drives attention, which drives learning and memory. We've never really understood emotion, however, and so don't know how to regulate it in school—beyond defining too much or too little of it as misbehavior and relegating most of it to the arts, PE, recess, and the extracurricular program.

"We measure students' spelling accuracy, not their emotional well-being. And when the budget gets tight, we cut the difficult-to-measure curricular areas, such as the arts, that tilt toward emotion. By separating emotion from logic and reason in the classroom, we've simplified school management and evaluation, but we've also then separated two sides of one coin—and lost something important in the process.

"It's impossible to separate emotion from the important activities of life. Don't even try."

Here's why it's **vital** to allow for the role of emotion in learning and education.

First, there are more neural connections going **from** the limbic emotional center **to** the intellectual cortex than vice versa. So emotion is often a more powerful factor in influencing our behavior than is logic.

Secondly, we've seen how the limbic/emotional system acts like a switchboard, sending incoming information from the senses to the thinking cortex. However,

> **Not even the universe, with its countless billions of galaxies, represents greater wonder or complexity than the human brain. The human brain is a mirror to infinity. There is no limit to its range, scope, or capacity for creative growth.**
>
> **NORMAN COUSINS IN *HEAD FIRST: THE BIOLOGY OF HOPE***

there's a faster route that sends emotionally laden information that could be threatening—not "up" for analysis, but straight down to the more primitive parts of the brain for a "gut" reaction.

This explains why situations that have previously caused pain or fear can cause such violent and unthinking "knee jerk" reactions. In evolutionary terms it makes sense. A fleeting glimpse of something that looks like a snake is best reacted to instantaneously, even if on closer examination it turns out to be a harmless stick. But the same process can happen, for example, when we "learn" to fear math problems.

That's why it's so important that as learners we learn how to control our state of mind. And why teaching students in school how to recognize, acknowledge, and control emotions should be on **every** school curriculum. But it isn't.

There's another major significance to allowing the role of emotion in learning. Our brains are very good at recognizing and reacting fast to sudden dangers. They are not good at recognizing danger brought about by gradual change. The brain has no sense of growing immediacy and therefore triggers no strong reaction. That's why we have difficulty motivating ourselves to deal with the creeping threats of diminishing resources, pollution, urban decay, overpopulation—even of large-scale job losses. They are too gradual to register as life threatening.

We need to find a way to make these problems urgent if we are to motivate enough people to take collective action. And we especially need to make these problems "come to life" with our students, for it will be their generation who will have to find the solutions or live with the consequences.

IT'S A JUNGLE IN THERE

Five kinds of memory. Eight intelligences. Three brains. Two brains. One brain. Four types of brain waves. What does it all add up to?

It adds up to the most complicated organism known to man. No wonder that in our vain attempts to describe the way the mind functions, many experts resort to the use of computer analogies. After all, we have astounded ourselves with the way the artificial intelligence of computers has revolutionized our lives. The computer analogy is a tempting proposition—but it's an entirely erroneous approach.

A somewhat controversial theory from an eminent source strongly disputes any suggestion that the brain operates using the same ordered procedure as do computers.

The source is Gerald Edelman, who won the Nobel prize in 1972 for a discovery that overturned conventional wisdom about the way in which the body's immune system functions.

The belief had been that generic antibodies *learned* to recognize harmful invaders such as bacteria and viruses. The immune system counterattacked, destroyed the antigens, and, in case of future assaults, remembered the profile of the attacker so it would be better prepared to respond.

Instead, Edelman found that we are each born with a tremendous number of *specific* antibodies that recognize and retaliate against a *specific* type of virus. If we don't have the natural immunity (such as to the AIDS virus), we may die if infected. Our immune system cannot *learn* how to destroy the attacker. We either have it or we don't have it as a result of natural selection processes that have occurred over eons.

Subsequently Edelman, chairman of the Neurobiology Department at the world-famous Scripps Research Institute in La Jolla, California, turned his attention to the functioning of the brain. His "Theory of Neuronal Group Selection" has been popularized as "Neural Darwinism."

In essence, he concluded that genetic processes over thousands of years have led to the development of a generic human brain fully equipped at birth with the basic "intelligence" and physical attributes to survive in the modern world.

There are basic neural networks operational at birth. The baby doesn't have to learn how to recognize specific sounds, for instance. We don't teach a child to walk or talk: the basic predispositions are genetically implanted— but if we don't *stimulate* those abilities they may never develop properly.

This is why it's **so** important to create an early rich environment

> It is the only example of evolution providing a species with an organ which it does not know how to use; a luxury organ, which will take its owner thousands of years to learn to put to proper use—if it ever does.
>
> **ARTHUR KOESTLER**

for children. If latent abilities aren't stimulated, they may literally be pruned away. Another case of "use it or lose it."

We know this is true of foreign languages. The window of opportunity for acquiring a native accent is before age twelve or thirteen. It may even be true of acquiring the ability to work collaboratively. If so, schooling—focused as it is on individual endeavor—may actually reduce our long-term capacity to work well together. That's dangerous when we realize that our success as a species comes not from our physical strength but from our ability to collaborate thoughtfully.

Edelman argues that it is wrong to use the computer as the model for the brain because a computer has to be programmed and run by something (someone) else. The computer analogy makes you think in terms of a neat, orderly filing system. And the brain just doesn't work like that. There's a preponderance of *parallel* processing in the workings of the brain, rather than linear activity.

Edelman turns to biology instead of technology for a better analogy. And, somewhat colorfully, suggests that the inner dynamics of the brain more closely resemble life in the jungle rather than the computer terminal.

The jungle, he says, is not controlled or directed by any one group or organism. The jungle is a rich, evolving system, with mutually dependent parts. All plants and animals perform a variety of important interrelated ecological jobs. A tree is a single living organism but has symbiotic relationships with insects, birds, vines, moss, etc. For instance, the tree doesn't deliberately grow limbs as a nesting site for birds, but birds take advantage of the limbs for that purpose.

Furthermore, the jungle environment doesn't instruct organisms how to thrive—for example by teaching trees how to position their limbs and roots to enjoy the benefit of sunlight and soil nutrients. All trees have the innate ability to do so—some succeed, some perish. Evolution works by selection, not instruction.

Says Edelman, "The circuits of the brain look like no others we have seen before. The neurons have treelike arbors that overlap in myriad ways. Their signaling is like the vast aggregate of interactive events in a jungle."

So—think of the phenomenally complex network of brain cells as the neural equivalent of the incredible, rich diversity of organisms in the jungle responding in various ways to a multitude of environmental challenges.

Think of our brain as being the result of natural selection and ecological principles operating both over eons and within our lifetime. The result: a magnificent human **mind** formed out of a basic human brain in which the neural networks we're born with adapt marvelously to a continuously changing and challenging environment.

The brain—like the jungle—is always teeming with life. The law of the jungle is survival. Similarly, the brain is best at learning what it needs to know to survive, socially, economically, emotionally, and physically. Edelman suggests that our brain does what it has to do to survive. It is neurologically prewired to learn.

A Blackboard Jungle?

But what are the implications of a "junglelike" brain adapted to respond to a challenging environment? How does it relate to our ability to learn? Perhaps it needs to be matched with a "junglelike" learning environment?

We are not suggesting a lawless, undisciplined school campus where students run wild. We are suggesting that a multiintelligence, multisensory classroom or training room with lots of color, art, music, role play, interaction, information on the walls, and sheer novelty is a more fitting response to the jungle brain. It is learning environment that focuses on **challenging** and thus drawing out and developing the students' innate, existing abilities.

We learn best by working things out, making *our own* meaning via our own preferred way of learning, not from being given answers delivered ready-made via the teacher's preferred way of teaching.

The brain **likes** complexity and challenge. It stays alert when it's trying to discover relationships, make sense of a rich environment, and when it feels that what

> Each of us is a living record of our own life experiences. The brain is very specialized—different parts do different things at the same time, which is where the brain is superior to a computer. Computers can be very fast—but work in series.
>
> LARRY SQUIRE, PhD,
> UNIVERSITY OF CALIFORNIA,
> SAN DIEGO

it is learning is important for its well-being. Motivation is a key to learning.

In some respects the image of a learning jungle isn't such a bad idea when one considers the unique talents and needs of each individual student, the mix of multiple intelligences, the preferences for left- or right-brain thinking—and so on.

What about the student who likes to listen to music while he's learning, or the student who needs to keep asking questions to fully comprehend and absorb the information, or the student who thinks better on his feet rather than "chained" to a desk?

The curriculum of tomorrow—if educators listen to Edelman and Sylwester—would focus more on the individual's needs. Educators would see classroom misbehavior as an ecological problem to be solved within the school structure rather than aberrant behavior to be stamped out. There would be increased attention to challenging, complex subjects such as the arts and humanities, which need interpretation, rather than a single-minded focus on basic linguistic and logical skills (left brain).

Says Professor Sylwester, "The brain is a biological system, not a machine. Currently, we are putting children with biologically shaped brains into machine-oriented schools. The two just don't mix. We bog the school down in a curriculum that is not biologically feasible."

Meanwhile, what's the relevance to you?

The metaphor of the brain as a jungle system is a thought-provoking way to open our minds; to stimulate the senses; to say that the rules have changed and are constantly changing; that the "disciplined" way in which you were taught may have been the wrong way for you and that—through acquiring Accelerated Learning techniques—you can make up for lost time.

And what if you have passed all of the exams in your life with flying colors, and the way you were taught suited you just fine? Don't be complacent. Accelerated Learning will show you ways to boost your brainpower and creativity by adding the elements for a rounded approach to learning.

USE IT OR LOSE IT!

But what if you're "getting on in years"? Studying is something you did when you were at school. You think you're too old to "go back to school." And surely, in any case, as you get older your memory inevitably fails you—isn't that the first sign of old age? So it's probably too late to worry about learning anything new, isn't it?

Taken at face value the statistics *are* downright depressing. The longer you live, the greater your chances of falling victim to Alzheimer's disease or other forms of dementia.

From the age of sixty the frequency of dementia doubles every five years. Only one percent of sixty- to sixty-four-year-olds are affected, but a staggering 30–40 percent of those of us over the age of eighty-five are affected.

But now experts from a variety of disciplines are all reaching the same conclusion: severe mental decline is not an inevitable companion to old age. They are finding that an old brain can have surprising abilities and strengths.

One study of more than 1,500 people, aged between twenty-five and ninety-two, testing such functions as math and reading, found that 25 percent to 33 percent of people in their eighties scored just as well as the younger participants. Some of the oldest people had exceptional scores that ranked them near the top of mental abilities for all ages, says Harvard University psychologist Douglas Powell.

Neurobiologists such as Gerald Fishbach at Harvard, who are now able to peer inside the living brain, are discovering the popular belief that 100,000 brain neurons perish every year is just not true. What they have discovered, however, is that many brain cells may shrink or grow dormant in old age.

"The standard teaching is that we lose massive numbers of neurons in the brain in the course of normal aging. Our data do not agree," says Robert D. Terry, MD, professor of neurosciences and pathology at the University of California, San Diego. "However, the number of large neurons does de-

> I must have a prodigious quantity of mind: it takes me as much as a week sometimes to make it up.
>
> **MARK TWAIN**

crease, while the number of small neurons increases to about an equal extent. Therefore, we came to a conclusion that large neurons are not dying but may be shrinking into a smaller-size class."

Researchers now say that from about the age of fifty, people of the same age begin to differ more and more from one another. Some experience a noticeable decline in mental performance, others hold steady or even improve. What's the difference?

Robert Ornstein of Stanford and Charles Swencionis of the Albert Einstein College of Medicine, Yeshiva University, provide an answer: "It now seems that the brain does not necessarily lose cells and can develop new dendrites through very old age. Brain cells grow new connections **as a result of stimulation** [our emphasis], and if we continue to stimulate organisms, dendrites continue to develop. The brain does not grow new cells, but the connections between cells may be important."

In other words, if an old mind is kept stimulated it can keep making those all important connections.

An old brain maintains a remarkable ability to rejuvenate itself. The older brain literally rewires itself to compensate for any losses. If one neuron can't do what's required, neighboring brain cells come to the rescue and take over, adding new dendrites and assuming the work of the lost cell.

PET scans now show that a stroke victim may recover at least some speech and limb movement even if the neurons in the affected part of the brain are permanently damaged.

Scientists like Dr. Lawrence Brass, associate professor of neurology at Yale, believe that the brains of stroke victims may form new dendritic connections, indicating that even an aging adult's brain can grow in response to injury. In some patients, scientists believe, nearby neurons enlarge their networks and take over for the damaged tissue.

The point is that the brain works a lot like a muscle—the more you exercise it, the more it develops. Too little exercise means a flabby brain.

In one famous experiment, UC Berkeley's Marian Diamond

placed rats in a superstimulating environment, complete with swings, ladders, treadmills, toys of all kinds—and other rats. Those rats who lived in the high-stimulus environment lived longer, surprisingly surviving until the age of three—the rat equivalent of ninety in a human. And, at the same time, their brains increased in size, sprouting forests of brain cell connections. They grew more brain! The rats who lived in bare cages stagnated and died younger. Their brains had fewer cellular connections.

Says Diamond, "A very simple principle, Use it or lose it, applies to stimulation for a nerve cell. We can show that the nerve cell can retain its healthy characteristics if it receives stimulation. Why do we bring this up?

"Because in essence, we are fighting old people's homes, where people are isolated from stimulation. The nervous system is not receiving much input. No wonder people become senile. Mental exercise helps the cerebral cortex as it does muscles, bones, and other organs of the body."

One thought-provoking study conducted by Ellen Langer and Rebecca Levy at Harvard points to a cultural bias. In China, where age is revered—and there is no negative cultural mind-set equating old age to mental infirmity—the elderly perform much better on cognitive tests than do Americans of the same age, and the incidence of Alzheimer's is very low.

The Super Sisters

Another fascinating study is being conducted with the aid of an order of nuns famed for their longevity. The School Sisters of Notre Dame not only live to an average age of eighty-five (many live far beyond that), they also do not seem to suffer from dementia, Alzheimer's, and other debilitating brain diseases as early or as severely as the general population.

Nearly seven hundred of the nuns agreed to donate their brains for medical research after their death. University of Kentucky professor of preventive medicine David Snowdon, who has so far studied more than a hundred of the nuns' brains, has already discovered one intriguing difference.

Those nuns who earn college degrees, who teach, and who constantly challenge their minds live longer than less educated nuns who clean rooms or work in the kitchen.

Professor Snowdon, who operates out of the university's Sanders-

Brown Center on Aging, anticipates proving that the better-educated nuns have far more nerve-cell connections, allowing them to cope better with brain disabilities.

In a study at the University of California at Los Angeles, researchers looked at the part of the brain devoted to word understanding—Wernicke's area—and found that the number of dendrites correlates to the individual's amount of schooling.

Those people who went through college had more dendrites than those who only finished high school, who had more than those who left school earlier. The clear inference: Education gives people practice in vocabulary, saying and hearing words, a particular kind of mental activity that enriches Wernicke's area with dendrites.

Moral: Learn to a high level and keep learning.

We shall return again and again to the importance of taking on challenging experiences as a means of building brain power.

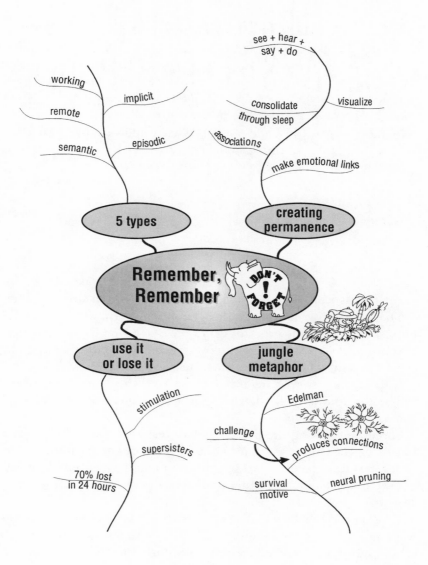

4

The Six-Step
M•A•S•T•E•R Plan

What if you knew you could not fail? What would you attempt to do?
ROBERT A. SCHULLER, AUTHOR OF
POWER TO GROW BEYOND YOURSELF

The young child wakes each day eager to discover what new delights the world has in store for him.

The child is a natural fearless explorer, born with an innate inquisitiveness about everything. Every day he embarks on a new adventure, a new voyage of discovery—encouraged, of course, by caring parents who celebrate each new accomplishment.

Setbacks are simply regarded as part of the learning process. When the toddler falls down, he just picks himself up and tries again.

Somewhere along the line the joy of learning often turns into a hard slog. Learning becomes equated with the acquisition of bits of information necessary to pass tests and achieve grades. Subjects get separated from each other and from the real world. It becomes stressful.

Why should this be so? Why can't learning be the pleasure it was when we were young—before "learning" became confused with schooling? Why can't education recapture something of the exploratory excitement of the young child when he is seeing, hearing, smelling, touching, and quite often tasting, the great uncharted world in which he finds himself—the critical time when he is trying to make sense of it all?

It can. *If we put into practice what we now know about the way the brain works.*

In our view the conditions for effective learning include a childlike (notice *childlike*, not childish), supportive, and playful environment.

It is a view promoted by eminent psychologist Mihaly Csikszentmihalyi, who for more than twenty years has studied what he calls "flow"—a state of

> **Accelerated Learning gives you the freedom to learn. It helps you to tap into that genius that all of us have.**
>
> **JEANNETTE VOS, PHD,**
> **COAUTHOR,**
> **THE LEARNING REVOLUTION**

concentration that leads to optimal experiences, a state of consciousness so focused that it amounts to absolute absorption in an activity. It's when an individual enjoys an exhilarating feeling of effortless control and is performing at the peak of his or her abilities.

Says Csikszentmihalyi, "During the first few years of life every child is a little 'learning machine' trying out new movements, new words, daily. The rapt concentration on the child's face as she learns each new skill is a good indication of what enjoyment is about. And each instance of enjoyable learning adds to the complexity of the child's developing self.

"Unfortunately, this natural connection between growth and enjoyment tends to disappear with time. Perhaps because 'learning' becomes an external imposition when schooling starts, the excitement of mastering new skills gradually wears out."

One reason children learn so well is that they haven't developed preconceptions of how they are supposed to learn. Also, they have not developed the notion that play and work are mutually exclusive activities. Play *is* an important part of the learning experience. When we enjoy learning, we learn better.

How do we make learning successful *and* enjoyable? Through

- creating a low-stress environment—one where it is safe to make mistakes, yet expectation of success is high.
- ensuring the subject is relevant—you *want* to learn when you see the point of it.
- ensuring the learning is emotionally positive—it generally is when you work with others, when there is humor and encouragement, regular breaks, and enthusiastic support.

- consciously involving all the senses as well as left-brain and right-brain thinking.
- challenging your brain to think through and explore what is being learned with as many intelligences as are relevant in order to make personal sense of it.
- and consolidating what is learned—by reviewing in quiet periods of relaxed alertness.

All of the above are included in our Accelerated Learning program. But no matter how much fun or how stimulating the learning process becomes, it's also vital to work to a cohesive, step-by-step plan.

The "structure" of our Accelerated Learning method falls into six basic steps. They can easily be remembered through the use of the acronym M•A•S•T•E•R—a mnemonic created by noted Accelerated Learning trainer Jayne Nicholl, author of *Open Sesame.*

1. Motivating Your Mind.

You need to be in a "resourceful" state of mind. That means being relaxed, confident, and **motivated.** If you are feeling stressed or lack belief in yourself or cannot see the point of what you are learning, you won't learn well.

Having the right attitude toward learning anything is an absolute prerequisite. You must want to acquire the new knowledge or skill. You must have the inner confidence that you are fully capable of learning—and that the information you acquire is going to have a meaningful impact on your life.

In other words: you need to see the personal benefit from your investment in time and energy. It's what we describe in the next chapter as your WII-FM—"What's In It For Me?" As Sir Christopher Ball, Director for Learning at the prestigious Royal Society for the Encouragement of Arts, Manufactures, and Commerce (RSA), puts it: "The three most important factors in learning are motivation, motivation, and motivation."

> **The best way to get a good idea is to get a lot of ideas.**
>
> LINUS PAULING,
> TWO-TIME NOBEL LAUREATE

2. Acquiring the Information.

You need to acquire and absorb the basic facts of the subject in the way best suited to *your* sensory learning preferences.

Although there are learning strategies everyone should implement, there are also key differences in the extent to which we individually need to see, hear, or get physically involved in the learning process. By identifying your Visual, Auditory, and Kinesthetic strengths you will be able to bring various strategies into play to make the acquisition of information easier than ever before.

3. Searching Out the Meaning.

To commit information to *permanent* memory requires that you search out the implications and significance—the full meaning—by thoroughly exploring the subject material. There's a big difference between *knowing* about something and truly *understanding* it. Turning mere facts into personal meaning is the central element in learning.

All too often we attempt to memorize information so it can be regurgitated to pass a test without any real attempt to understand what it really means. Facts don't require much interpretation. That's why multiple-choice testing is such a weak method. It only tests the acquisition of facts (i.e., what we cover in Stage Two of our Learning Model). But it doesn't test whether you've created your own personal meaning from those facts. You don't, for instance, have to understand that Paris is the capital of France—you just have to remember it. It's a comparatively low level of learning performance.

No one will pay you very much for having "mastered" this type of skill. In the same way, knowing that the date of the French Revolution is 1789 is factual. But understanding **why** the French Revolution was important and how it influenced European and American history requires interpretation. It requires you to respond to a jungle of information and make sense of it. That's a skill for which the world pays handsomely. The distinction between fact finding and "meaning making" is what distinguishes shallow from deep learning.

Turning facts into meaning is where your eight intelligences come into play. Each is a resource upon which you can draw as you explore and interpret the facts of the subject.

4. Triggering the Memory.

Very often there is a large amount to remember in a subject. You now need to make sure that the subject matter is locked into your long-term memory.

Conscientiously apply all of the previous steps and you will have truly learned the subject because you understand it. But you also have to be sure to "lock it down" so that you can recall it on demand.

There are numerous memory techniques detailed in Chapter 7—the kind of strategies used most effectively by the professional "memory men" who astound audiences around the world on TV and stage. They include the use of association, categorization, storytelling, acronyms, flash cards, learning maps, music, and review.

5. Exhibiting What You Know.

How do you know you've really understood what you've learned? First of all, you can test yourself—prove to yourself that you fully know the subject, that you have a deep, not surface, knowledge.

Better still, try sharing the information with a learning partner or a "study buddy." Rehearse a presentation in your mind, or on paper, and then try teaching it. It's easy to think you've understood something, only to find you can't explain it to someone else. If you can "teach" it, you're really showing that you fully comprehend it. You don't just know it—you "own" it.

Using these five steps should become a matter of habit. But to make that happen you need to practice them over and over again. You need to actively seek situations in which you can implement them and test yourself.

6. Reflecting on How You've Learned.

You need to reflect on the learning experience. Not upon what you learned, but *how* you learned it. What lessons can you draw for the next time?

In this step you are examining the process of your own learning and reaching conclusions on which techniques and ideas work best for you. Gradually, you evolve an approach to learning that's custom-made for your own unique brain. And you're in control—you've become a self-managed learner.

The final step in your learning plan is to stop and reflect and ask yourself:

- How is the learning task going?
- How could it have gone better?
- What's the significance of this for me?

This is, in reality, the final step of a "learning loop." Reviewing and reflecting on the learning experience can help you convert any stumbling block into a stepping-stone. You'll be able to drop ideas that don't work and experiment with new ones. You can begin the next learning undertaking with the benefit of your self-analysis.

As a result you will have discovered the customized method of learning that works best for the unique individual that is you. Think of your true potential like a combination lock. Once you've learned your personal combination of intelligences and learning preferences, your learning potential truly springs open.

As Brian Tracy puts it: "Accelerated Learning techniques are like the master program of a computer. They are not the program itself, but you can run all other programs on them. They are the tools you use to achieve your goals faster and with greater certainty."

Most people use only a tiny fraction of their brain's capacity, not because the capacity is not there, but simply because they have not been taught how to use what they already have. The next six chapters will show you how to become a true master of your own mind.

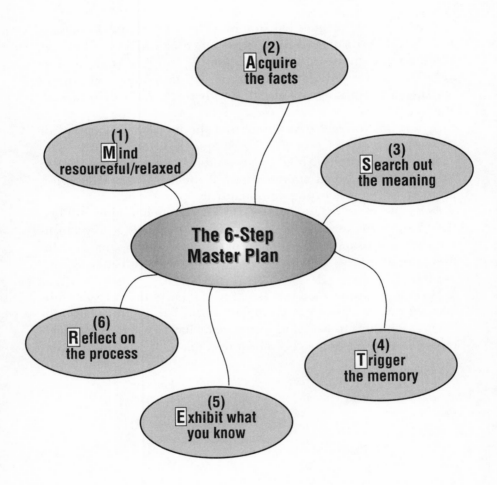

5

Getting in the Right
State of Mind

Whatever the mind can conceive and believe, the mind can achieve.
NAPOLEON HILL, AUTHOR OF *THINK AND GROW RICH*

World-class pentathlete Marilyn King lay in a hospital bed. The Olympic trials were fast approaching, but her injuries prevented her from getting out on the track.

Such a disruption at such a critical time in an intensive training schedule would have ruined the career of many a promising athlete.

But Marilyn had a secret weapon at her disposal. She dared to imagine. She practiced in her mind—because she couldn't practice on the field.

From the confines of her hospital bed she substituted mental imagery for physical training. Over and over in her head she reran her winning performances, imagined herself actually training—and going on to compete in the Olympics.

Amazingly, when she did resume "real" training, her coach said she was almost completely fit. She had developed her powers of visualization to such an extent that Marilyn's state of mind told her she was fit—and so *she was fit.*

Today, the three-time Olympic star is putting those powers to good use in the community. She is now running a "Dare to Imagine" project with at-risk students in East Oakland, California.

At the end of the first two years thirteen of the original group of fifteen were still in school and completing "success contracts"

> **A funny thing about life. If you refuse to accept anything but the best, you very often get it.**
>
> **SOMERSET MAUGHAM**

based on creating an "ideal image" and designing their own "success maps."

Like Marilyn, many world-class athletes, from all sports, have the ability to get in the right state of mind. They visualize breaking records, crossing the finishing line first, having the gold medal draped around their necks, hearing the roar of the crowd.

And such ability is certainly not limited to sports superstars. In fact, all other great achievers in life—scientists, businesspeople, politicians, educators—have a crystal-clear vision of the end result of their labors. They make a commitment to get there. They are overwhelmingly positive about their efforts. They know where they are going.

But what's the relevance to you? What has this got to do with learning? First of all, you must ask yourself if you really want to learn. Are you ready for the experience of absorbing new knowledge? Have you thought through the benefits of mastering a new subject and acquiring new skills? Do you have a positive desire to tackle the subject? Do you want to be a peak performer? Do you want to achieve your academic gold medal?

If you have a negative attitude, if you are disinclined to be receptive to what is being taught to you, if you regard learning as a necessary chore, you are almost certainly setting yourself up to fail.

It is only natural to have some doubts, fears, and uncertainties when venturing into unexplored territory, but you can overcome those predispositions—if you want to.

Sometimes it only takes a small change to make important shifts in attitude. For instance, the word *Impossible* can easily become *I'm possible* with the insertion of one small apostrophe.

You can change a negative to a positive with just one quick stoke of the pen:

— +

In a similar way, you can choose to change your feelings and attitudes toward learning. You can—and should—choose to take control of your learning, to be an active participant in your own education rather than a passive consumer. You need the will as well as the skill to learn.

And before you get started you need to know what a successful end result is going to mean to you. So now's the time to tune in to Radio Station WII-FM.

Switch to WII-FM

It stands for "What's In It For Me?"

It's not a selfish question. It's an essential first step. There is very little motivation to tackle anything if you don't perceive a positive reason for doing so. So, let's apply the question to this book. Why should you read another page? What's it going to do for you? What's in it for you?

Here's your WII-FM:

- You'll learn how to learn—a skill that will last for the rest of your lifetime. Remember, *what* you learn can become outdated, *how* to learn lasts forever.
- When you become a true Accelerated Learner you'll earn better grades or acquire skills that will improve your work performance.
- Generally speaking, the more you learn the more you earn. The better educated you become the more likely it is that you will command a higher income. You'll be more flexible, more productive, a greater asset to your current employer— and should be rewarded accordingly.
- You'll be able to help your entire family. Knowing how to learn, gaining an appreciation that each of us has a different learning style, and understanding that what works for you may not work for your partner or children, will enrich your home life and your most personal relationships.
- It's the beginning of a whole new life! Learning is an accumulative process. This book is the first important foundation stone in building your brainpower.

As Charles Handy puts it, in *The Age of Unreason,* "Those who learn best and most, and change most comfortably, are those who:

a) take responsibility for themselves and for their future;
b) have a clear view of what they want that future to be;

c) want to make sure that they get it; and

d) believe that they can."

Almost certainly, you have your own personal reasons for wanting to become an Accelerated Learner. List them now. Many people may feel inclined to skip this exercise—and carry on reading. Please don't. That would be a mistake. Thinking about—and responding to—these questions will keep you on the right track.

Posing questions to yourself, debating information presented to you, asking yourself questions such as "Does this sound right? Does this make sense?" are essential parts of learning because they maintain your attention and focus. So compile your list before continuing.

I want to improve my ability to learn because:

_____

_____

_____

_____

_____

_____

You have a positive attitude toward learning. You're motivated. You know *why* you want to learn. You have identified the benefits you are going to enjoy when you achieve your goals. What now?

Method One——Creating a Resourceful State of Mind

It's important to approach the learning process in a relaxed manner. Take a few deep breaths, filling your lungs with air, and then exhale deeply, pushing out your stomach. Consciously let your jaw and neck muscles go slack. Play some relaxing (maybe classical) music. Your brain needs to be in the right "mood."

> **To become what we are capable of becoming, is the only end of life.**
>
> **ROBERT LOUIS STEVENSON**

As you discovered in "The Awesome Brain" chapter, our

brain does not function very well when it is stressed. Tension or fear can literally make your mind go blank.

When you're relaxed, spend a few minutes visualizing what it will be like when you've become an Accelerated Learner and have achieved your personal goals.

- **See** yourself confidently tackling a future learning task.
- **Feel** a sense of pride in knowing you can master the subject.
- **Hear** the kind of approving comments people will make about your newfound abilities.

To make the most of the learning experience you need to be in a comfortable mental environment. Trying to properly absorb information while fighting your way through freeway traffic or elbow-to-elbow on a congested commuter train is not ideal. You can, of course, create your own "mental cocoon" and insulate yourself against the physical environment, but it would be preferable to find a quiet corner in your home. Kick back and relax. Take your shoes off. Put your feet up. Choose some pleasant music. (Rock may be fine for doing the housework or washing the car—but almost certainly not for learning.)

Other recommendations: Have favorite artwork on the walls. Plants on the table or floor. Fresh, clean air in your study area (or step outside for regular breaks). Natural sunlight (work close to the window). Then follow this seven-step plan.

Step 1 Recall a moment of success in your life—a time when you did something that was exceptional. Something of which you are proud.

Everyone has been successful at something. Perhaps it was a sporting event? Or when you got high marks in an examination at school—a grade higher than you had expected. Or the precise moment in a business negotiation when you realized you were getting the deal you wanted? Perhaps it was a joyous family event or an accomplishment with your favorite hobby or leisure activity? In other words: a peak moment.

Step 2 Intensify the memory. Remember exactly what it was like at that moment of success. What did you see? What did you hear? What did you feel? Use all of your senses to fill your mind with a vivid impression of your triumph.

Take some time. Avoid seeing yourself in the scene from a distance. It is essential that you look out at the successful picture through your own eyes—recreating the same exultant feeling of competence and achievement that you had at the time.

You have learned how to recall a powerful state of resourcefulness. All you need now is a way to call up that feeling, whenever you wish.

Step 3 Having recaptured your moment and feeling of peak experience, think of one word that sums up the original event. This is your "cue" word. The "cue" word is the direct link to the feeling.

Step 4 Sit up straight and straighten your body. Pull your shoulders back. Look up and take a deep breath. This is important, because at moments of peak experience we automatically breathe deeply.

Step 5 Clench your fist—a natural thing to do when you feel powerful.

Step 6 Now intensify your memory of that original experience. Close your eyes to shut out other influences. Really revel in the powerful feeling.

Step 7 Unclench your fist and open your eyes.

Repeat this seven-step sequence as often as you can over the next two days. The more you repeat the sequence, the stronger the stimulus/response pattern becomes. Later you will be able to return to this resourceful state of mind whenever you wish by merely clenching your fist and saying the "cue" word. This is not just a skill for learning, it's a skill for life.

You can use a similar approach to overcome negative feelings using a technique from a learning strategy system known as Neuro-Linguistic Programming (NLP).

You think about the event that has disturbed or embarrassed you, conjuring up the way you felt at the time. Allow yourself to really feel the unease, the nervousness, the hurt. Play it back in your mind—and feel just as uncomfortable all over again.

But now into the scene you vividly visualize a brass band marching past, playing "Seventy-six Trombones"—cymbals clashing, drums beating. This happy, upbeat, intense image begins to drown out and replace your original negative feelings. So much so that whenever you remember the unhappy event, it will now be fused with the sight and sound of the brass band. It helps turn a negative into a positive. You can invent similar upbeat scenarios to eclipse the negativity—just so you don't grow to hate brass bands!

Method Two——My Lists of Successes

So, what have you been successful at? What are your proudest moments? Recognizing one's accomplishments is an integral part of building self-confidence. You've been successful before—you can be successful again.

It's a good idea to record below your most rewarding achievements in life—from all aspects of life. Family. Social. School. Work. Sports.

Here's the kind of thing we're talking about:

- Becoming a parent and learning tolerance!
- Passing the driving test.
- Getting an A in math instead of the usual C.
- Meeting a deadline to complete a major business proposal.
- Hitting a home run.

Personal Record of Learning Successes

_____

_____

_____

_____

_____

Method Three——Positive Affirmations

You can boost your chance of success by thinking and saying really positive things about yourself—by creating and using *affirmations.* Easily satirized (most notably on *Saturday Night Live),* affirmations are widely acclaimed by those individuals willing to overcome any initial self-consciousness about using them.

You use affirmations to describe yourself as the person you would like to become. For instance:

"I am a confident learner." "I am a good manager." "I am qualified to handle the XYZ account."

You say the affirmation to yourself (or out loud) over and over again. And you make the statement in the present tense.

You don't say "I wish I were able to . . ." or even "I hope to be-

> **An affirmation is a strong, positive statement that something is *already* so.**
>
> SHAKTI GAWAIN AUTHOR OF
> *CREATIVE VISUALIZATION*

come . . ." You simply tell yourself that you are *already* capable and confident at whatever it is you desire to become. Don't make it complicated or lengthy. Short, snappy affirmations are more easily remembered—and, therefore, actualized.

Many people find it difficult to do this. After all, if you talk to yourself you must be a little crazy. Right? The same people often have no difficulty in understanding how negative comments have a very real impact on people's thoughts and behavior. If you tell people often enough that they are stupid or irresponsible, don't they come to act stupidly and irresponsibly? Negative programming works all too well. So why not "program" yourself positively?

Accentuate the positive; eliminate the negative. A catchy enough line for a jingle!

Repetition is the way to embed the affirmation into your subconscious. Try saying the affirmation to yourself frequently and at regular intervals—for example, ten times first thing in the morning; ten times at your lunch break; ten times immediately before dinner; ten times when going to bed.

Repeat the affirmation if you are confronted with a challenge to your goal. As you get more comfortable with the idea, say it out loud. And imagine how good you feel as the affirmation comes true.

SETTING CLEAR GOALS

You won't hit a target you can't see. Learning is like setting out on a journey. You need to know your final destination. And you need to know how you're going to get there.

What is it you really want in life? To achieve it you must:

1. Have a clear vision of what it is you want to achieve.
2. Have a firm belief that you can achieve that vision.

Researchers have proven that one of the common denominators of peak performers is that they possess an above-average ability to consciously practice a task in their minds, using imagery or visualization. They "start with the end in mind."

A university study of two groups of basketball players showed that one group who split their time evenly between the physical practice of free throws and mental imagery outperformed a second group who used physical practice only. Not surprisingly, both groups did better than a control group who did not practice at all.

Imagery can include all of the senses. It can mean seeing images, hearing sounds, experiencing feelings, and even smelling or tasting in the mind. Deliberately invoking all the senses becomes a powerful and effective learning tool.

If you have not previously used imagery, it can be a bit of a culture shock. But surely you have imagined something in your head that you wanted to happen? And surely you worry about things? If you worry—you are good at imagery. Because worry is imagining and acting as if something you don't want to happen has actually happened. If you can worry, you can visualize. So let's use it positively to learn.

Imagery/visualization works because the mind cannot distinguish between an actual event and one that is "only imagined." This is because the same electrochemical neural pathways in the brain are activated.

Let us give you a practical example of what we mean:

Imagine you are in the kitchen of your home. You take a fresh lemon from the fruit bowl. It is cool in your hand. The yellow dimpled skin feels waxy. The lemon comes to a small green conical point at either end. As you look at it in the palm of your hand you realize it is firm and quite heavy for its size.

You raise the lemon to your nose. It gives off such a characteristic, unmistakable citrus smell, doesn't it? You take a sharp knife and cut the lemon in half. The two halves fall apart—the white pulpy inner skin contrasting with the drops of pale lemon-colored juice that gently ooze out. The lemon smell is slightly stronger.

Now you bite deeply into the lemon and let the juice swirl around in your mouth. That sharp sour lemon flavor is unmistakable.

> **Imagination is more important than knowledge.**
>
> **ALBERT EINSTEIN**

Stop a minute! Is your mouth watering? Did you purse your lips? Maybe you winced a little? If so, you have achieved synesthesia, because you imagined the feel, sight, smell, and taste of the lemon. You have used your imagination well.

The implications are fascinating because, of course, nothing actually happened—except in your imagination! Yet your mind communicated directly to your salivary glands and told them to wash away the sour taste. You puckered your lips and grimaced.

The words you read were not reality. But they created reality. *The subconscious mind cannot differentiate between what is real and what it believes is real.*

Yet it directly controls your actions in a very tangible way.

The Will to Succeed

We talk about people having the willpower to succeed. Ask most people to define *willpower* and you will find that they use expressions such as "grim determination" or "gritting your teeth and sticking with it." There is an interesting implication in such a definition. It implies a struggle. And presumably that struggle could only be with yourself. Does that sound like a healthy state of mind?

We prefer to define willpower in this way:

WILLPOWER = A CLEAR VISION +
BELIEF IN YOUR ABILITY

A vision is important because if you don't stand for something—you can fall for anything. You need to create in your mind a successful outcome. Napoleon, for instance, played out all of his battles in his mind before they took place. He expressed it well: "Imagination is stronger than willpower."

The power of determination was vividly illustrated in a five-year study of 120 of America's top artists, athletes, and scholars, led by University of Chicago education professor Benjamin Bloom.

The key element that all the peak performers had in common was not an innate talent but an extraordinary drive and determination that came from a vision of what they would become.

We will either find a way, or make one.

HANNIBAL

Says Dr. Bloom, "We expected to find tales of great natural gifts. We didn't find that at all. Their mothers often said it was their other child who had the greater gift." But what the high achievers had was vision.

Dare to Imagine

At her "Dare to Imagine" project Marilyn King seeks to inspire her youngsters by promoting what she feels are the three traits shared by most successful people.

1. They are motivated by something that really matters to them, something they really want to do or be. King calls this "Passion."
2. They can see a goal really clearly, and they can imagine taking all the steps to achieve it: "Vision."
3. They are willing to do something each day, according to a plan, that will bring them one step closer to their dream: "Action."

Passion + Vision + Action = Success!

The former champion has students identify their passion and create the vision in their mind. Then they put a photograph or make a drawing of it in the center of a piece of paper. The students draw lines radiating from the image and they write down the traits or skills needed to achieve their vision, rating them from one to ten. The most important skill is circled. The students' success maps also include action steps needed, names of advisers and cheerleaders, obstacles that must be overcome and ways to overcome them, resources available, accomplishments and awards, and creation of a success statement. King suggests reading the statement in front of a mirror ten times, morning and evening, for ten days.

Many of her students have experienced dramatic improvement both in their schoolwork and behavior, and the program is enthusiastically supported by the mayor and local realtors. King is now training mentors for the at-risk kids and expanding the program to include many more students.

Creating Your Own Vision

Your involvement in a learning program—the fact that you're reading this book—is clear evidence that you have a desire to improve yourself and/or help others to do so. You know the rewards of learning and the penalties of ignorance.

It's essential, however, that you are now specific in the goals you wish to attain. It is simply not good enough to want to "do better." It's important to have a life plan of which your educational and career goals form an integral part.

As Gus Tuberville, president of William Penn College, puts it, "For learning to take place with any kind of efficiency, students must be motivated. To be motivated they must become interested. And they become interested when they are actively working on projects which they can relate to their values and goals in life."

What are your values and goals in life? What do you want in your relationships with the people who matter most to you—your spouse, partner, parents, children, relatives, friends, close business associates? What do you want your state of health to be? What action do you need to take to accomplish that? Do you need to change your eating and exercise habits?

What do you want to do to grow as a well-balanced person? What hobbies and sports would you like to pursue? Do you want to travel? Write? Paint? Hang-glide? Learn to play a musical instrument? What would make you feel proud? Concentrate on what you *feel* is right, rather than what you think you *ought* to do.

Your first step is to create the vision. You need to decide exactly what you want to be. You need a vision you can see clearly, a goal you can actually see yourself reaching. Beware of words such as *wish* and *try*.

When people say, "I wish I could . . ." what they really mean is "I'd like to . . . but it's too much trouble and hard work." When they say, "I'll try to . . ." what they usually mean is "I'm warning you now that I may fail."

Wish and *try* lack conviction. The only words to use are **"I will . . . !"**

Once you have your vision, your ultimate long-term goal, you need to be specific and you need to organize the steps to get you there. Write it down. It's a simple thing to do, but very powerful. Just the act of committing to paper the goal you aim to achieve makes it "real." When you put it in writing, you can't be vague. You are clearly stating your intentions.

If it's a really important goal, write it on a Post-it sticker and place it where you will see it every day.

So—you want to put together a step-by-step action plan. What do you need:

- Money? How much? Where do you get it?
- Time? How do you take time out of your already busy schedule?
- Knowledge? Where do you acquire it?
- Skills? Where do you get them from?
- Support? Who, from among your family, friends, colleagues, and superiors, can and will help you?

Making a "To Do" List

People who succeed always create a list of what they are going to do. They update it each month, each week, and often each day. The list they make is simple and it is in order of priority.

A list achieves two things. It concentrates your mind on what needs to be done in order to realize your plans and, therefore, achieve your goals. And it gives you a sense of satisfaction when you check off a task that has been completed. Sensing progress is an important part of motivation.

You should carry your "to do" list with you and prioritize it into A's, B's, and C's.

A's are "must do's."
B's are "should do's."
C's are "nice to do's."

Don't be seduced into doing C's first because they are easier. And make sure that having some fun is on your A list. Even Einstein took time out to go sailing and play the violin.

Create your own "to do" list NOW to ensure you begin working on your action Plan.

> There is no guarantee of reaching a goal at a certain time, but there is a guarantee of never attaining goals that are never set.
>
> DAVID MCNALLY IN
> EVEN EAGLES NEED A PUSH

Planning Your Time

Time is the sole capital of people whose only fortune is their intelligence.

HONORÉ DE BALZAC

We talk about going to prison as "doing time" for a very good reason. When you deprive people of their right to allocate their time, you are imprisoning them.

We talk, too, about "spending" time. Time is even more precious a commodity than money. How you invest your time determines how rich and rewarding your life is going to be. And time can't be bought. It's free. It's something we all have in common with the richest, wisest, and most powerful men and women in the world. We all have 1,440 minutes in our day and—apart from the jail inmates—we're free to decide what we do with that time.

It is one of our most valuable—if strictly limited—assets. While you can never physically create (or buy!) time, you can waste it or lose it. It is a resource you cannot renew. Time is money. Are you spending it wisely? Are you making deposits or withdrawals?

Whether you are already in the workplace or still at school, you should ask yourself, How much am I worth? How valuable is my time? What's my hourly rate? The time you spend learning something new is worth more than your regular salary. So make the most of it.

Controlling Time

Take charge! You can control your time only if you plan your time. And the time you initially take to plan will pay dividends. To control your time means recognizing that it is a limited resource and needs to be spent wisely. When we budget our financial resources, we don't find it strange to say, "I'd like to go to Hawaii, but I can't afford it." In the same way, we need to be able to say no to expenditures of time that don't meet our goals or priorities.

Ask yourself the question, Is it important or merely urgent? At first, that may sound like a silly question, but think about it. You should differentiate between the two. Here are some examples to put you in the picture:

Important but Not Urgent

- Thinking of and doing something specific each week for the people you love.

- Taking thirty minutes for physical exercise three times a week.

- Deciding what you want to achieve in life.

Urgent but Not Important

- Answering the telephone only to find it's a sales pitch.

- Unexpected visitors on your doorstep.

- A colleague at work interrupts your project to discuss last night's football game.

Do you notice the underlying difference between what is important and "merely" immediate or urgent? *You* decide what is important. *Other people* decide what is urgent. Of course, there are times when something is both urgent and important—an accident, for example.

But generally, the most important things in life are seemingly the easiest to postpone. Quite often, we allow other people's immediate needs to detract from our own schedule. We find it hard to ignore the ringing of the telephone or a work interruption, but we are able to decide to start an exercise regimen—and then postpone it. Or decide to sit down and list our goals in life and then not get around to it because "something keeps cropping up."

The answer to managing your time, rather than allowing time to manage you, is:

1. Decide what your goals are.
2. Create an Action Plan to achieve them.
3. Make a regular "to do" list that sets down your priorities.

This way, your life will have a sense of direction and purpose. The goals, of course, will not stay fixed. You will change and modify them as time goes by, but any change will be deliberate and made by you.

Three final thoughts to get the most out of your time.

> **Dost thou love life, then do not squander time, for that's the stuff life is made of.**
>
> **BENJAMIN FRANKLIN**

1. **Use "downtime."** We all have unavoidable times when we are at the mercy of someone else's schedule—while waiting for a bus or train or in the dentist's office, for instance. Make sure you use such "downtime." Just fifteen minutes a day adds up to over ninety hours in the course of a year. You could, for example, learn ten words of a foreign language during each downtime—over three thousand words in a year. (Tip: Write the words on flash cards so you can easily refer to them.)

2. **Set your own deadlines.** Have you ever noticed how people may complain about being given a deadline to accomplish a task—and then make sure they do so? Meeting a deadline becomes a triumph and a cause for celebration. It's just as important to set deadlines for yourself so that projects don't "drift." Your deadlines—and achieving those deadlines—are more important than other people's deadlines. Meeting your own personal deadlines means that you continually achieve your goals.

3. **Share your goals.** When you discuss your aspirations and specific goals with someone else, you automatically increase your own motivation. You have gone "public" with your commitment and, therefore, won't want to let yourself down. You're much more likely to achieve the goal.

So write down what you plan to learn, the date by which you will have learned it, and who is going to be your mentor. Your mentor's role is to support, advise, and motivate you. A mentor is of fundamental importance.

Catch Yourself Doing It Right

You know better than anyone else when you've done something right, when you have successfully completed a project or a task. You're much more likely to appreciate those minor accomplishments—the ones that might appear inconsequential to others.

A good manager always acknowledges and praises the successful performance of his or her subordinates. So why not congratulate yourself—especially for the seemingly trivial achievements that you can't expect others to notice? Give yourself a pat on the back in the same way that you would give others a pat on the back.

Notice and value each of your small triumphs—and praise yourself. All you need do is say something straightforward to yourself like "Hey, John, you did a good job. Well done!"

Overcoming Inertia

Discouragement blocks action. This is because discouragement is a state of low arousal. The antidote is to create a state of high arousal, playing music or a game, or running, for example.

The Ten-Second Stress Control: When stress strikes, your teeth are gritted and your whole body is tense. Try this guaranteed relaxant: Let your jaw drop, your shoulders sag, and breathe in slowly from the bottom of your stomach. Try it now—the effect is instantaneous.

The Last Word on State of Mind

You have been introduced to several practical and proven ways to create a confident yet relaxed attitude toward learning.

We call this a "resourceful" state of mind because your attitudes and feelings become a resource, a strength to draw upon. That strength replaces the apprehension that exists in so many people's minds.

In other words, you now have useful, positive methods for getting ready to learn. What underlies all these ideas is the simple, powerful belief in the possibility of change.

We may not choose the events that happen to us—but we can *always* choose how we react to those events. We can control our mind and our destiny. As Marilyn Ferguson, author of *The Aquarian Conspiracy*, puts it so well, "Your past is not your potential."

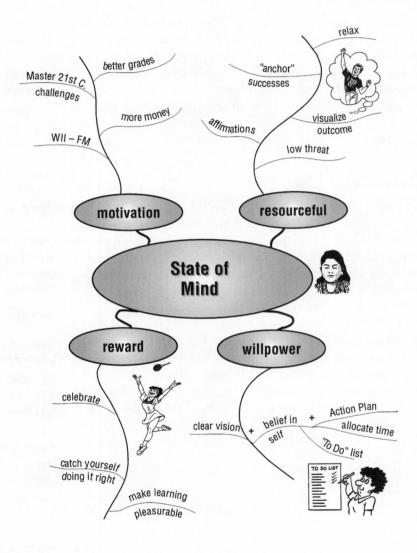

6

Acquiring the Information

Learning is not a spectator sport.
ANONYMOUS

The Dalai Lama is bending over a desk. Sunlight reflects the icy peaks of the Himalayan mountain range. With one hand the exiled Tibetan leader presses a jeweler's loupe to his eye; the other hand twirls a screwdriver inside the mechanism of an old-fashioned watch.

"It is my nature," he explains to the documentary maker. "As soon as I get a play toy . . . few minutes later, I try to open . . . see what is inside." He holds up the watch, chuckles contentedly, and says with some deliberation, straight into the camera lens: "That's the way to learn something."

Well, that's certainly one way to learn. And, as we'll discover, the eminent Dalai Lama could, therefore, be simplistically labeled as a kinesthetic learner. But it is only *one* way to learn. You may be completely different.

Have you ever consciously thought about *how* you prefer to learn?

Are you aware of the ways in which you absorb new information most effectively?

Some people, for instance, learn best when they're left to their own devices. Some people are stimulated when they have an opportunity to interact with their peers. Others find that the impact of an authority figure such as a teacher, lecturer, supervisor, or parent is more meaningful.

Some students enjoy background music; others require silence. Some need a neat, orderly work area where everything has its place; others favor the "organized chaos" of a cluttered, paper-strewn desk.

Some people prefer to sit back in a comfortable chair; others feel the need to walk around as they ponder the answer to a puzzle.

Successful learners may learn in many different ways—but the one thing they have in common is an active approach to learning. They never sit passively listening or reading. They are always asking themselves questions and doing something to ensure that they take in the facts in the way that best suits their sensory preferences.

You do need to get the facts to suit yourself. It's up to you to make sure that you acquire information in the way that you're most comfortable—in the way that gives you the best chance of attaining and remembering that new knowledge.

We will shortly explore ways to identify and work with your individual preferences, but first we will share with you some universally recommended strategies.

Get the Big Picture

One of the best approaches *everyone* can take is to get an overview of the entire project. Otherwise, it's like trying to put a jigsaw puzzle together without knowing what the picture looks like.

Let's use the reading of this book as an immediate convenient example. Flip through all the pages. Mentally note chapter headings, subheadings, illustrations. Stop and speed-read anything that particularly intrigues you. This is the way you read a newspaper. And it is an effective way to start learning. You'll form a pretty good picture of what Accelerated Learning is all about.

Establish the Core Idea

Every subject has a core idea. Once you understand it, everything else makes sense and adds to your knowledge and understanding of the subject.

For example, the core idea that makes the study of history so significant is that it helps identify recurring patterns of human behavior in order to predict the future. It is only indirectly about dates. Once you've grasped the core idea, the whole subject becomes interesting. It is like a detective novel. Learning about apparently unrelated incidents and dates is merely confusing and seems pointless.

The core idea in Accelerated Learning is found in a box on page 19. Did you spot it as the central concept around which everything else is built?

Sketch Out What You Know

Don't walk blindly into a learning experience. Make some notes to get started.

First of all, jot down what you already know. It's rare that you launch into any learning session without knowing *something* about the subject matter. Not only does the fact you have some basic knowledge work wonders for your self-confidence, but it also highlights the gaps in your knowledge. You'll then be alert for information that fills these gaps.

Record what you need to discover more about. This will make you start formulating questions in your mind, for example: "What do I need to know more about ?" You then start to look for the answers and are consequently fully involved.

One Small Step at a Time

Opening a two-hundred-page training manual can be a daunting, overwhelming experience. Many learners fail before they start because they are initially discouraged by the perceived enormity of what they are undertaking.

You deal with this by consciously breaking down what you are trying to learn into small "bite-size" segments. By devouring the information portion-by-portion you will experience a continuing number of small successes—without mental indigestion. Your motivation and confidence will remain high.

For example, if you are learning a foreign language, it is not difficult to master ten new words a day. It may not seem like much, but over the course of a year you would learn 3,650 words—

> **Through action you create your own education.**
>
> **DAVID B. ELLIS IN *BECOMING A MASTER STUDENT***

enough to give you a degree of competency in the language of your choice.

Ask. Ask. Ask.

Keep asking questions. When you find the answers, they'll be particularly significant and memorable—because they directly relate to issues you have personally raised. You'll stay interested in the subject matter while you look for the answers.

One of the first things a journalist is taught is that a story is not complete unless these questions have been answered: Who? What? When? Where? Why? How?

Applied to a learning experience you could ask:

Who is the source of the information? (Is it credible?) Who will benefit from it?

What is the meaning of . . . ? What can I do with that knowledge? What are the implications of what I'm learning?

When was this discovery made? When can it be implemented? When could I use it?

Where was the research conducted? Where will the results be utilized?

Why is there a need for this work? Why are the conclusions true?

How can I use this information? How does it impact what I'm already doing?

Continually questioning what you don't know keeps you focused.

Asking questions is also the key to continual personal growth. When you see someone who is particularly good at something, ask him how he does it. What's the secret of his success? How can you emulate it? Then put those discoveries into practice in your life. In art, there have always been "schools" of painting—apprentice painters emulating the techniques of the master by watching, asking, and imitating. It's a powerful way to learn.

Now let's begin to explore your personal learning style.

The VAK Attack

When something is explained to you, how do you respond? Are you more likely to say:

a) "I *see* what you mean" • "I get the *picture*" • "That *looks* right to me."

OR

b) "That *sounds* about right" • "I *hear* what you're saying" • "That's *music* to my ears."

OR

c) "That *feels* right." • "That hits the nail right on the head." • "I can handle that."

Perhaps you're beginning to recognize yourself? Extensive research, particularly in the United States, by Professors Ken and Rita Dunn, of St. John's University, in Jamaica, New York, and Neuro-Linguistic Programming (NLP) experts Richard Bandler, John Grinder, and Michael Grinder, has identified three distinct communication and learning styles:

a) **Visual.** Learning through seeing. We like to see pictures or diagrams. We like demonstrations or watching video.
b) **Auditory.** Learning through hearing. We like to listen to audiotapes, lectures, debates, discussions, verbal instructions.
c) **Kinesthetic.** Learning through physical activities and through direct involvement. We like to be "hands-on," moving, touching, experiencing.

All of us, to some degree, utilize *all* three types—but most people display a preference for one over the other two. A study of over five thousand students in the United States, Hong Kong, and Japan, grades 5 through 12, showed the following learning preferences:

Visual: 29 percent
Auditory: 34 percent
Kinesthetic: 37 percent

By the time they reach adulthood, however, visual preference dominates, according to Lynn O'Brien, director of Specific Diagnostic Studies of Rockville, Maryland, who conducted the study.

It is not surprising when you consider the fact that 70 percent of our body's sensory receptors are located in our eyes. To absorb light rays the retina has 120 million rods and 7 million cones, with each rod or cone focusing on a small, specific segment of the visual field.

> **Don't make me walk when I want to fly.**
>
> GALINA DOLYA, INSPIRATIONAL UK EDUCATOR

In practice, when visual aids were used to teach vocabulary, students improved up to 200 percent, according to a University of Wisconsin study.

Identifying and understanding all of the ramifications of your personal learning style—and, just as important, the styles of other people—opens the door to improved performance and more enriching experiences in all aspects of your life.

You'll be able to absorb information faster and more easily. You'll be able to identify and appreciate the way that those around you prefer to receive information. You'll be able to communicate much more effectively and boost your rapport with them. You'll be able to get on the same wavelength as people whom you never seem to understand and people who never seem to understand *you*.

To do this takes practice, persistence, and time. You have to look for things you were not seeing before, listen for things you were not hearing before, feel things you have not felt before. And ask questions you did not previously know to ask. You need to be able to match your message to the way in which the mind of the person to whom you're trying to communicate works.

What are the odds involved? According to neuro-linguistic proponent Michael Grinder, author of *Righting the Educational Conveyor Belt,* in a typical group of thirty students, twenty-two have enough Visual, Auditory, and Kinesthetic tendencies that they are able to learn *no matter how the lesson is presented.*

Two or three students have difficulty learning, regardless of the presentation style—owing to factors outside of the classroom. The others—some 20 percent of the group—favor one modality so heavily that they have extreme difficulty learning anything unless the subject is presented in their preferred mode.

Grinder refers to them as VO's, AO's, and KO's ("visual only," "auditory only," and "kinesthetic only"). And he points out, "It's not just a coincidence that the initials *KO* stand for 'knockout.' These kids are 'knocked out' of the educational system. In every study I have seen regarding 'kids at risk,' kinesthetics make up the vast majority of the twenty-six percent dropout rate."

Are you a Visual, Auditory, or Kinesthetic type?

Visual	Auditory	Kinesthetic
• Enjoys reading, watching television, going to the movies, crossword puzzles. Would rather read than be read to. May watch the expressions on your face when you speak or read to him.	• Enjoys listening to the radio, music, plays, debates. (Auditory children love having stories read to them with a lot of expression.)	• Enjoys active pursuits, both social and sporting, such as dancing and hiking.
• Remembers people by sight—"never forgets a face." Remembers words by sight and is usually good at spelling—but has a hard time remembering the order of the alphabet unless she recites it from the beginning.	• Remembers people's names. Good at recalling facts. Likes to talk and has extensive vocabulary.	• Remembers events; things that happened.
• When giving or taking directions would rather use a map.	• Gives verbal directions—"Make a left and go two blocks before turning right." Happy to receive instructions the same way.	• Gives directions by leading the way—"It's easier if you just follow me."
• Dress sense: stylish. Appearance is important. Color coordinated.	• Dress sense: The label is important! Knows who the designer is and can explain choice of clothing.	• Dress sense: Comfort and the feel of the material is more important than style.
• Reveals emotions through the expression on his face.	• Reveals emotions verbally through a change in her vocal tone.	• Reveals emotions through her body language—muscle tone/movement.
• Uses words and expressions such as: *look, see, picture,*	• Uses words and expressions such as: *sounds right, rings a*	• Uses words and expressions such as: *feels right, touch, get a*

Visual	Auditory	Kinesthetic
point of view, enlightening, perspective, reveal, appears to me, tunnel vision, clearcut, focus, bright, colorful, bird's-eye view, shortsighted, showing off, under your nose, up-front.	*bell, hear what you say, music to my ears, tell, listen, tuned in, hidden message, call on, loud and clear, idle talk, reason, afterthought, earful, express yourself, hold your tongue, manner of speaking, pay attention to, to tell the truth, tongue tied, unheard of.*	*handle on, start from scratch, lay cards on table, underhanded, grasp, grope, pull strings, boils down to, come to grips with, hand-in-hand, hold on!, sharp as a tack, stiff upper lip, topsy-turvy.*

- Creative activities: writing, drawing, painting, designing, doodling.

- Handles projects by planning ahead, looking at the overall "big picture." Organizes game plan by compiling lists. Detail oriented.

- Talks quickly—but may be quiet in class.

- Relates to others by making eye contact and by facial expression.

- During quiet time doodles or stares into space.

- Likes to conduct business on a personal face-to-face basis.

- Has very good visual recall—re-

- Creative activities: singing, telling stories, making music, telling jokes, debating, philosophizing.

- Handles projects by talking through procedures, debating problems, coming up with verbal solutions.

- Talks at a medium pace. Likes to talk—even in class.

- Relates to others through dialogue, open discussion.

- During quiet time hums or talks to himself.

- Likes to conduct business over the telephone.

- Tends to memorize well and recollect

- Creative activities: handicrafts, gardening, dancing, sports.

- Handles projects on a step-by-step basis. Likes to roll up his sleeves and get physically involved.

- Talks at a slower pace.

- Relates to others through physical contact, coming close, touching.

- During quiet time fidgets restlessly; can't sit still!

- Likes to conduct business while doing something, going for a walk, while playing golf.

- Remembers better through the use of

Visual	Auditory	Kinesthetic
membering where she left something days earlier.	spoken words and ideas.	three-dimensional learning aids, such as flash cards.
• Responds better when you show him rather than tell him.	• Responds better when hearing information rather than reading.	• Learns concepts well through being able to manipulate objects (e.g., the Dalai Lama and his watch).

The way we use words is one of the best giveaways of our preferred learning style. Compare these further examples:

Visual	Auditory	Kinesthetic
See you later.	Let's talk later.	Let's keep in touch.
It looks to me as if . . .	I'm telling myself . . .	The way I feel about it.
Clearly we have different perspectives.	He's talking out of both sides of his mouth.	I just can't get a handle on this.
I want you to take a look at this.	I want to make this loud and clear.	I want you to get a grasp on this.
I know beyond a shadow of a doubt that is true.	That information is . . . accurate word for word.	That information is . . . solid as a rock.
That is pretty hazy to me.	That does not really ring a bell.	I am not sure that I am following.

It would be extremely unusual, of course, if you found yourself positioned in just one column, because we all display some elements of all communication and learning styles. But the chances are that you will easily identify your *preferred* method.

The point is that if you use techniques that best suit your sensory preferences, you will be taking in the facts efficiently.

Of course, different learning tasks will dictate using different learning methods, so you have to be flexible. And we don't normally have a choice as to how information is presented to us. However, when you have a reper-

> **They know enough who know how to learn.**
>
> HENRY ADAMS

toire of techniques to convert the source of your information (no matter whether it's a book, video, lecture, or audiotape) to your preferred way of acquiring information—then you're going to be learning well.

Here are the main techniques. Test them all out and find the ones that work best for you. Try to use a combination of techniques, because we know that we store visual (V), auditory (A), and kinesthetic (K) memories in separate parts of the brain. So a multisensory way of learning will be the most effective. VAK it!

VISUAL STRATEGIES

LEARNING MAPS

Learning maps are a dynamic way to capture significant points of information. They use a global format, allowing information to be displayed in the same way that our brain functions—in many directions simultaneously.

Research by Robert Ornstein and others has shown that the process of thinking is a complex combination of words, pictures, scenarios, colors, and even sound and music. Thus the process of presenting and capturing lesson content in learning maps closely approximates the natural operation of thinking.

The brain can be regarded as a formidable forest hosting tens of thousands of trees with hundreds of thousands of large branches, millions of smaller branches, and billions of twigs. Learning maps are created in the same way with information stored on offshoots of the central theme—albeit on a significantly smaller scale! In creating learning maps the processing styles of the left and right hemispheres of the brain are fully involved.

When new information is absorbed using learning maps, retention is increased. The format appeals strongly to the Visual learner and the Global learner and, of course, the "emotional" brain is more involved through color. Furthermore, the information is personal—it's specific to you.

Visual note-taking, of course, has been around throughout human history. Just look at the cave paintings of primitive man and the hieroglyphics of ancient Egypt. Left to their own devices, most children sketch and doodle when presented with new ideas.

Says master artist Nancy Margulies, author of *Mapping Inner Space* and *Yes, You Can Draw,* "Before we establish language, we visualize pictures in our minds and link them to concepts. Unfortunately, we often block the creative channels by training children to write only words, monochromatically, on lined paper."

Indeed, for many of us, the traditional style of writing ideas in linear fashion, on lined paper, using one color, a monotone (usually blue, black, or gray), is a deeply ingrained habit. It also becomes monotonous—and it's no accident that *monotone* is the root of *monotonous!*

Asks Tony Buzan, developer of the learning map technique that he calls Mind Mapping, "And what does a brain do when it is bored? It tunes out, turns off, and goes to sleep. So ninety-five percent of the literate human population is making notes in a manner designed to bore themselves and others to distraction, and to send many of them off into a state of unconsciousness.

"We need only look at libraries in schools, universities, towns, and cities around the world. What are half the people doing in those libraries? Sleeping! Our places of learning are becoming giant public bedrooms!"

Retraining the brain to draw ideas radiating from a central image takes practice and patience. The trick is to practice the skill until it becomes automatic.

You will notice that a learning map allows you to record a great deal of information on one page and to show relationships among various concepts and ideas. This visual representation helps you to think about a subject in a global fashion and lends to the flexibility of your thinking. On a map you can literally see the structure of the subject in a way that isn't possible with outlines. You can see separate themes **but also the relationship between themes.** Linear *note-taking* can't keep up with our complexity of thought. *Note-making* through learning maps can.

CREATING LEARNING MAPS

Start with the Topic in the Center

Begin by putting the central theme in the middle of the page. This forces you to define the core idea of your subject—the start point of effective learning.

Keep this core central theme reasonably small so you have room to clearly display the subthemes around the center. They can be connected to the central theme by lines, like the spokes of a wheel.

Use Key Words

The point of learning maps is to capture only the essential facts that, when reviewed, will trigger recall for the whole lesson. You will find that this mainly means using key verbs and nouns. Everything else is "fill-in" information that your mind will supply when it has been "jogged" by the learning maps.

Work Outward

Work from your central theme outward in all directions. Limit your main branches to between five and seven.

Use Symbols, Colors, Words, Pictures, and Other Images

The combination of many styles makes the learning map more memorable. For added variety, vary the size of the words throughout the map. Write key words or phrases in bold capital letters. Keep the words to a minimum. Use easily identifiable symbols— crosses, check marks, exclamation points, question marks, stick men, hearts, triangles, and so on.

Make It Like a Billboard

Use plenty of white space between the information so that all of the words and images stand out. Make it bold, startling, and "memorable." Make it as outrageous as you like. Make important words jump off the page.

Make It Colorful

Highlight various key points or themes using colors that link them together. Make it as vivid as you like.

Practice Makes Perfect

Don't expect to get it right the first time. In fact, it's better if you have to redraw your learning map. Doing it a couple of times will help you remember the details.

Doing Your Own Thing

You don't have to be a graphic artist to excel in the creation of learning maps. The important thing is to develop a style of your own. By all means, use as much visual imagery as you can. Tony Buzan, for one, strongly emphasizes the need for pictorial representations.

But, to repeat, it is not necessary to have an artistic flair. It is far more meaningful to develop your personal style, to create maps that *you* can understand and which will help you embed information into your long-term memory. Try to get a little more creative with every new learning map you draw.

Learning Maps Become Memory Maps

We use the term *learning map* to describe the use of maps as input devices. We use the term *memory map* to describe their creation and use as revision or summary devices.

Why Learning Maps Make Sense

You'll save time because you will only be noting—and subsequently reading and reviewing—key words rather than sifting through unnecessary or peripheral material. The connections between various points will also be clearer. And the visual, multifaceted nature of the maps makes it easier for your brain to absorb and remember. That's why we end each chapter with a summary memory map.

Use a Hi-Liter Pen

If the book is your own, using a Hi-Liter can be helpful. When you look back on the material a day, a month, or even a year, later, you will have highlighted the important bits of **new** information.

Notice the emphasis on the word *new.* Many people highlight all the important ideas in a paragraph. That sounds logical, but it isn't. The point about learning is that you are acquiring **new** information or **new** ways of looking at old information.

So to highlight something you already know is only going to increase your work when you come back for a quick review later. And a quick review of what you have been learning is an essential part of really "locking it all down."

Result? You can review your knowledge of a whole book in fifteen minutes or so.

Sit Quietly and Visualize

Most of us need to sit and think quietly over what we have just seen, read or heard. Go over it in your mind's eye and make a "mental movie" of it. It's a bit like an instant replay in a sports program. It helps to store the information in your visual memory.

TWA flight attendants taking a safety test used images to boost their pass rate from 70 percent to 100 percent with the following sequence.

1. They toured the plane, noting the safety locations.
2. Then they identified on diagrams the locations they could remember.
3. They checked them against the master diagram.
4. They then sat, closed their eyes, and visualized the original tour in their mind's eye. Finally, they filled in the location diagram again.

How can **you** add mental imagery the next time you learn something?

Simply Draw It

Very often the simplest visual strategy is to draw a sketch or design a chart, graph, or diagram.

AUDITORY STRATEGIES

Read It Dramatically

We remember what's dramatic. A pastel floral dress may be pretty, but it probably isn't memorable. A single crimson flower on a black dress would be memorable.

Just as visual images can be memorable, so can sound. So if a passage is crucial or difficult, try reading it out loud dramatically. You can use a foreign accent or whisper it. (We often whisper what's important!)

Putting this kind of auditory emphasis into the material will definitely help imprint it in your mind.

Summarize It Out Loud

Do you remember the statistics we have quoted so far? We tend to remember more than twice as much of what we say aloud as of what we merely read.

So stop regularly and summarize out loud passages that you read in this book. The sound of your own voice adds to the memorability. Tape recorders are great for auditory learners. Tape your summary notes and play them in the car.

Dr. Win Wenger of Project Renaissance in Gaithersburg, Maryland, makes the observation that a key to learning is what he calls detailed articulation. The very act of describing something that is new to you sharpens your perception and memory of it. The more detail you uncover, the more associations you form and the easier it is to remember.

Dr. Wenger recommends that when you read something new, you should close your eyes and then describe what you've learned out loud. The reason it works so well is that you will have read it, visualized it (when you recalled it with your eyes shut), and described it out loud. So you've automatically learned and stored it in a multisensory way. Simple but powerful.

> **If I could say it, I wouldn't have to dance it.**
>
> ISADORA DUNCAN

KINESTHETIC STRATEGIES

Walk About While You Read or Listen

At school we were usually told not to fidget. That was before we realized that learners with a preference for physical learning **need** some way to express that preference.

Try walking about. Certainly get up and move every twenty-five to thirty minutes. Doodle, underline in color, jot notes, and make learning maps. If it's appropriate to the subject, draw a chart or graph or even stop and mock up a simple model.

Experiment with how much **you** need a physical element for the way in which you assimilate information. For example, a desk or table may not work as well for you as a lap board.

Make Notes on Post-its or Index Cards

Stationary shops sell Post-its—the little yellow sheets of paper made up into pads. Each small square sheet has a sticky patch on the back.

Because these yellow Post-its are small, they force you to reduce your notes to a very brief form. The key words jump out at you when you look back at them. If you stick them all on a large sheet of paper in logical order, they allow you to sort out your thoughts physically.

Index cards work equally well. And you can put them on the wall as reminders.

Write

Writing and any form of note-taking converts auditory input (a lecture) into a physical form.

Learn in Groups

Probably the single best learning strategy is cooperative learning—learning with someone else or in

> **Ah. If you could dance all that you've just said, then I'd understand.**
>
> **NIKOS KAZANZTAKIS IN**
> ***ZORBA THE GREEK***

a group. There's a considerable amount of information about group learning in Chapter 18, "Accelerated Teaching," and Chapter 19, "Corporate Learning."

Tick It Off

If you have a textbook or large instruction manual to tackle, make a light pencil mark at the end of each paragraph to show that you have fully understood it. This is a sort of signal to your brain to lock that information away. What's more, you can identify exactly where it was you started to get lost. Just after the last tick!

Reread

It's a **good** thing to read and reread a difficult passage. Sometimes read aloud. Instead of feeling overwhelmed by a whole chapter, you can concentrate on understanding small chunks at a time.

Even people who have learned the most complex subjects start with the simple basics and work up.

THE VAK ATTACK STRATEGY

The best idea is to find a combination of ways to learn. Multisensory learning can be as simple as:

- Read and visualize the material....................you have **seen** it.
- Make up questions and record the answers aloud................. you have **heard** it.
- Write out the major points on index cards and arrange them in a logical order....................you have **physically** handled it.

Spelling

It has been discovered that good spellers **invariably** bring to mind an image of the word (V) and can "feel" (K) if it is right. Bad spellers don't use this sequence. Instead, they try to check the work phonetically (A) and—with English—that is a poor predictor of correct spelling!

Consequently, it is much more productive to teach a bad speller the sequence of V, then K, than it is to ask him or her to laboriously memorize the specific spelling of thousands of words. You have then taught the correct principle, and that principle holds true in thousands of different situations.

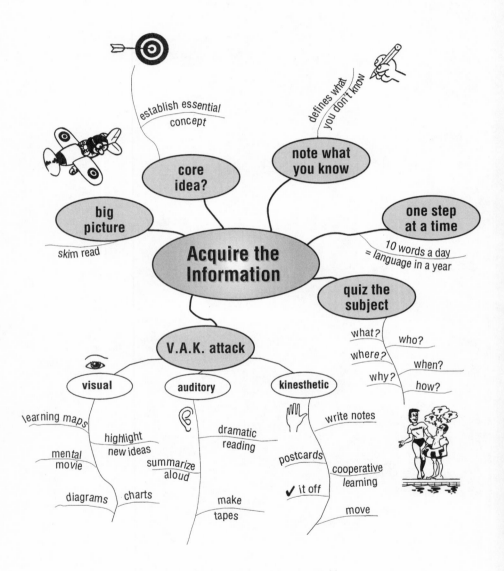

7

Searching Out the Meaning

A person who has a cat by the tail knows a whole lot more
about cats than someone who has just read about them.
MARK TWAIN

FBI chief J. Edgar Hoover was one
of the most feared men in America. He dominated the crime-fighting agency during his long reign, ruling with an iron fist that could
not be ignored. To risk the wrath of Hoover was to risk "exile" to
the least-desired postings in the Midwest.

Renowned for being fastidious, Hoover demanded neatness in
all of his correspondence. On one occasion he was infuriated by
the sloppiness of a memo he had received concerning the potential danger of terrorist groups in U.S. cities. It was badly typed and
the margins poorly laid out.

Hoover, therefore, wrote the vital instruction *Watch the borders*
across the top of the page and dispatched the memo back to the
offending executive. Hoover's command was quickly obeyed.
Within two weeks hundreds of FBI agents were staking out the
Mexican and Canadian frontiers!

The moral of the story is that taking a subject at face value, without stopping to ask or explore what it really means, can be very
costly. Unlike Hoover's unfortunate subordinates you need to fully
explore information to get the right message.

And to fully search through information it is necessary to use
ways that suit your unique combination of intelligences. This way

you will be using your full range of mental powers—using whole-brain Accelerated Learning.

Do you remember your eight intelligences from Chapter Two, "The Awesome Brain"? Well, they represent your "team" of eight ways to explore and fully understand anything you're trying to learn.

PUTTING YOUR EIGHT INTELLIGENCES TO WORK

Consciously developing and using your full range of intelligences leads to balanced learning—learning that not only suits your current strengths but that also enables you to develop and grow as a person.

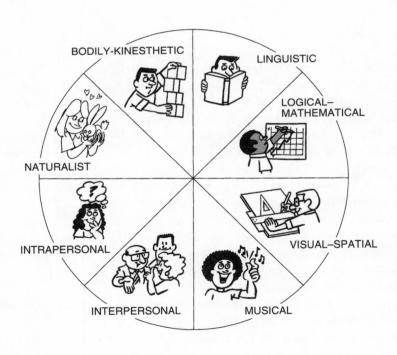

Using your full range of intelligences will also prompt you to think in new ways. The result is that you can become more creative.

Schoolteachers and corporate trainers typically impart knowledge using linguistic and logical-mathematical intelligences. So, if your brain is naturally inclined to function best through the use of words and figures, you are more likely to do well in a formal education environment.

If you like a teaching style that reveals subject matter bit by bit in a logical, step-by-step manner, you will like the way most textbooks and lectures are formatted.

If these approaches *don't* suit you, you are not well served by traditional teaching—what Howard Gardner calls "the single-chance theory of education." When the material is available or delivered in such a way as to engage all or most of the eight intelligences, there is, says Gardner, a "multiple chance" to understand it.

You need to explore the learning process using the forms of intelligence that you prefer—even if the educator is not catering to your needs—to create "deep" rather than "surface" learning.

"The 'single chance' practice of education has resulted in a depressingly large number of people who have concluded that they have little talent for learning," says Gardner.

A powerful way to learn is to use *as many* of your intelligences as is practically possible. This way you experience what you are learning in a well-rounded way.

Teachers don't have to worry about identifying each individual student's preferred learning style. That would be too much to ask! Instead they should cycle through a range of activities incorporating as many of the intelligences as they possibly can.

This way they should be reaching out to their entire class—not just to those whose intelligences are predominantly linguistic and logical-mathematical. But at the same time as they are reaching wide, they are also teaching in-depth, because each person has several ways to "get it."

> **It is increasingly difficult for traditional teaching techniques to capture and hold the interest of a child who has been reared on video games and MTV.**
>
> **LINDA A. TSANTIS, PhD, IN**
> **CREATING THE FUTURE**

THE MI QUIZ

Which of the intelligences do you favor? What are your strengths?

By answering the following questions you will be able to gauge which forms of intelligence are your strongest—and weakest. This will enable you to focus on making sure you make the most of your existing abilities and—if you so desire—see if you can develop some of the others.

Let us emphasize again that most of us have a mixed portfolio of intelligences and that there is no purpose in trying to simply label someone as a "logical-mathematical" type or a "bodily-kinesthetic" type. The checklist is designed to help you develop a fuller appreciation of the intelligences you enjoy.

Check each statement that applies to you and add the totals.

Linguistic

1. You enjoy wordplay. Making puns, tongue-twisters, limericks. You enjoy poems, stories, and rhymes.
2. You read everything—books, magazines, newspapers, even product labels.
3. You can easily and confidently express yourself either orally or in writing, i.e., you're a persuasive debater and a good storyteller or writer.
4. You pepper your conversation with frequent allusions to things you've read or heard.
5. You like to do crosswords, play Scrabble, or have a go at other word puzzles. You can spell well.
6. You have such an excellent vocabulary that people sometimes have to ask you to explain a word you've used. You enjoy using the precise word in context.
7. In school you preferred subjects such as English, (language and literature) history, and social studies. You are conscious of the need to build your child's vocabulary.
8. You can hold your own in verbal arguments or debates, and you give clear directions and explanations.
9. You like to "think aloud," to talk through problems, explain solutions, ask questions.

10. You can readily absorb information by listening to the radio or audiocassettes or lectures. The words are easily imprinted in your mind.

Total:

Logical-Mathematical

1. You enjoy working with numbers and can do mental calculations.
2. You're interested in new scientific advances, and like to experiment with things to see how they work.
3. You can easily balance your checkbook; do the household budget. You create numerical targets in your business and private life.
4. You like to put together a detailed itinerary for vacations or business trips. You often prepare, number, and implement a to-do list.
5. You enjoy the challenge of brainteasers or other puzzles and games that require logical and statistical thinking, e.g., checkers, chess.
6. You tend to readily identify the logical flaws in things people say and do.
7. Math and science were among your favorite subjects in school.
8. You can find specific examples to support a general point of view, and feel comfortable analyzing situations and arguments.
9. You take a systematic, step-by-step approach to problem-solving. You like to find patterns and relationships between objects or numbers.
10. You need to categorize, group, or quantify things to properly appreciate their relevance.

Total:

Visual-Spatial

1. You have an appreciation of the visual arts and enjoy painting and sculpture. You have a good color sense.
2. You tend to make a visual record of events with a camera or camcorder.
3. You find yourself doodling when taking notes or thinking through something. You can draw quite accurately.

4. You have no problem reading maps and navigating. You have a good sense of direction.
5. You enjoy games such as jigsaw puzzles and mazes.
6. You're quite adept at taking things apart and putting them back together. You can assemble kits quite easily and can follow diagrams to do so.
7. In school you liked lessons in art and preferred geometry to algebra.
8. You often make your point by providing a diagram or drawing and can interpret charts easily.
9. You can visualize how things look from a different perspective or how a building might look from a plan.
10. You prefer reading material that is heavily illustrated.

Total:

Bodily-Kinesthetic

1. You take part in a sport or regularly perform some kind of physical exercise. You enjoy walks, swimming, and the sensation of using your body.
2. You're quite adept at "do-it-yourself."
3. You like to think through problems while engaged in a physical pursuit such as walking or running.
4. You don't mind getting up on the dance floor.
5. You like the most thrilling, body-contorting rides at the fun fair.
6. You need to physically handle something, to grasp it and manipulate it, to fully understand it. You enjoy jigsaws and model-making.
7. The most enjoyable classes in school were sports, PE, and any handicrafts lessons. You enjoy sculpture as an art form.
8. You use hand gestures or other kinds of body language to express yourself.
9. You like rough-and-tumble play with children.
10. You need to tackle a new learning experience "hands on" rather than by reading a manual or watching a video.

Total:

Musical

1. You can play a musical instrument.
2. You can manage to sing on key.

3. Usually you can remember a tune after hearing it just a couple of times.
4. You often listen to music at home and in your car, and you sometimes go to concerts. You like—even need—a musical background when you're working.
5. You find yourself tapping in time to music. You have a good sense of rhythm.
6. You can identify the sounds of different musical instruments.
7. Theme music or commercial jingles often pop into your head.
8. You can't imagine life without music. You find that music easily evokes emotions and images for you as you listen to it.
9. You often whistle or hum a tune.
10. You often use rhythm (or rhyme) to remember things, e.g., saying a telephone number rhythmically.

Total:

Interpersonal

1. You enjoy working with other people as part of a group or committee.
2. You take great pride in being a mentor or advisor to someone else.
3. People tend to come to you for advice. You could describe yourself as sympathetic.
4. You prefer team sports—such as basketball, softball, soccer, football—to individual sports such as swimming and running.
5. You like games involving other people—bridge, Monopoly, Trivial Pursuit.
6. You're a social butterfly. You would much prefer to be at a party than home alone watching television.
7. You have several very close personal friends.
8. You communicate well with people and can help resolve disputes.
9. You have no hesitation in taking the lead; showing other people how to get things done.
10. You talk over problems with others rather than trying to resolve them by yourself.

Total:

Intrapersonal

1. You keep a personal diary or log to record your innermost thoughts.
2. You often spend "quiet time" reflecting on the important issues in your life.
3. You have set your own goals—you know where you're going.
4. You are an independent thinker—you know your own mind, make up your own mind.
5. You have a private hobby or interest that you don't really share with anyone else.
6. You like to go fishing by yourself or take a solitary hike. You're happy with your own company.
7. Your idea of a good vacation is an isolated hilltop cabin rather than a five-star resort and lots of people.
8. You have a realistic idea of your own strengths and weaknesses.
9. You have attended self-improvement workshops or been through some kind of counseling to learn more about yourself.
10. You work for yourself—or have seriously contemplated "doing your own thing."

Total:

Naturalist

1. You keep or like pets.
2. You can recognize and name many different type of trees, flowers, and plants.
3. You have an interest in and good knowledge of how the body works—where the main internal organs are, for example—and you keep abreast of health issues.
4. You are conscious of tracks, nests, and wildlife on a walk and can "read" weather signs.
5. You could envision yourself as a farmer, or maybe you like to fish.
6. You are a keen gardener and are familiar with the effects of the seasons.
7. You have an understanding of, and interest in, the main global environmental issues.

8. You keep reasonably informed about developments in astronomy, the origins of the universe, and the evolution of life.

9. You are interested in social issues, psychology, and human motivations.

10. You consider that conservation of resources and achieving sustainable growth are two of the biggest issues of our times.

Total:

Compare the totals from all eight intelligences and you will readily see your greatest strengths and weaknesses. The higher your score, the more you favor that particular intelligence.

EIGHT WAYS TO EXPLORE WHAT YOU ARE LEARNING

Linguistic Exploration

Your words are more powerful than anyone else's. You are obviously more attuned to the way you prefer to describe situations and events. It is hard to learn a series of words written by someone else—the lines of a play or a poem, for instance. Learning the words "parrot fashion" certainly does not mean that you understand them either.

But "translating" what you have heard or read into your own words not only proves to yourself that you understand the subject, it also means that you are more likely to remember it long-term.

Why not start right now by putting into your own words what you have already learned about Accelerated Learning? Here are some ways to make it easier.

1. "Brainstorm" all of the key points. Talk into a tape recorder, saying everything that springs to mind so far. Or just write the key points down. Then, feel free to skim through the pages of this book to jog your memory and add further thoughts. Be sure to put these into your own words. Don't copy verbatim. You will now have a list of key points. Organize them in any

> **An ounce of experience is worth a ton of theory.**
>
> BENJAMIN FRANKLIN

way that is meaningful to you. Write them on flash cards, for instance.

2. Write a newspaper article. Pretend that you have to write a story for your local paper explaining the main concepts of Accelerated Learning. Create the headline first, e.g., "Learning Secrets Exposed!" Then write a punchy introduction . . . "You can unleash the genius in you through a six-step master plan that says . . ." etc. Alternatively, write a letter to a friend explaining what Accelerated Learning is all about and how it is changing your attitude toward learning and how it can do the same for her.

3. Fill in the following section with a short summary of what you have discovered about the three stages of learning we have covered so far. Making a summary is a very useful skill, because you have to reduce what you have learned to its core essentials. That means deciding what is really important. This entails a deeper level of thinking about the subject, which leads to better memory.

Getting in the Right State of Mind

_____

_____

_____

_____

Acquiring the Information

_____

_____

_____

_____

Searching Out the Meaning

_____

_____

_____

_____

Logical-Mathematical Exploration

List the main points of what you are learning in a logical, numbered sequence. The very act of selecting the key points means that you have to think carefully about what you are learning.

Analyze what you are learning. Don't take anything at face value—go beneath the surface. The following systematic approach should help. Use the vowels A•E•I•O•U to remember the following five questions.

A   1. What _Assumptions_ are being made? Has anything been taken for granted? Has anything been left out? Has the author used an isolated example to arrive at a general or sweeping conclusion?

E   2. What's the _Evidence_ for this? Are we dealing with facts or opinion? If it's opinion, can I trust the source? If it's fact, is this always true? What other explanation could there be? If this is true, what else follows?

I   3. Can I think of a good _Illustration_ or example of this? Does this fit any other category or class of things I'm familiar with? Is what I'm reading or hearing consistent with my experience?

O   4. What _Opinions_ or conclusions can I draw about this? Are they justified?

U   5. What are the _Unique_ points in this? What are the key and new points? What is essential to know—and what is just padding?

These questions make sure you always stop and think about what you're learning, rather than jump to initial conclusions. You can also make a flow chart or diagram that expresses in a step-by-step manner what you are learning.

Visual-Spatial Exploration

Throughout this book at the end of each chapter you are presented with a Learning Map—a powerful visual reminder of what you have learned.

The Learning Map is even more dynamic when you create it yourself. When you lay out the information yourself, it is personal and much more meaningful to you as a unique individual. It becomes yours. You "own" it.

Why not make a large Learning Map right now of everything you have gleaned to date from reading this book? Leave plenty of white space so you can insert new information from upcoming chapters.

Alternatively, it can be very effective to simply make a brief sketch of something you're learning. Many mathematical problems are also easier to solve when you find a way to visualize them.

Other visual explorations include designing a colored poster, a cartoon, making a video, or a timeline. Use symbols instead of words.

And certainly don't forget the impact of visualization.

Bodily-Kinesthetic Exploration

Some people just don't learn very well when they are forced to sit still. They need to be more physically involved in the learning process.

For them, acting out what they are learning allows them to turn theory into something more memorable. "Role play" helps them explore material in a way that is meaningful to them. It's especially important to switch roles so you can see the world from the other person's perspective.

This is hardly surprising. It is generally accepted that only about 20 percent of what we communicate is the content of what is said—the words. Up to 80 percent is nonverbal—the tone of how it is said and the accompanying body language. It follows that there will be many concepts that are truly understandable only if we add a nonverbal element to the explanation. Let's look at two examples to make the point.

We "know" that the moon affects the tides because the physical mass of the moon creates a gravitational pull. But do we really understand how? Or, put another way: we've "found the facts" but have we "made the meaning"? Try this now.

Assuming you are wearing a shirt or a blouse with a sleeve, hold your right arm out. Now pull your sleeve firmly upward at about the elbow and watch what happens at the cuff. The sleeve moves up your arm, doesn't it? This is exactly what happens when the moon goes over the middle of the ocean. The mass of the moon creates a gravitational force that **pulls** the water upward in the center of the ocean. Result? Water at the edge of the sea flows outward, **and the tide goes out.** When the moon moves away again, the gravitational pull disappears, the "bump" in the sea flattens out, and the tide flows back in again.

Which was more powerful, the words or the physical representation?

Peter Kline is a brilliant Accelerated Learning trainer. In his book *Ten Steps to a Learning Organization,* written with Bernard Saunders, he introduces the idea of "Kinesthetic Modeling" to help illuminate relationships in companies. The idea is simple; the impact is profound.

How do you get people to understand how the separate departments in a company all relate to one another? Using kinesthetic modeling in a seminar, you might challenge people to role-play the processing of an order from a customer. Each delegate would represent one department (or one process) between the arrival of the order and its ultimate dispatch. The acting out and description of what's happening by the participants illuminates not just the process, but the hidden relationships, and what can go wrong.

When one person describes something to another, he is trying to translate his mental picture of that subject into words—so it is already a secondhand representation. Then, he hopes that the words he uses will mean exactly the same to the other person as they do to him—in order for the other person to have the same mental picture. Of course, the words often do not translate to the same image, which is the cause of so much misunderstanding.

If you find a way to pictorialize the idea, you have cut down the chance of miscommunication. Better still, if you find a way that the other person can also **experience** the idea—then you can both share the same experience of an otherwise abstract idea. That's why role play and kinesthetic modeling are so important.

When we have used a similar process, we have found that the greatest value is the challenge of finding a way to physically model a process or a complex set of relationships. At first it can be difficult, but the effort of working out how to do it produces deep insights and lasting memories.

Not for nothing did Confucius say:

"I hear and I forget. I see and I understand. I do and I remember."

You can also use role play to uncover attitudes. Peter Kline gives a good example of how he invited members of a team to silently position themselves in relationship to one another to represent their feelings of how they were working as a team.

As they formed their "tableau," each person was to think about what was happening and what the positioning of his or her body vis-à-vis the others meant. Were they grouping in a circle? Or a hierarchical structure? Were they shaking hands? At the end each person was invited to contribute his observations on a flip chart.

After a break the same group was now asked to model how they would like their team to operate in the future. After modeling the new "tableau" they were again invited to explain their thoughts and feelings on the flip chart. The difference between what had been and what could be thus became a shared learning experience. It helped to bring their ideas for improvement dramatically to life in a way that no "mere words" could do.

"Actions," as Peter Kline and Bernard Saunders say, "often speak not only more loudly but more clearly than words."

We learn best from doing and observing—yet most teaching uses abstract words.

Sometimes the role play can be very specific—acting out words and phrases when learning a foreign language, for instance. Role play is also good for learning history. Imagine you are the character you are learning about. What would he or she say, do, feel, see? Talk about that person in the first person. "I am Henry VIII. I have had six wives."

There are many other ways to physically explore a subject. You could write all of these explorations on a large sheet of paper and cut it into irregular shapes. By piecing the paper back together—

like assembling a jigsaw puzzle—you then get to see how everything "fits together."

You could also make up index cards of the main ideas and sort them into a logical sequence. Carry them with you and refer to them from time to time. Or you could pin the cards on a notice board and look at them regularly.

Writing is a physical exercise, so we should not be surprised that when we write something down, we learn it better. We have added a physical element (writing) to sight (reading) and sound (inner speech). There are also many other examples of how physical representation can boost learning in Chapter 16, "Successful Schooling: The Theory."

As an interesting side note, there appears to be the beginning of an appreciation of bodily-kinesthetic intelligence in its own right.

In the UK, the Associated Examining Board (AEB) is now offering A-levels (the exams taken as a prerequisite for university entrance) in physical education and sports studies.

Says George Turnbull of the AEB, "If you are good at mathematics, you take an A-level in it. We see nothing wrong applying the same principle to sports such as football."

Adds Kevin Wesson, who helped design the soccer syllabus, "I believe this will be one of the harder A-levels. In physics you study only one subject. In football you are combining practical ability and theory of the sport with science as well. It will be tough."

There is some criticism, of course, from educational traditionalists who don't regard this as a sign of intelligence.

Musical Exploration

Music is a much more powerful learning tool than is normally appreciated.

Think how many songs you know—yet have never consciously learned. Often you only need to hear the first few bars to trigger the words of an entire song. Radio and television commercials use catchy jingles that you just can't get out of your head.

> "Why," said the dodo, "the best way to explain it is to do it!"
>
> LEWIS CARROLL IN
> ALICE IN WONDERLAND

All human interactions are opportunities to learn or to teach.

M. SCOTT PECK, AUTHOR OF
THE ROAD LESS TRAVELLED

The melodic and rhythmic patterns of the music really ease the task of remembering. Music stimulates the emotional center of our brains, and as you've discovered, our emotions are strongly linked to our long-term memory. So playing some background music—especially quiet classical music—is a very effective strategy for many people.

You don't have to be musically gifted to benefit from musical exploration. The important thing is that you're doing it yourself so it is relevant to you. Here are some ways to learn via music.

1. Choose a memorable jingle from a radio or TV advertisement. Take some key information that you've already read in this book and try to fit it to the jingle.
2. Listen to some rap songs and notice how the words are just chanted to the rhythm of the music. At first, try reading actual points from the book. Once you're comfortable doing that, invent some simple verses of your own. Children seem to have a natural knack for doing this—so ask them to help!
3. Make up some simple verses about the Accelerated Learning process. The rhythmic quality of the words will help you learn.
4. Take a well-known song and write your own words to the familiar melody.

It is interesting to note that exploring a subject through one's musical intelligence is one that many people find a little strange. Yet years ago, before the advent of newspapers, radio, and then television, it was common for knowledge to be passed from generation to generation in rhymes and song. Even today, some cultures such as the Maoris of New Zealand pass down much of their history in song.

Research from test schools indicates that when one hour of music, art, and drama is added to the timetable, grades in ALL the other subjects can be improved by as much as 20 percent.

Interpersonal Exploration

Discussing what you are learning is an excellent way to check your understanding of something new. You will also gain from the other person's experiences, insights, and views. It is particularly helpful if the other person can ask you questions and even challenge your opinions.

> **Many ideas grow better when transplanted into another mind than in the one where they sprang up.**
>
> OLIVER WENDELL HOLMES, JR.

We suggest you encourage friends or colleagues to get together on an informal basis—perhaps, at coffee breaks or mealtimes. Casually discuss what you have learned: "I found this interesting . . . what do you think?" Prompt open debate by asking someone to share points of disagreement.

As Stephen R. Covey says in *The 7 Habits of Highly Effective People,* "The person who is truly effective has the humility and reverence to recognize his own perceptual limitations and to appreciate the rich resources available through interaction with the hearts and minds of other human beings. That person values the differences because those differences add to his knowledge, to his understanding of reality. When we're left to our own experiences, we constantly suffer from a shortage of data."

All of this highlights an important element. Learning does not have to take place in a formal environment while sitting in a classroom. Some of the most valuable learning of all can take place sitting around a family dinner table. You could do nothing more valuable for your family than to regularly discuss what each of you is doing, and how you can all learn from these experiences.

Find a study buddy; interpersonal exploration can be conducted very efficiently on a one-to-one basis. Team up with a colleague or school friend. You each agree to learn the same section or chapter independently. When you next meet, summarize to each other what you have learned and note and discuss differing interpretations.

Full-time students: Involve your parents—they will quite probably bring an entirely different perspective to what you're learning.

Parents: Ask your children what they think of some of the ideas in the Accelerated Learning program. If they're being taught the "traditional" way, it will be a real eye-opener for them.

Intrapersonal Exploration

What is your favorite hobby? Whatever it is, no one had to pressure you to learn how to do it. You had a built-in desire. You had an extremely personal interest. But what can you do when you're faced with a subject that you find boring?

In one study students' memory for paintings was tested. Some just looked at the artwork; others were given information about the paintings and the painter. The latter group remembered the paintings twice as well.

They remembered better because they created their own interest in the subject by digging deeper. They did not take it at face value. They explored the subject on a personal level. They were able to reflect on the material, weighing it up in their mind.

Ponder all of the aspects that went into the subject you are studying. What was in the mind of the creator or the developer? What makes his work so different? What new technique was used? What were the steps she went through before reaching her ultimate conclusion?

If, for example, you're reviewing an historical event, visualize the personalities who were instrumental in making political or social changes. Approach it as you would a novel, looking for the ambition, power struggles, weaknesses, strengths, loves, hates, and quirks of character of the people involved.

Get your emotional brain involved. Ask yourself which side you would have supported: allow yourself likes and dislikes. If you start thinking of history in terms of characters, headlines, and political skulduggery, it also becomes real. Look how much history people learn by reading the fact-laden historical novels of James Michener. He's an excellent history teacher!

It's entirely possible that a student accused of daydreaming is simply absorbing the lesson by personalizing it!

You always learn better if you can make the subject interesting. Ask yourself:

- Why does this matter to me?
- How can I use this idea?
- What significance can I find in this for me?

Why not ask your teacher, lecturer, or trainer what he finds so interesting about the subject you are studying? After all, he chose to do it full time, so he should be able to share his passion with you.

And keep a diary or a "learning log" recording your personal reactions to the information you are learning. Make notes evaluating how it has helped you toward your goals. How may your future be changed by it? Reflect—and learn.

Howard Gardner says that in the school system not enough attention is given to intrapersonal intelligence. "Intrapersonal needs are unfortunately neglected in every area of education. It's terribly important that people living in a complex world understand themselves, their abilities, and their options," he says.

A Sign of Genius?

Have you ever noticed that a remarkable number of successful men and women kept diaries and journals and wrote detailed letters to their family and friends?

In the 1920s researcher Catherine Cox studied three hundred geniuses from history. She scrutinized the lives of luminaries such as Sir Isaac Newton, Thomas Jefferson, and Johann Sebastian Bach. One sign of genius, she noted—and that was displayed not only by aspiring writers but also by generals, statesmen, and scientists—was a predilection for eloquently recording thoughts and feelings in diaries, poems, and letters to friends and family. Starting from an early age this was a discipline that the "greats" continued throughout their lives.

Edison, for instance, produced some three million pages of notes and letters. And we're all familiar with da Vinci's multidimensional, voluminous notebooks filled with sketches and diagrams as well as his thoughts and ideas.

Researcher Dr. Win Wenger poses an interesting question: "Why did these gifted men and women start keeping diaries in the first place? Was it because they knew in advance that they would someday be famous and wanted to leave behind a record for future historians? Was their

> I shall the effect of this good lesson keep, As watchman to my heart.
>
> **WILLIAM SHAKESPEARE,**
> **HAMLET, ACT I, SCENE 3**

writing simply an irrelevant by-product of a highly expressive mind—or a highly inflated ego? Or was the scribbling, in and of itself, a mechanism by which people who were not born geniuses unconsciously nurtured and activated a superior intellect?"

Wenger favors the last interpretation and it is certainly worth thinking about!

Naturalist Exploration

We think that the naturalist intelligence offers less of a way to explore the subject than to provide an "ecological" check on the social value of what one is learning.

For example:

- What are the environmental implications of what you are learning?
- Has it any implication for conservation of resources?
- Will it help or hinder social fairness? Does it have anything to say on solving any of the major social problems of our times?
- Does it help you better understand the mind of individuals or social behavior?
- Does it exploit or harm anyone or anything else?
- Does it guide you to any action or social purpose?

Clearly for much learning these questions are not relevant. But when they do become relevant, you know the subject is worthwhile.

Summary

We don't expect you to follow ALL of the above advice. But we're sure that you will find a combination of explorations that appeal to you, enabling you to utilize a wider range of intelligences. The result: a full, balanced learning experience.

Remember, the whole purpose is to bring information to life, to make it memorable, to enable you to *interpret* the facts, to turn it from surface knowledge into deep understanding. To relate what is new to what you already know. To make comparisons, draw conclusions, see the significance, and make it all usable and meaningful for you personally. That's true learning.

I keep six honest serving men,
They taught me all I knew,
Their names are What and Why and When,
And How and Where and Who?

RUDYARD KIPLING IN
"THE ELEPHANT'S CHILD"

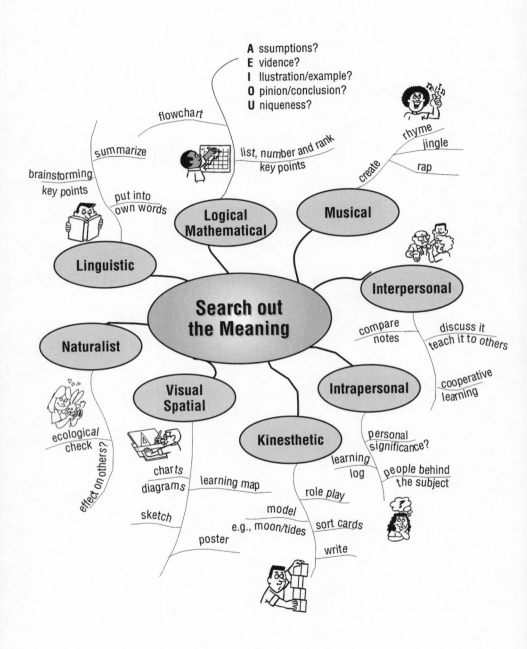

8

Triggering the Memory

The true art of memory is the art of attention.
SAMUEL JOHNSON

Russian journalist Solomon Veniaminovich Sheresheveskii was famous for having a "perfect memory."

Prompted to recall what happened on a particular day fifteen years earlier, he would simply pause for a moment before asking, "At what time?"

Sheresheveskii was studied for more than twenty-five years by the famed psychologist Aleksandr Luria, who reported his findings in a book entitled *The Mind of a Mnemonist*.

In test after test of increasing complexity "S"—as the journalist was identified—was able to recall with hundred-percent accuracy long lists of nonsense syllables that were confusingly similar.

Even more remarkably, "S" demonstrated perfect recall when asked to remember the lists some eight years later. He was also able to recollect what Luria had been wearing at the time and other environmental factors.

Extraordinary feats of memory like those of "S" have been reported throughout history and throughout different cultures.

Mehmed Ali Halici of Turkey was able to accurately recite over 6,500 verses of the Koran.

Hideaki Tomoyori of Japan memorized the first 10,000 decimal places of the value of pi and recently, according to Japanese researcher Mayumi Mori, extended his record to an amazing 40,000 decimal places.

Maori Chief Kaumatara of New Zealand was able to recount the

> **The number-one reason we forget is because we aren't paying attention in the first place.**
>
> LYNN STERN, COAUTHOR OF
> *IMPROVING YOUR MEMORY*

entire thousand-year history of his tribe—a feat that took three days.

Blind John Milton composed *Paradise Lost* in his mind—forty glorious lines at a time. The great conductor Arturo Toscanini knew every note of more than four hundred scores. And Julius Caesar could simultaneously dictate as many as seven different letters to his secretaries without losing the thread of what he was saying.

In the modern age Microsoft chairman Bill Gates still remembers hundreds of lines of source code for his original BASIC programming language. Investment genius Warren Buffett can quote financial details of companies he investigated years ago.

All of these great achievements of recollection, however, were possible only because the individuals concerned employed particular *strategies.*

"S" had an incredible capacity for visualization and synesthesia— the ability to express a memory, generated in one sense, in terms of another. Sounds expressed as colors, for example.

In this chapter you'll discover many strategies that you can successfully apply to help lock anything you learn into your long-term memory. In fact, if you've been paying attention to the previous three chapters, you've already learned three key stages to improve your ability to remember.

Stage 1. If you are in the right state of Mind, feeling relaxed and confident about learning, the parts of your brain that create memories can actually work better.

Stage 2. If you Acquire new information in ways that suit you, then that information is immediately more memorable for you.

Stage 3. If you Search out the meaning of the material in a variety of ways, then you will understand the meaning of what you are learning. We remember what makes sense; we forget nonsense phrases.

How Quickly We Forget

Studies show that 70 percent of what you learn today can be forgotten in twenty-four hours if you do not make a special effort to remember it.

You can think of your memory as resembling the moving of sheep into a big field. Short-term memory is like a holding pen at the entrance to the field. To transfer the sheep into the field (long-term memory) you need to deliberately drive them in. You need to make a specific effort.

And remember: just as different people have various types of intelligence, different people have different abilities to remember. Some people are good at remembering names or faces or numbers but not all three. But virtually all kinds of memory can be improved with the right kind of training.

Your Memory Is Already Good

During the course of your lifetime your brain has already stored an immense number of memories. Just, for instance, consider one small example.

Imagine walking into your kitchen. Now, starting with the wall on your left, mentally note everything in the room. The position of the cupboards, pictures, kitchen utensils, refrigerator, oven, microwave, storage jars, etc. etc. Mentally open the cupboards, one by one, and recall what is there. The amount of detail you can remember is incredible. And that's just the kitchen. You could do the same for every other room in your home.

Explore How Your Memory Works

Here is a list of words. Relax, then focus on the words and read through them slowly—just once. When you have finished, follow the instructions below the words.

Grass	Truth	Blue
Paper	Table	Sheep
Cat	Fork	Meaning
Knife	Zulu	Field

Love	Radio	Pencil
Bird	Wisdom	Stream
Tree	Flower	Pen

ACTION

Now cover up the list and write down as many of the words as you can recall, in any order.

————	————	————
————	————	————
————	————	————
————	————	————
————	————	————
————	————	————
————	————	————

Now you have finished (and it doesn't matter how many or how few you have remembered), let's see what conclusions we can draw. Compare your written list to the full printed list and we suspect you will notice the following:

You probably remembered the first words. You tend to remember more of the beginning of any learning session. So you probably recalled *grass* and maybe even *paper.*

You probably remembered the last words. You also tend to remember more of what you learn at the end of each learning session, so you probably recalled *pen* and maybe *stream.*

Put these two conclusions together and you have a typical pattern of recall for a learning session as follows:

Create initial Learning Map.

Recreate it from memory.

Compare the two. The mind instantly focuses on what was missed.

Now here's an interesting tip. If you want to keep your recall high, make sure you have plenty of beginnings and endings to your learning sessions.

The way to do that, of course, is to keep taking breaks. Most people find it difficult to really concentrate for longer than twenty minutes. Stop frequently, take brief breaks—and you'll boost the amount of material you retain.

Level of recall

One long session

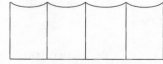

A session with 3 breaks

You Normally Remember What's Unusual

You probably remembered the word *Zulu*. Why? Because it stood out from the rest of the list and a vivid mental image almost certainly sprang into your mind of a Zulu warrior with shield and spear.

We remember what is odd, bizarre, comical, or rude. Therefore, if you want to remember something, try really hard to associate it with a funny or unusual mental picture. This is exactly what the professional "memory men" do. And we'll show you exactly how to do the same.

You may also have recalled the word *radio* or even *fork*—because they benefited from the extra attention you paid to the word *Zulu*. They were next to it or associated with it.

You Remember Information That Is "Organized"

You may have automatically written down some words in groups— objects and subjects that have associations or fall into the same category. In fact, the list did have some fairly obvious groups:

animals — cat, bird, sheep
countryside — grass, tree, flower, field, stream
office — pencil, pen, paper, table

Organizing what you are learning into groups or categories definitely works. It works because you are actively doing something with the information, not just passively looking at it. And you are forming meaningful associations.

You Remember "Real" Things More Easily

The list also contained words such as *love, truth, wisdom,* and *meaning*. These are the least well remembered because they are not specific or concrete. They are not things; they are ideas.

"Real" things are easier to remember than abstract ideas because you can picture them in your mind's eye. We remember pictures many times better than

> **It is impossible even to think without a mental picture.**
>
> **ARISTOTLE**

words—so find a way to make a picture of what you are learning, either literally or in your head.

Visual memory *is* very strong. A picture, as the old aphorism tells us, is worth a thousand words. And a study at the University of Rochester, New York, shows just how true that actually is.

In the study a group of people were shown 2,500 separate photographs—one every ten seconds. Three days later they were

> **You can remember any new piece of information if it is associated to something you already know or remember.**
>
> **HARRY LORAYNE AND JERRY LUCAS IN *THE MEMORY BOOK***

shown 250 pairs of photographs. The photographs in the pairs were deliberately similar. One they had seen; the other picture was new. Yet the participants could tell—with over 90 percent accuracy—which of the photographs they had seen before, and which they had not.

It is because of the strength of visual memory that we have emphasized so many visual tools of learning: making a mental picture of the learning material, making a diagram, chart, sketch or cartoon; using color, highlights, and underlining; and constructing your own personalized learning maps.

When you create your own diagrams or charts you begin to see the pattern in the information. Here's an example: Suppose you were studying the countries in the Far East. Most people only have a hazy idea where they are located in relation to one another.

Draw a simplified map of the area, copying it from an atlas. Then draw the map again from memory and compare it with your original effort. Now you begin to "own" the information.

The Importance of Making Associations

Think of your memory as a library storing thousands of books (i.e., facts). If the books are stored in a haphazard manner or illogically—such as by size or color—it becomes virtually impossible to locate a specific book.

However, if the books are arranged in an organized way (by subject and author), then retrieval becomes easy and quick. So, to remember well, create strong connections and associations.

Two studies highlight the value of active linking to create powerful memories.

In one study three groups of students were each asked to learn ten new words.

Group 1 just read the words. Group 2 sorted the words by type of word (category). Group 3 formed sentences that contained the words. The result? The students in Group 3 remembered two and a half times better than those in the first two groups.

In the second study, students were asked to learn pairs of unconnected words such as *dove* and *car.* Group 1 read the words silently. Group 2 read a sentence aloud that contained the words. Group 3 made up their own sentence and read it aloud. Group 4 made a vivid mental picture where the words interacted with each other, for example, "The dove just missed a speeding car."

Each group did better than the previous group and the final group learned three times better than the first group. Is there a way that Group 4 could have done even better? Yes—by describing *out loud* the mental image they had created. In this way you would have a story with interactive pictures and sound. Multimedia learning!

Storytelling Stores Memories

A story is always a good memory aid because it links words together in a sequence and because it's easy to picture in your mind. Here's an example.

Let's say you want to remember the names of Snow White's Seven Dwarfs. Make up a story like this:

I'm usually still SLEEPY at seven o'clock in the morning, but when I awoke today I was immediately wide awake and GRUMPY because I knew I had to visit the DOC. I'm normally quite BASHFUL about going but my friend told me to stop being so DOPEY, and as an allergy had made me very SNEEZY, I simply had to go. After I'd been given some medication I felt better and was really very HAPPY.

ACTION

Read the story to yourself and then read it aloud.

Then see if you can write down the names of the Seven Dwarfs from memory. You could also invent your own story. This way it's personal to you and even more memorable.

The fact that stories make it easier to remember facts is behind our decision to base our home-study language courses on a series of specially constructed radio plays. Language is much more easily learned in the context of a story.

Associations Create Meaning

We remember, too, things that have a meaning for us. And things have meaning when we can connect or associate them with what we already know. When we learn a foreign language, for instance, it is useful to start with the points of similarity to our native tongue.

Our self-study Accelerated Learning language courses contain an idea we call the "Name Game." The principle behind the Name Game derives from the fact that English has evolved from both Old German and Latin. Indeed, eight hundred years ago Old German and Old English were very similar languages.

Naturally, over time, German and English began to look and sound different—as do dialects in modern-day Britain and America. However, in an hour or so it is possible to uncover many of the underlying similarities between the two languages. Learning German then becomes an intriguing game and the fact that it is possible to recognize thousands of words of German after just a few hours' study is a major motivation.

Here are some examples to show you just how easy it can be:

1. If *Malz* in German = *malt* in English, and if *Zinder* in German = *tinder* in English, what might you conclude? That the *z* sound in German has, over the years, sometimes changed into a *t* in English.

   If that is true, what do you think the following words mean?

Katze	**Zweig**	**zu**	**Zinn**	**Zoll**	**Salz**
(cat)	(twig)	(to)	(tin)	(toll)	(salt)

2. If *Bein* in German = *bone* in English, what might you conclude?

   That sometimes (obviously not always) an *ei* sound in German has developed into an *o* sound in English. So figure out the meaning of:

Stein	**ein**	**Eiche**
(stone)	(one)	(oak)

Now, here's the game. Knowing the above, what do you think the German word *zwei* means?

3. If *danken* in German = *to thank* in English what might you conclude?

That *d* in German is sometimes *th* in English. So figure out the meaning of:

Dorn	**Ding**	**dick**
(thorn)	(thing)	(thick)

This "principle" even works for words that look different. So *Dach = roof.* It makes sense when you realize that roofs used to be thatched!

4. In many European languages the *b* sound and *v* sound can easily be transposed. So *ich habe = I have*. Armed with this principle you can see why *ich gebe = I give*.

It even gives you an intriguing insight into why the German word for *to die* is *sterben*. You have to be a bit of a detective to unravel this one, until you realize that *to starve* is a specialized form of dying!

The Name Game makes an effective "entry point" into learning a language for these reasons:

1. It creates meaning fast. All of a sudden what looked like a huge learning task begins to shrink to realistic proportions.
2. You see that there is a pattern, a connection, between the languages. That suits the "global" learner, yet it also suits the logical learner who likes to know the rules involved.
3. It creates a good, optimistic frame of mind at the outset. Not only do you get a fast start, but the language is no longer so strange or forbidding.
4. It is actually fun—and you get involved.

In short, it is meaningful—and when something has meaning for you, it is much more easily remembered. There is more on the Accelerated Learning approach to learning a foreign language in Chapter 11.

ACTION

Whenever you have to learn something, ask yourself what connections or associations it has to things with which you are already familiar.

Go for the Long Haul

Your ability to remember depends upon the length of time you spent studying a subject.

Psychologist Harry P. Bahrick of Ohio Wesleyan University tested one thousand high school graduates to see how well they recalled their algebra.

For some of the graduates it had been as long as fifty years since they had studied the subject; others had been in algebra classes as recently as the previous month. The students who recalled the best were—contrary to what might be expected—not those who had studied it most recently but those who had spent *more time* studying it in the first place.

In a study of people who had learned Spanish, Bahrick discovered similar results. Students who had taken several courses spread over a couple of years could recall—decades later—60 percent or more of the vocabulary they had learned. Those who had taken just one course retained only a trace, three years later.

Message: if you want to learn something, you would do better taking one lesson a week for a year rather than two weekly lessons for six months. And instead of practicing the piano for seven hours on Sunday, practice one hour a day, seven days a week.

Do Your Own Thing

Designing your own memory aid may be the very best approach for you. Rearrange something or leave something in an unusual spot, so when you see it, it will prompt the memory. Tie a bow to the refrigerator handle to remind yourself to buy milk—or better still, attach a cowbell. The quirkier the memory aid, the more likely you are to remember!

Sleep on It

Often we "forget" because the information was never really registered in the first place. Sometimes, however, information just seems to fade from our memory. Indeed, researchers once thought that memory gradually faded, rather in the way a piece of curtain can be faded by the sun.

As mentioned earlier, several studies now show that when you sleep you are actually recording and filing away things you have learned during the day.

Back in the early 1970s Vincent Bloch, of the University of Paris, showed that when rats were being trained in a maze-learning task, the time they spent in REM sleep increased. Conversely, several studies have shown that when both rats and humans have their REM sleep interrupted, they have much poorer recall of the previous day's events.

Salk Institute neuroscientist Terrence Sejnowski, reviewing two of the most recent studies published in *Science,* commented that together the findings provide "evidence that something important is happening [during sleep] with regard to learning and memory."

One study was carried out with human volunteers at the Weizmann Institute in Rehovot, Israel. Researchers, led by Avi Karni and Dov Sagi, showed that during the Rapid Eye Movement (REM) phase of sleep their subjects improved at skills learned by repetition.

The volunteers had been given training in the evening before "going to bed." Then they were awakened by the ringing of a bell every time their brain waves indicated they were entering REM sleep—about sixty times a night. Another group had their sleep similarly interrupted—but during slow-wave (SW) sleep. The results were amazingly clear cut.

> **I've known countless people who were reservoirs of learning yet never had a thought.**
>
> **WILSON MIZNER**

The subjects who underwent REM deprivation did not learn anything; the others showed definite improvement in what they had learned over the previous night.

What happens during REM sleep to embed information in the brain is not completely understood, but in studies of sleeping animals a flow of the neurotransmitter acetylcholine from sub-cortical neurons into the cerebral cortex has been noted.

A key element in Karni and Sagi's work is the fact that they may have extended the idea of memory consolidation during REM sleep to include procedural memory—memories of a simple repet-itive task. Previous tests have focused on declarative memory—the locking down of one-time events.

Meanwhile the other study, by Matthew Wilson and Bruce Mc-Naughton of the University of Arizona in Tucson, looked into the brains of sleeping rats and found neuronal activity that may help strengthen the animals' spatial memories.

They noticed that the identical groups of brain cells active when rats were learning a task became active again during sleep—al-though at a faster speed. Researchers now believe that sharp wave bursts of neuronal activity compress hours of activity into a split second.

The findings of these two new studies—taken together—lend considerable weight to the long-held belief that something that happens during sleep, and in particular during REM sleep, may play a role in the strengthening of memories.

As researcher Chris Evans speculates: we sleep in order to dream. And, in turn, we dream in order to sort and integrate our new experiences into the existing networks of our memory.

The implication for improved learning is to follow this pattern:

1. Learn.
2. Review the material briefly before sleep.
3. Sleep.
4. Briefly review the previous day's learning again.

Researchers Jenkins and Dallenbach tested this pattern. They had two groups of students spend the same amount of time learn-ing a list of words.

One group was tested after eight hours of daytime activity. They scored only 9 percent recall. The second group was tested after eight hours of sleep. Their score was a 56 percent correct recall!

Remembering What You've Forgotten

When we forget something we tend to single-mindedly try to re-member it by concentrating on what we've forgotten. In other words, we try to dredge up the specific entity as if it were the only fish in the sea.

But that's illogical. We can't expect the missing thought (the single fish) just to jump up and conveniently attach itself to our fishing line. We have to go fishing—by using the power of association.

Retrace in your mind what led up to and what followed the forgotten event, name, fact, or article. What were you doing, thinking, feeling, saying? Whom were you with? What were your physical surroundings?

Trawling through all of the surrounding "fish" will usually lead you to the one you want to catch. You will find that you make a connection that helps the answer "pop" into your brain. Of course, the answer was always there in your memory—you just had to find the way to retrieve it.

Sometimes it's a help to add another association by slowly going through the letters of the alphabet. You may well find that you get a strong feeling for which letter the forgotten item begins with— and that triggers the memory.

A POINT TO PONDER

The more you can see it, hear it, say it, and do it, the easier it is to learn. It has been said that, on average, we remember:

20% of what we read

30% of what we hear

40% of what we see

50% of what we say

60% of what we do

90% of what we see, hear, say, and do.

So, how can you can learn in ways that combine seeing, hearing, saying, and doing? Answer this question and you are well on the way to a super memory.

YOUR MEMORY ACTION PLAN

There are many ways to make sure you can remember. Here are some tools for remembering both complex and simple information. As with the entire Accelerated Learning program, you will need to explore these tools to find those that work best for you.

Decide to Remember

You can remember anything you want to remember. The operative words here are *you want to.* You must make a conscious decision that *you want to* remember something.

The reason witnesses of an accident are so unreliable is that they had never planned on having to remember the scene. If you want to learn something, you must elect to do so. You have to make the choice—the decision—to remember or not to remember. Some experts say that to insert information into long-term memory you need to focus on it for at least eight seconds.

Take a Break——and Often

Have you ever sat through a class, lecture, or training seminar and found your attention wandering? Or perhaps you've been physically uncomfortable sitting in one place for so long? You probably know from personal experience that lengthy working sessions do not enhance the learning process.

You need to take a break at least every thirty minutes. It need only be two to five minutes long—but it should be a complete rest from what you are learning. Try drinking water at each break. Our bodies are more than 70 percent water and a regular glass of water can keep us more alert.

"Review" During and After

Throughout this book we constantly ask you to think about what you have just learned and repeat it in your own words. Review and repetition are essen-

> **We sometimes think we have forgotten something when, in fact, we never really learned it in the first place.**
>
> **FROM *IMPROVE YOUR MEMORY SKILLS***

> **Memory is the diary that we all carry about with us.**
>
> OSCAR WILDE

tial stages in creating long-term memory.

And that's why you will find many essential elements repeated in different ways in the pages of this book.

You should review material frequently, albeit briefly—after an hour, one day, one week, one month, and six months. All you need do is look at the notes that you made or the sections that you highlighted. This review sequence has been shown to improve the recollection of material by some 400 percent.

Create Multisensory Memories

We have learned that we have a separate memory for what we see, hear, say, and do. Multisensory experiences, therefore, broaden and deepen our potential to remember. So make sure there are Visual, Auditory, and Kinesthetic experiences in the way you embrace knowledge.

Remember to:

a) Make notes or a Learning Map as you learn from a talk. You listen (Auditory), make the notes or drawing (Kinesthetic), and see what you have produced (Visual).

b) Remember the steps in a process. You watch someone else's demonstration (Visual), say the steps out loud (Auditory), and then "walk through" or act out the steps yourself (Kinesthetic) before actually attempting it for real.

c) Make visual images interact. Visual memory is normally the strongest—especially if you can make the mental images "larger than life" and connected. Picture a horse galloping rather than standing still. Add color and brightness. Imagine something funny or bizarre. If you park your car in 4F, think of four frogs.

Invent an Acronym

One of the most common—and useful—memory aids is an acronym. An acronym is a word made up of the first letters of the word, phrase, or sentence that you are trying to remember. SCUBA (as in scuba diving) stands for Self-Contained Underwater Breathing Apparatus.

You can recall the four voices in a quartet if you think of them each receiving a stab in the back. *S* for Soprano, *T* for Tenor, *A* for Alto, and *B* for Bass. Children are often taught to remember the Great Lakes with the acronym HOMES—for Huron-Ontario-Michigan-Erie-Superior. The government bureaucracy loves acronyms—NASA, FBI, CIA, HUD, etc.

We've used Jayne Nicholl's acronym—M•A•S•T•E•R—for Accelerated Learning's six-step master plan for learning. As you have already discovered, it stands for: Mind-Acquire-Search-Trigger-Exhibit-Review.

Another approach is to make up an odd sentence such as Keen Aunt Agatha Can Cut All Felicity's Nails. It's a way to lock into your brain the letters for various chemicals: K = Potassium; Au = Gold; Ag = Silver; Ca = Calcium; Cu = Copper; Al = Aluminum; Fe = Iron; Na = Sodium.

Most budding musicians are taught to remember the notes on the lines of the treble clef with the sentence:

Every   Good   Boy   Deserves   Favor
(or Fruit or Fun)

We've seen various versions of the above. "Every Good Boy Does Fine" is one. Choose the one that you prefer or, better still, invent one to suit yourself. Making your own mnemonics makes more permanent memories!

Memory Flashing

This exotically named way to remember is extremely powerful and simple. In fact, when we've used it in classrooms, students have voted it the single best memory strategy. Here's how it works.

1. Make notes in learning-map form—or a brief list.
2. Study them carefully for one or two minutes.
3. Then set your notes aside and recreate them from memory.
4. Now compare the two learning maps or two sets of notes (i.e., your original and the one just made). You will immediately notice anything you missed.

5. Now make a third learning map or set of notes and again compare with the original.

When the original and the new notes become the same, you will have created a very strong memory of these notes. Almost a photographic memory. Moreover, because a learning map is itself a way of concentrating a large amount of information into a few brief notes, you may well have recorded an entire book or learning program in one easily remembered form. The KEY words will trigger your memory for lots of other detail.

An even better idea is to tie together the power of Memory Flashing with an acronym. Take all of your memory maps for a whole course. Let's say it's a year with twelve maps. Give each one a title, creating an acronym in the process to remember the titles. Result? You could bring the memory maps to mind one by one and thereby review a whole one-year course in just an hour or so. Or bring the items to mind, one by one, in an exam room!

Flash Cards

Some subjects are ideal for flash cards—scientific formulae or foreign words, for example. Make use of spare time—traveling, for instance—to review and test yourself.

Whole Learning

What if you need to learn a lot of material by heart—a complete poem or a part in a play? Don't tackle it line by line—learn it as a whole.

1. Read it all the way through—thoroughly. Make sure you understand it. Go over any particularly difficult passages, making sure that you comprehend them. You won't easily remember what you don't understand.
2. Reread it, quite quickly. And again.
3. Now reread it aloud and hear the words in your mind.
4. Reread aloud with as many visual pictures as you can produce. Imagine everything as clearly as possible.
5. Reread again—aloud—adding action or movement as far as it is appropriate.
6. Repeat steps 1–5 above.

Yes, this is a lot of repetition. But it has been proven that this whole-to-part method is at least 50 percent faster than the "part to the whole" method. The reason? It starts with the big picture, the whole pattern, and it is multisensory.

Wordplay with Numbers

You can use words to represent figures. For example:

1616   The year of Shakespeare's death.

Generally, with years you can afford to drop the one thousand—assuming the date is after the year 1000. So you want to find three funny or relevant words to represent 6-1-6—a six-letter word, a one-letter word and another six-letter word.

How about . . .

Writer a Genius

6   1   6

You can use the figures-with-words strategy to remember passport or social security numbers. One of us had a passport number that was 311216. Since humor or vulgarity are good memory triggers, he never forgot it through inventing a phrase containing words made up of three, one, one, two, one, and six letters. The phrase: "sex-o-I-am-a-maniac!"

A REAL-LIFE EXAMPLE

We applied many of the above techniques when we were asked to put together an Accelerated Learning version of a best-selling negotiating course—"The Secrets of Power Negotiating"—developed by one of the country's foremost experts in the negotiating field, Roger Dawson.

Acronym

We came up with an acronym to help us remember some of the key techniques to utilize when in a negotiating situation. We actually used the word

NEGOTIATE.

The letter *N* stands for *Navigate.* You need to take charge of the negotiation, like a ship's captain steering it in the direction you want it to go.

The *E* represents *Eyes and Ears* because you need to keep your eyes open and your ears alert for giveaway body-language clues and for the hidden meanings in what your negotiating counterpart says and doesn't say.

The *G* is for *Grimace.* One of the principal rules in a negotiating situation is that you should always flinch, always pull a face, when you're first made an offer to show that it is not acceptable.

The *O* is for *Outrageous!* You always find someone else's first offer outrageous—unacceptable—while you yourself should make your demands somewhat outrageous. So you have room to maneuver.

The first *T* in NEGOTIATE stands for *Trade-off.* Whenever anyone asks you for a concession you automatically and immediately ask for something in return.

The *I* is for *Impersonate.* There are many times during the course of a negotiation when you will take a position you don't really believe in. You may represent yourself to be a reluctant buyer or a reluctant seller, for instance. Or you may bring up an issue that doesn't really matter to you—it's a decoy or a red herring. Or you may pretend to be dumb when you know you're really smart. You're "impersonating."

The *A* is for *Agree.* Always agree up front with the other side. "Yes, I see your position, I understand

> **When using comedy make sure that all humor arises out of the teaching points . . . if they remember the joke, they've remembered the training point.**
>
> **JOHN CLEESE, TV AND MOVIE STAR TURNED TRAINING EXPERT**

what you're saying, but . . ." You can employ the "feel, felt, found" strategy. "I know how you feel, others have felt the same way, but what they found . . ."

The second *T* is for *Teasing*. You tease extra concessions from the other side, most probably when you've reached agreement on the main issues. After you've shaken hands on the $50,000-a-year salary, agreed on the health benefits and vacation package, then is the time to say, "Oh, yes, and by the way, I do have membership in the country club, don't I?"

The last letter *E* in NEGOTIATE is for *Easy Acceptance*. You want to make it easy for the other side to accept the deal and not feel badly about having conceded so many points. So you offer something that makes them feel better even if it isn't of major significance. "Okay, George, well, next time I'll definitely come to see you first before anyone else."

So there you have the key elements of negotiating, which can be remembered with the acronym NEGOTIATE.

Turn It into a Story

You can add another dimension by creating a story to help you remember the key points. Think of it, if you like, as a cartoon strip.

In this instance you would visualize a ship's captain Navigating his ship into a port. He's at the helm; he's in charge. Our captain has got big Eyes and big Ears. He's arriving in the port and meeting with a trader. He's Grimacing because he's unhappy with the Outrageous offer being made by the importer. The captain is willing to trade and he's saying something like "I can accept fifty dollars a barrel, but if I do, I need an extra month to deliver." That's the Trade-off.

The captain goes on to say, "Actually, I don't know if I can live with the fifty dollars." He's Impersonating, pretending to be a reluctant seller. Then you see the captain adding, "I know how you feel about the price. Other customers have felt the same, but they found they were able to make a good profit." He's finding ways to Agree. In the next scenario the captain is saying to the importer, "Okay, it's a deal . . . and you will take care of the port tax, won't you?" He's Teasing or nibbling for that extra concession.

And finally, Easy acceptance. The captain says, "You've been really fair. Next time I'm in town I'll definitely make sure you have first choice."

Set It to Music

Rhythm and music make it easy to remember. Just think of all of the old songs whose words come flooding into your mind as soon as you hear them. You could really embed the negotiating tactics into your mind by continuing the seafaring theme.

Change the words to a sea chantey such as "What Shall We Do with the Drunken Sailor?" and make it "What Shall We Do When Negotiating?" It may be silly and humorous—but that's what makes it memorable.

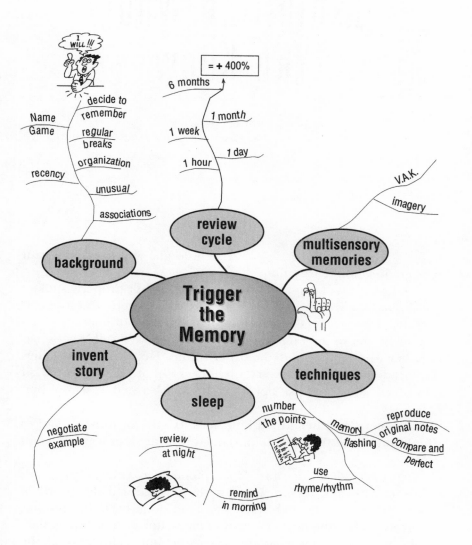

9

Exhibiting What You Know

Not I, but the city teaches.
SOCRATES

The little girl was struggling with her grade-school curriculum.

She had always been a slow learner. She hadn't properly spoken until she was five years old. She had since been diagnosed as dyslexic. Her teachers were beginning to despair of her.

Luckily, the young woman—a friend of ours we'll call Mary—had a father who really cared about her future. He rescued her faltering academic progress. Every evening, without fail, he would sit down with Mary and ask her what she had learned at school that day.

He encouraged her to tell him. And to write or draw it. And to think what were the most important things she had learned—and why.

Not only did this ensure Mary mentally rehearsed the day's learning activities, this meant that she created a daily record of them. At the end of each week she could look back and see her progress. Reflecting on her learning made her progress tangible.

She was exhibiting what she knew—an important part of the learning process. And now she has obtained a PhD from a leading U.S. university.

Exhibiting what you know, demonstrating what you have learned, is when you begin to discover if you have been successfully applying the first four stages of the Accelerated Learning M•A•S•T•E•R plan:

1. Getting in the right frame of **Mind**—relaxed, confident, and ready to learn.
2. **A**cquiring the information in ways that best suit you.
3. **S**earching out the meaning, implications, and personal significance.
4. Being able to **T**rigger the memory of it whenever you need it.

Now you have to prove to yourself that you have totally comprehended the material you have learned and that you can put it into practice. You must "show you know." In other words, now is the time to test, practice, and use what you have learned.

Test Yourself

Have you really "got it"? Have you really locked down the information you have been learning, the skills you have been trying to acquire? Fully explore what you know. Find the outer limits of your knowledge. Testing yourself should be an automatic and straightforward check on your ability. Use the learning tools that you have come to favor.

- Reconstruct a learning map.
- Test yourself with flash cards.
- Create a "mental movie" of what you have learned.
- Recreate a flow chart.
- Make a logical, numbered list.
- Say it out loud to yourself.

When you make testing yourself an automatic part of the learning technique you can become more matter-of-fact about making mistakes. You come to see that mistakes have a role to play, rather than dreading the thought of "getting it wrong."

You see that any errors, in fact, are useful feedback. They are stepping-stones, not stumbling blocks. They clarify areas of doubt or inability. They highlight where you will have to spend more time or what areas you might have to explore more thoroughly. As long as you are determined to learn from your errors, you can't go wrong.

This kind of testing is designed to show you where you are, and it's an essential task for the self-managed learner. It's designed to be a natural part of any learning rather than the judgmental examination feared by so many students.

Students' fear of testing seems to have grown in proportion to the steady increase in the volume of testing in schools. Over a forty-year period almost every significant educational reform has either expanded existing tests or mandated entirely new tests—a staggering increase of 10 percent to 20 percent *per year.*

Say authors Haney and Madaus, who wrote an academic paper on the subject entitled "Searching for Alternatives to Standardized Tests: Whys, Whats, and Whithers": "Learning and teaching are corrupted when most of the instruction becomes merely preparation for testing."

So concentrate not on how many mistakes you make but *what kind* of mistakes they are. And remember: "Mistakes are merely the staging posts on the road to success."

Practice What You've Learned

Moving from being a beginner to being an expert depends upon practice. Experts tend to make it "look easy." But that's because they have persistently and patiently worked at acquiring a skill until it becomes second nature.

Top athletes and sportsmen are the easiest example. Most of us don't see the hours and hours of painstaking practice that they made the commitment to do; we just see the prize-winning event.

Some learners are happy to jump in with both feet and immediately try to apply what they've learned. Others feel the need to practice by themselves or with a friend.

If you are in the latter category, try Mental Rehearsal. Use your imagination to see yourself actually using what you have learned. Build up a full and detailed picture of yourself in a real-life situation and then see yourself, in your mind's eye, performing well.

The man who makes no mistakes does not usually make anything.

BISHOP WILLIAM CONNOR MAGEE

Try Role Play too—either by yourself or with your partner, friend, or colleague. If what you are going to tackle involves other people, this is a very effective form of practice. You can hear and check out what you are going to say, and it's a good confidence builder.

Consider the following two possible ways to communicate a point:

Statement

"Power corrupts and absolute power corrupts absolutely."

OR

Role Play

A class was divided into two groups. They were told to imagine the classroom was a jail. The first group took the role of wardens. The second played the part of the prisoners.

After some hours the experiment had to be discontinued because many of the "prisoners" were in severe mental distress due to the bullying behavior of the "wardens"!

Which approach makes the point about the corruption of power more strongly? The Statement or the Role Play?

Role play also lets you see how someone's else's learning style may differ from yours and why "two heads are usually better than one."

You Are Your Own Best Judge

One of the things that happens with "formal" learning is that we get used to other people judging us—giving us grades. However, it is obviously more satisfying when we judge the quality of our own work. That's why exhibiting what you know to yourself is so important. You set your own standards and you check your performance against those standards.

If you are a student, get into the habit of looking at your own work before you hand it in. What grade would you honestly give it? Is it up to your own best standards? When the work is re-

> **Practice doesn't make perfect. Perfect practice makes perfect.**
>
> **VINCE LOMBARDI**

turned to you, if you didn't get the grade you thought you deserved, ask the teacher or trainer what you could have done better to achieve it.

And why not put yourself in the movies? Make a video of yourself presenting what you've learned, or role-playing. You'll be able to judge your performance more critically. By seeing yourself on the screen you can see yourself as others see you.

Use It

You really have succeeded when you can use what you have learned independently and distanced from the learning environment. That's why this show-you-know step is essential. Using what you have learned in different ways, developing and improving on it, is true mastery.

It's one thing to learn how to use a computer in a course, and an entirely different matter implementing that knowledge in the workplace when you may be under pressure to prove yourself—and the helping hand of the tutor is no longer there. (Remember what it was like after passing your driving test and then actually driving alone for the first time?)

And, of course (like Mary with her father), it's another level of challenge to explain what you've learned to someone else. The advantage of the learn-then-teach format is that it forces trainees to marshal their thoughts and to articulate their learning.

This was clearly proven in a trial with a group of students. One group studied printed material, knowing that they would later have to present a summary of it out loud. A second group studied the same material without expecting to make a presentation.

Afterward both groups were split into thirds. One third in each group presented oral summaries, another third listened to the presentations, while the "third third" did not have the benefit of either review activity. The best results were achieved by those students who actually gave the summary *or expected to have to do so.*

> **The self-controlled and self-motivated learner is one who can plan, regulate, and evaluate his or her own skills and strategies.**
>
> **BARBARA L. McCOMBS,
> UNIVERSITY OF DENVER**

Note that research shows you should try to use whatever you've learned within the following twenty-four hours. You are much more likely to retain the information long-term if you begin to apply it immediately.

Take every advantage to learn from others who are successful. Watch how they learn the same sorts of material and take careful note of how they do it. Ask them to explain their approach to the learning task.

Research again shows that when you learn strategies from more than one person, you become a much more flexible learner, able to apply skills in many different situations.

Indeed, one of the most important skills in life is to analyze what makes others successful and adapt their winning strategies to your own circumstances.

Getting Support from Others

Learn with Your Family
Make a serious attempt to involve your family. For example, if you recruit their help by asking them to listen while you explain what you have learned, they are also likely to gain from it. They will also come to realize how important it is for you to be acquiring and developing new skills and will not resent the time you need to spend on the learning process.

Study Buddies
Find yourself a learning partner—somebody who is also trying to understand and use what you are learning. You can offer each other support as you explore the subject, and regularly quiz each other to check your progress. This way you get immediate feedback on the accuracy and effectiveness of your own learning and the way you present it—as well as a different perspective on the subject.

Study buddies help not only by testing each other but also by having different styles to compare. Studies show that having a partner is most useful when you and your study buddy take regular turns being the presenter and listener.

Cooperative learning of this kind is informal teamwork—a skill valued highly by all modern organizations.

Learning Circles

Learning circles are groups of people tackling the same subject who get together informally to share their experiences, questions, and findings. A very effective idea—especially in the workplace.

Mentors

Find yourself a mentor—someone highly skilled in the subject under consideration and who would be encouraging and supportive as well as a source of further information for you.

A mentor should be someone with whom you feel comfortable and who can offer positive feedback, constructive criticism, and ideas. You can also gain from the mistakes he has made during his career. Get him to open up to you.

The experiences he has had—good or bad—can dramatically cut down the time it takes for you to become proficient. But only if you ask!

The whole of human progress is founded on learning from the mistakes and successes of those who have gone before. That's why the Internet and the information superhighway are so significant. They put the experience and knowledge of the world instantly and literally at your fingertips.

10

Reflecting on How You've Learned

Learning is not just knowing the answers.
CHARLES HANDY IN *THE AGE OF UNREASON*

The Emperor Napoleon, victorious in battle, strides across the battleground. In his moment of triumph the diminutive figure walks through the bloody aftermath with a keen analytical eye.

The "little general" is more interested in assessing the thrust and counterthrust of the battle than he is in celebrating the hard-fought conquest.

It was a scene played out time and again. After every victory Napoleon would waste no time in walking the battlefield, while the strategies of the encounter were still fresh in his mind.

First he would look at the battle from the perspective of his opponent.

Wherever his vanquished adversary had made an important decision, Napoleon would put himself in the same position, asking himself how he would have conducted the battle from his opponent's standpoint.

Napoleon's reflection went even further. He then imagined how he would have fought the battle against himself—rather similar to trying to play chess against yourself. This was a continuing learning process that gave him valuable insights for future battles.

Reviewing and evaluating not just what you have learned but especially **how** you learned it is at the heart of becoming a self-sufficient, independent, and successful learner.

If you develop a habit of automatically thinking through and evaluating how you learn and how you think (or how you do anything), you gain control over your life, and you have the information to keep improving.

Continuous self-monitoring, self-evaluation, and introspection are the key characteristics of the self-motivated learner. Strengths and weaknesses need to be recognized so that action can be taken.

A failure from which you learn some important general principles for the future is more valuable than a one-time lucky success from which you learned nothing to guide you in the future.

Introspection is not just "talking to yourself" (an alleged sign of early senility!). It's what's called "metacognitive" behavior. It's our ability to know what we know and what we don't know. To think about how we think. To be conscious of what steps and strategies we are taking during the act of learning or problem solving, and to constantly improve on these steps and strategies.

Most people rarely take time to reflect on their experience in a way that helps them improve. Self-analysis is not a quality many people seem to have instilled in them. And although it requires meaningful thought, this kind of evaluation does not have to take much of your time—and its rewards will pay you back many times over. The simple truth is that you can't improve a process of which you are not conscious.

David Perkins, a senior research associate at the Harvard Graduate School of Education, argues for greater recognition of what he calls "reflective" intelligence.

He believes it offers "the greatest hope for an all-around improvement in people's intelligent behavior."

Says Perkins, "Hardly anything in conventional educational practice promotes, in a direct and straightforward way, thoughtfulness and the use of strategies to guide thinking. Those students who acquire reflective intelligence build it on their own, by working out personal repertoires of strategies.

"Or they pick it up from the home environment, where some parents more than others model good reasoning in dinner table conversation, press their children to think out decisions, emphasize the importance of a systematic approach to schoolwork, and so on. In general, neither the ordinary school nor the ordinary workplace models or promotes the stand-back strategizing that is the hallmark of reflective intelligence."

Reflecting on the learning experience should not be confined to adults. It is important for students of all ages—and not just their parents and teachers—to understand their own intellectual profiles.

In some "multiple intelligence" classrooms students as young as four years old are asked to identify the activities that they like most, as well as the ones they think they do best. Toward this end we recommend that teachers regularly introduce activities involving reflection.

Older students can write in journals, create charts, or discuss their strengths with other students. Such reflection fosters the development of intrapersonal intelligence, a capacity that enables students to draw more readily on their strengths when solving future problems.

As a self-managed learner, three simple but powerful questions to ask yourself are:

- What went well?
- What could have gone better?
- How can I do it better next time?

Keep asking those questions and you've mastered the essence of self-assessment.

It is precisely because the process of Reflection is so rarely taught, while so important, that we have written this book.

Our whole philosophy is that the process of learning, and the process of thinking analytically and creatively, are not mysterious activities done well by some people and not by others. In each case the successful strategies can be captured, written down, and then learned and followed. So that anyone can become good at them. It is a big gap in schooling that we hope to help fill.

> **If you plunge into a learning task without first considering your purpose, you may be wasting your time. And if you don't reflect on it afterward, you almost certainly will.**
>
> **DEREK ROWNTREE IN**
> **LEARN HOW TO STUDY**

PERSONAL PROGRESS PLAN

Monitoring your own ongoing performance provides a constant honest evaluation of your current capabilities: you record areas where you have made improvement and signal other areas where you "could do better."

Be ready to record the "downs" as well as the "ups." Stumbling blocks can be expected when you try something new. They are part of life and should be seen as helpful feedback, not as destructive and negative events. You can turn stumbling blocks into stepping-stones when you see them this way.

The Personal Progress Plan is a useful tool for self-assessment. It allows for rewards for success. Don't forget to pat yourself on the back and celebrate so that learning becomes a pleasurable habit.

It calls for you to analyze which of the learning strategies in the first five steps works best for you and your personal learning style. And it allows for recording ways to improve next time.

Sit quietly after you have completed the learning task. Savor the feeling of accomplishment. Notice how your body feels when you have performed successfully. Make a note of it. You'll want to recreate that feeling as part of a "resourceful state."

The master-mind learner is always willing to evaluate himself and his behavior. He regularly examines his life.

Here are some questions to guide you as you reflect on a learning experience:

1. Was it successful? If so what were the main factors?
2. Did I prepare well for it?
3. Did I find out everything I needed to know? If not, why not?
4. Which learning strategies were especially useful? Which weren't?
5. Is there a **pattern** in my successes; that is, do I learn better in certain circumstances than in others? What type of thing do I learn well/less well? What lessons can I learn from this for the future?
6. How can I do better next time?

7. I can expect this difficulty in implementing what I learned today _____
but I will overcome it this way:

_____

_____

8. What personal "reward" would be appropriate to celebrate a success?
9. Who else might help next time?

The six-step model of learning we have developed is designed, of course, as a comprehensive blueprint to learn *anything*. It is the "learn-how-to-learn" skill that we believe is one of the two core 21st century skills.

It seems astonishing—even outrageous—that most schools persist in teaching *what*, but not *how*. Especially since you will see in later chapters that learning how to learn can have dramatic results in companies, schools, and homes.

The six-step Accelerated Learning M•A•S•T•E•R plan has also provided us with a structure to create a series of home study courses. Let's therefore look at a practical application of the M•A•S•T•E•R plan in the learning of foreign languages so you can see how it works.

We learn by thinking and the quality of the learning outcome is determined by the quality of our thoughts.

RONALD R. SCHMECK,
DEPARTMENT OF PSYCHOLOGY,
SOUTHERN ILLINOIS UNIVERSITY

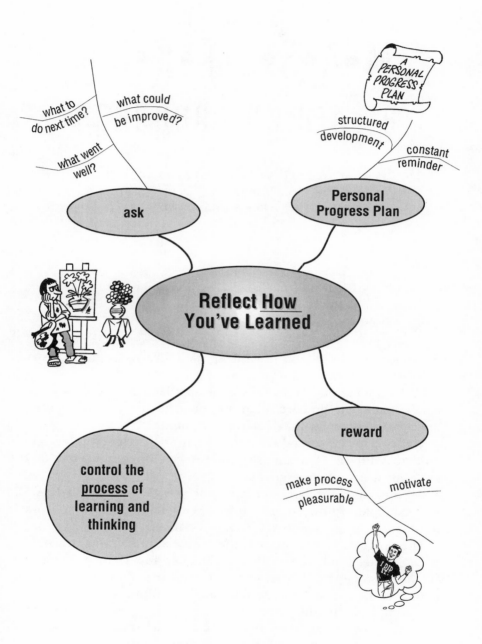

11

M•A•S•T•E•R•ing
a Foreign Language

*I am referred to in that splendid language [Pidgin]
as "Fella belonga Mrs. Queen."*
PRINCE PHILIP OF ENGLAND

Close your eyes, relax, listen to
the sound of music—and learn to speak a foreign language easier
and faster than ever before.

In developing our Accelerated Learning language courses we've
been careful to practice what we preach! It's a multisensory,
multiple-intelligence way of learning a language.

The course has several elements, each one designed to accom-
modate a different learning style, so you can emphasize those that
suit your learning preferences.

We introduce the basics of it to you now because it provides a
real example of how the principles of Accelerated Learning work
in practice. In other words, it brings the theory to life.

The program incorporates music, video, audio, drama, learning
maps, games, and many other techniques for a comprehensive
"theater-of-the-mind" experience. It recreates the rich, sponta-
neous learning that happens naturally in childhood when you're
acquiring your "mother tongue."

You don't just watch a video, for instance. Instead you observe
the action and physically follow the tutor, acting a role yourself
and repeating the words. On audiotapes you listen to your new

language in a series of entertaining radio plays. You become absorbed in the story line and the interesting characters, and you want to discover how the plot unfolds. So it provides ongoing motivation.

Some sequences are spoken dramatically to a background of classical music; others to the measured rhythm of Baroque music to effect a relaxed and receptive state of mind and to fully involve the right hemisphere of the brain.

Although the courses were originally designed for businesspeople to learn at home, they are now widely used in schools. Typical is British teacher Val Duffy-Cross of Bridley Moor High School in the West Midlands, who pioneered the use of our courses in an Accelerated Learning pilot program in her school.

"Many staff started off being skeptical, but some are surprised, even shocked, by the progress these youngsters are making. Their level of confidence is unprecedented," says Mrs. Duffy-Cross.

After only six weeks of the Accelerated Learning trial period, the "pilot" youngsters (thirteen- and fourteen-year-olds) were already very confident—both orally and aurally; so much so that they wrote and performed a three-act play in German in front of astounded older students. Twenty-three out of the twenty-six children in the pilot group opted to continue their German studies the following year.

When it came to exam time, 67 percent of the students who learned German using the Accelerated Learning program scored marks of 80 percent or more. Only a little over 10 percent of pupils following traditional methods achieved such high marks. Thirty-eight percent of the "accelerated learners" actually scored over 90 percent versus just 3.6 percent of the "traditional" learners. That's ten times more top grades.

And the verdict from the English students themselves: "Exciting." "Fun." "Relaxing." Not the kinds of words fourteen-year-olds normally use to describe the learning experience.

But what about their parents? Although initial funding came from the school's PTA, many parents were concerned about the unorthodox approach. "But the children themselves sold the idea to their parents eventually," says Mrs. Duffy-Cross, "and now parents want to know why their children aren't doing enhanced learning techniques in other classes."

We'll come back to more results at the end of this chapter, but let's first explain some of the ways in which language learning can indeed be speeded up by a factor of at least three—and some have found that even a ten-time acceleration is possible.

The Core Idea

Remember: every subject has a core idea, and once you understand it everything else makes sense.

The core idea in the Accelerated Learning language courses is that to learn a language you must build a "mental model" of how it is structured, and then be exposed to numerous natural situations so you absorb the vocabulary.

That's how you learned your native language. Children are surrounded by language and make sense of it. So, for example, a toddler will often say "I breaked it" rather than "I broke it." Because they have *unconsciously worked out* that to say something that happened previously they normally add an *-ed*. No one ever tells them that "the general rule for making the simple past in English is to add *-ed." They work out the structure (grammar) and the vocabulary for themselves.*

We have reproduced the same type of challenging situations in the Accelerated Learning foreign language courses.

> It is in foreign-language teaching that the amazing results of the Accelerated Learning methodology have been best assessed. In this field one soon ascertains how fast a person learns and develops his personality as a whole.
>
> LUIZ MACHADO DE ANDRADE,
> PROFESSOR OF LANGUAGE
> STATE UNIVERSITY,
> RIO DE JANEIRO

The Name Game

We introduced the idea of the "Name Game" in Chapter 8, "Triggering the Memory." It challenges you to work out for yourself (with a little help) the many ways in which, for example, German and English are similar. English also has common (Latin) roots with Spanish. Understanding the similarities is a tremendous motivator—because you come to realize there are thousands of Spanish words you can immediately identify through just twenty-six simple principles.

For example, if you spoke no Spanish whatsoever you would

still almost certainly be able to translate the following simple sentences.

El profesor es inteligente.	=	The professor is intelligent.
La decisión es final.	=	The decision is final.

These deceptively little sentences are packed with helpful associations and clues enabling you to work out the structure of the Spanish language. You can see that *the* is *el* or *la*—masculine or feminine. And that many words in Spanish are virtually the same as their English counterparts with merely a single rather than double letter, or the addition of a final letter. So:

efecto = effect	*attención* = attention
communicación = communication	*necesaria* = necessary
completo = complete	*crédito* = credit
no importa = not important	*no idéntico* = not identical

By gradually working through plenty of examples you are not only learning a lot of vocabulary very quickly, but you are also building up a mental picture of how Spanish is constructed.

So, for example, you learn that *beber* (to drink) is related to *beverage* (because *b*'s and *v*'s are often swapped around in European languages) and if *bebo* is "I drink," then you work out for yourself that if *amar* is "to love," then "I love" must be *amo*.

In this way, you begin to build up the grammar (structure) of Spanish, not by being given long lists of words to memorize (yawn) but by being challenged to work it out for yourself—often at the subconscious level.

Here's just a few more for fun!

When you discover that:	means:	You can figure out that:	means:
e*scorpión*	scorpion	*esponja*	sponge
e*spacio*	space	*estimular*	stimulate
*cha*qu*eta*	ja*ck*et	*esquí*	ski
*posibili*dad	possibil*ity*	*autoridad*	authority
*profundi*dad	depth	*velocidad*	speed
c*alidad*	quality	*cuadrangula*	quadrangle
pirámide	pyramid	*himno*	hymn

pitón	py*th*on	*mito*	myth
Habana	Ha*v*ana	*probar*	prove or try
cuerda	c*o*rd	*puerto*	port

Where it really gets intriguing is when you see the direct connection between the Spanish words and an English word derived from Latin.

So	*sol* (sun)	relates to	solar
	flor (flower)	relates to	floral
	fuerte (strong)	relates to	fortify
	mirar (look)	relates to	mirror
	diente (tooth)	relates to	dental
	libro (book)	relates to	library
	vida (life)	relates to	vital
	decir (say)	relates to	dictation
	caballero (gentleman)	relates to	cavalier
	mueble (furniture)	relates to	movable
	hablar (to speak)	relates to	fable
	enviar (to send)	relates to	envoy
	tenir (to have)	relates to	tenable
	palabra (word)	relates to	parable

Fun, isn't it?

Seeing, Hearing, Doing

How did you learn your own language?

In your earliest years you watched your parents and listened to what they had to say. You then imitated their actions, followed "commands," and you came to understand, and repeat, the words and sentences. This is pure hands-on learning. The language is physically registered in your brain and it becomes instinctive.

We have put together what we call a "physical learning" video to accomplish the same aims. You watch an actress miming commands, which you hear in the language you are learning—"Stand up," "Sit down," "Walk," "Knock on the door," etc.

You watch and follow, physically performing the actions yourself. The commands are also superimposed on the screen—providing another visual "clue." Finally, you repeat the sequence out loud, additionally following the commands in a booklet if you wish. The foreign and English language texts are printed side by side. Then you do it all over again.

You've achieved a perfect introduction to your new language, combining visual, auditory, and kinesthetic input. You *saw* it, *heard* it, *read* it, *did* it, and *said* it. It duplicates the way you learned as a child, and it is the next best thing to being dropped in Madrid or Mexico. It's experiential, whole-brain learning.

The "Name Game" and the "Physical Learning Video," however, are really the warmup to the heart of the Accelerated Learning courses—the Radio Plays.

Once again we've tried to duplicate the process by which you learned your native language so easily as a child. So we devised a story, presented in twelve acts through twelve radio dramas on audiotape—but with the text also printed in an accompanying booklet.

As the story unfolds, you are listening to real-life dialogues in the same situations you face when traveling. There's a genuine motivation to see what happens so you become involved in the story line. Without realizing it you're absorbing the three thousand–plus most needed words and you are automatically and unconsciously absorbing the grammatical structures—exactly as you did as a child.

As with the programs used in a classroom setting the at-home program starts with an audio relaxation exercise. We learn best, of course, in a stress-free environment, and you enter a state of relaxed, focused alertness—an ideal condition in which to learn.

Visualize

You're invited to familiarize yourself with the story. By reading the act in your own language first, you get an overview of the whole lesson. In no time you are engrossed in the story of the American student from Omaha delivering a package to a Señor Alvarez in Guadalajara, Mexico's second city.

You visualize yourself being there with him, you see and hear the sights and sounds of the city. You smell and taste the food and drink. The better you can visualize the reality of the scenes, the more easily and enjoyably you learn.

Read

The text is presented in a special way. Sentences are rarely longer than seven words, so they are easier to remember. This is called "chunking" and follows a Harvard University study that shows we best remember words, numbers, or bits of information when they are delivered in short bursts of about seven elements. The English text is on the left, and read first, so you always know what the Spanish means. And even when you are reading the Spanish words, the side-by-side presentation means that the English is in your peripheral vision. So subconscious learning takes place too.

You absorb the grammar as you proceed. This is a much more natural sequence than trying to learn the rules of grammar first. Although we do explain the rules of the language later, we minimize complicated terminology like *dative* or *gerund*. They are inhibiting and not the way you learned your native tongue.

Finally, as you will be listening to the radio play and following the text at the same time—you will have linked visual and auditory input.

Here's an example:

ACT 1	ACTO 1
SCENE 1	**ESCENA 1**

Peter looks at the house.	**Peter mira la casa.**
It is big and very pretty.	**Es grande y muy bonita.**
He walks up slowly	**Camina lentamente**
to the door.	**hasta la puerta.**
He rings the bell and waits.	**Llama al timbre y espera.**
An old lady opens the	**Una señora mayor abre la**
door.	**puerta.**

There's a significant point to make about the use of these "radio plays." You are immediately learning from complete sentences. There is, quite deliberately, no slow, analytical buildup of individual words. If one starts simply and works up to longer sentences, it suggests that the subject will get harder and harder. In Accelerated Learning courses the "formula" of short, real sentences is used throughout. So the "suggestion" being presented to the learner is that it will never get harder. Master the first lesson (or Act 1) and you are destined to succeed—which is true. Notice that Act 1

Scene 12 does not appear to be much more difficult than Act 1
Scene 1.

ACT 1	ACTO 1
SCENE 12	**ESCENA 12**

It was exactly two minutes	**Faltaban exactamente dos**
before six o'clock	**minutos para las seis**
when Peter stepped out of the taxi.	**cuando Peter se bajó del taxi.**
On the front door	**En la puerta de entrada**
there was a sign with the name	**habia una placa con el nombre**
of the person Peter was looking for:	**de la persona a quien Peter** **buscaba:**
Eduardo Rodriquez, Lawyer,	**Eduardo Rodriquez, Abogado,**
third floor.	**tercer piso.**
The elevator was not working and	**El ascensor no funcionaba y**
Peter climbed up the stairs.	**Peter subió las escaleras a pie.**
He knocked on the door	**Llamó a la puerta**
and he was received by	**y lo recibió**
a secretary.	**una secretaria.**

The role of suggestion in Accelerated Learning is very important. Everything should be orchestrated to suggest success and to
lower threat. So, for example, in a classroom, students assume a
typical person's name from the target language. So Jayne Jones,
the student, becomes Consuela López, the actress. Not only does
this encourage role play, but Jayne Jones naturally dislikes making
mistakes—they threaten her ego. As Consuela López, however, she
doesn't mind. So this apparently simple device means that the student is more willing to jump in and experiment using the new language—without fear of failure.

But we digress. Let's return to the language courses.

Mental Movies

The radio play has sound effects enabling you to easily create pictures in your mind. The association helps you to remember the
words. They can also be played in the car for practice.

You can reproduce this idea yourself. Simply record the language you are learning, leave a gap to give yourself time to mentally translate, then give the translation.

First Learning Map from the Spanish language course

Memory Maps

The spoken dialogue is turned into mental images—the strongest form of memory there is. By providing unusual, sometimes humorous, pictures, you visualize the words in your mind's eye. By replaying the radio drama while looking at the memory map, you harness the power of your right brain, simultaneously linking it to your left brain, which is primarily processing the spoken words.

Active Concert

While following the written text, you again hear the radio play—but the words are now read over a background of classical music. The speaker tries to harmonize with the music—almost as if the voice were another instrument in the orchestra.

Often the words are exaggerated or slowed down. The effect is deliberately dramatic and theatrical, because we remember words spoken in this manner. Again, you are synchronizing the two hemispheres of the brain—as well as its emotional center. The music, therefore, has a number of functions. It helps keep you focused and alert, it gives your new vocabulary an emotional dimension, and it links left and right brainpower.

Passive Concert

At the end of your first learning session you hear the text repeated once more over a background of different music. For this purpose we use Baroque music at about sixty regular beats per minute. The reading is at normal speed. This type of music, as explained in Chapter 12, increases meditative brain wave activity, a state of mind conducive to quietly absorbing your new language.

The radio play and physical learning video constitute the "Input" stage of acquiring a language through the Accelerated Learning method. You will have

> My philological studies have satisfied me that a gifted person ought to learn English (barring spelling and pronouncing) in thirty hours, French in thirty days, and German in thirty years.
>
> **MARK TWAIN**

absorbed considerable vocabulary, and you will recognize the words but so far be able to use only a portion of them. Turning what we call "passive" vocabulary into active, usable vocabulary is what you will achieve in the subsequent Activation sessions.

The Activation Phase

A color coding system in the text is recommended to emphasize various verbs and tenses. Underline or highlight the words so you have a colorful, easy-to-use grammar reference system. It makes review fast and effective. Add words or phrases to the memory maps—or add your own drawings, making them personal and, therefore, even more significant.

You will listen to the act whispered, line by line, in your own language. Then you speak it aloud in Spanish. Each time a correct model is provided on tape for your reference. This is an ideal show-you-know exercise that you can practice in the car.

Two sections of dialogue encourage you to turn the passive vocabulary you've acquired into active vocabulary you can use. We invite you to act out the various roles of the dialogue. You can have loads of fun with this. Be as theatrical and outrageous as you like. Gesture. Walk around. You'll be satisfying the physical learner in you.

Games, games, and more games. There is a whole series of games and activations designed to stimulate each style of mental processing. Some are "doing" games, some are analyzing activities, some appeal to visual learners, some to auditory learners, others to bodily-kinesthetic learners.

In short, Accelerated Learning attempts to reproduce that childlike (not childish!) state where you really get involved in the learning process. You look forward to learning. It's fun. And it's memorable.

Learning How to Learn a Language

We have tried to "lay bare" the structure of our language courses— for a reason. A language learner should not simply be learning Spanish. She should be learning how best to learn a language.

If schools explicitly invited students to reflect on what language-learning techniques were working best for them, they would make it increasingly easy to learn more languages. In that sense it doesn't matter which actual foreign language you learn first—as long as you learn the meta-skill of learning a foreign language.

Thumbs Up from 'Down Under'

Australian TV recently reported on two Sydney high schools that have been trailblazing the use of our Accelerated Learning courses, with students confidently speaking French after only eight weeks of lessons and becoming fluent in the language in less than six months.

Beverley Clark, language teacher at Balmain High, says her Year 11 beginners French class condensed three years' work into three months.

"I'm amazed at their level of proficiency. It's extremely rewarding to hear them carry out fluent conversations in French. What's really beneficial is the relaxation and music played at the beginning of every lesson," she says.

The school is now extending the Accelerated Learning system into other age groups.

At the Beverly Hills Girls' High, teacher Beverley Buckley is equally impressed and enthusiastic: "After only eight weeks the students were able to perform a play in French. That's amazing. I think a lot of schools will come on-line after they see the results of the test programs."

The TV reporter covering the students' success commented, "Their attitude toward French and school has been revolutionized."

Also in Australia, at the Sandgate District High School in Queensland, Accelerated Learning principles are being applied on a wider scale after a successful trial with foreign-language students.

Says teacher-librarian, Elizabeth Burridge, "The students learn to take control of their learning and when they feel more in control, they do better."

Higher Up, Down Under

At a higher level of education Graham Patterson, a lecturer in the Faculty of Education at the University of New England, conducted a twelve-and-a-half-day residential school using the Accelerated Learning German course. The school was attended by ten teachers and business trainers with no previous knowledge of German.

Mr. Patterson reports: "After four days the learners were able to write and perform short dialogues without referring to their scripts. After eight days they were able to introduce a friend in German with a three-minute speech on professional background and interests. After twelve days they confidently performed short plays lasting fifteen to twenty minutes." They had achieved a standard, according to Graham Patterson, of close to university entrance–level from a zero base just twelve days before.

The learning of German, however, was not the main purpose of the exercise. The main goal was to prove to the attendees—through an experience in which a substantial amount of information could be learned—the benefits of adopting a total Accelerated Learning approach to teaching. The course participants' verdict: they unanimously gave the program a 5 out of 5 rating.

Says Graham Patterson, "The course has many parallels in countries around the world. From preschool to adult education, from schools in city slums to multinational company training, Accelerated Learning is challenging our paradigm of learning."

Talking the Same Language

Today's shrinking world and global economy makes it more important than ever for businesspeople to be able to "speak the same language." As U.S. Senator Paul Simon, author of *The Tongue-Tied American,* succinctly puts it: "You can buy in any language; but to sell you need to know the language of your customer."

Many companies are now finding that learning a language through Accelerated Learning gives them the competitive edge that they need. The ideal way to inspire the right learning culture within a company is to marry the advantages of self-study at home with interaction in a "Team Language Learning" group.

Each student uses the self-study courses as the main way to acquire the language, but then the activation of that language is in groups or teams.

The "team" element is a once-a-week ninety-minute class held on the company's premises and conducted by a foreign-language tutor. Each weekly session ensures that the students put into practice the vocabulary and language they learned during the previous week. We provide the teacher with a complete pack of color flash cards, wall posters, and a full curriculum of enjoyable activities.

Knowing that they will be interacting with their peers ensures that each student does his or her homework.

Reporting on the experience at Crosfield Electronics in the UK, participant Trevor Burdett says, "Does it work? I can give an unequivocal yes. The secret is that it is downright FUN. The big advantage to each weekly session is that you all stay motivated to keep learning. You get a chance to actually communicate in your new language straightaway, which is what most business people want.

"Our group of ten finished the whole course in twelve weeks and we all feel competent in German. We have all noticed a big difference in attitudes when we deal with overseas people."

Perhaps the most significant success is in a school in Westminster, England. A class of students wanted to take Italian but teacher time was limited. So the school provided each one with one home study course and gave them just one lesson a week for two terms. After these twenty-four weeks they took the GCSE examination in Italian—normally taken after at least three years of schooling. All passed, and 63 percent with an A grade! Why? The students took active control of their own learning and worked in their own preferred way.

Foreign Language Learning as a Thinking Skill

Studies have shown that children who receive instruction in a foreign language tend to be better at solving complex problems—and more sensitive to cultural diversity.

The most successful foreign language programs in school don't just teach the language—they *use* the target language as a tool of learning. So, for example, it's worthwhile for teachers to consider the benefits of running the whole of the history or art class in Spanish.

We have paid special attention to applying Accelerated Learning to language learning because we know that it and mathematics are the two subjects that the average student feels least comfortable about.

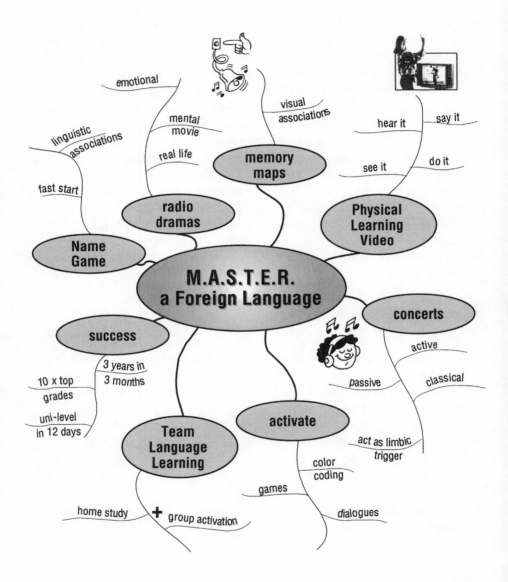

12

The Magic of Music

Music is the mediator between the life of the senses and the
life of the spirit.
BEETHOVEN

The great Albert Einstein is strug-
gling with a complicated formula. The answer to his ruminations is
eluding him.

A passionate violinist since he began playing at the age of six, he
picks up the instrument and is soon lost in a different world, ex-
hilarated by the emotion and genius of Beethoven and Mozart
sonatas.

Suddenly, he stands up, the answer to a physics problem having
entered his mind, declaring, "There, now I've got it!"

"A solution had suddenly appeared to him," his sister later rem-
inisced, noting that playing music seemed to "put him in a peace-
ful state of mind, which facilitated his reflection."

His oldest son recollected, "Whenever he felt that he had come
to the end of the road or into a difficult situation in his work he
would take refuge in music, and that would usually resolve all his
difficulties."

Einstein himself, discussing his
love of music and his ground-
breaking physics research, stated,
"Both are born of the same
source and complement each
other. . . ."

Music, then, was a powerful
catalyst in the creative process of

> **Music is the art of
> thinking with sounds.**
>
> **JULES COMBARIE**

one of this century's greatest geniuses—in the development of scientific breakthroughs of world-class magnitude.

From the Sublime to the Ridiculous?

Charlie Brown . . . Lucy . . . Snoopy. It's quite a mental transition to switch from the lofty research of Einstein to characters in one of the world's most famous cartoon strips—*Peanuts*.

But it's strikingly relevant, inasmuch as cartoonist Charles Schulz credits music as the inspiration behind many of his whimsical observations on life through the famous characters he created.

Says Schulz, "I've thought of countless ideas at concerts. And I think all of us experience the mesmerizing feeling of watching the conductor as he leads the orchestra and our minds begin to wander. The next thing we know, the symphony is half over and we never heard it.

"It makes you so mad because here you've been waiting for three months to hear Brahms's Second Concerto performed and all of a sudden you realize you've been thinking about something else. And you think, *What a waste of time.*

"But in that thinking, your mind begins to travel from one thing to another, and all of a sudden you're inspired by the music—by the emotion—and from that I will get some of my very best ideas."

It Isn't All Greek . . .

Centuries before the physicist and the cartoonist discovered the creative inspiration of music, it was described by Plato, no less, as "a more potent instrument than any other for education."

He believed that children should be taught music before anything else. He felt that in learning to pay attention to graceful rhythms and harmonies their whole consciousness would become ordered.

In the Middle Ages monks used music to help them memorize lengthy Scriptural passages. And Dr. Georgi Lozanov, in his pioneering work, illustrated the brain-boosting power of music to great effect.

Lozanov found that rhythmi-

> **When words leave off, music begins.**
>
> HEINRICH HEINE

cal, soothing Baroque music has a mighty impact on our ability to absorb information and remember it. Between the years 1600 and 1750 Baroque composers such as Handel, Vivaldi, Corelli, Telemann, and Johann Sebastian Bach—perhaps its most celebrated proponent—specifically set out to create music to lift the spirit and free the mind from earthly concerns.

Baroque music's steady, stately tempo of about sixty beats a minute parallels the brain's wavelength when in a state of "relaxed alertness"—the alpha brain wave pattern. The state of "relaxed alertness," claims Lozanov, becomes the receptive state for learning.

Accelerated Learning proponents who specialize in the use of music obviously agree. Dr. Ivan Barzakov, a former student of Lozanov, who swam all night to escape to the West in 1976, feels Baroque music is extremely powerful because of its structured stability and peace. "The memory thrives on the sense of stability and a sense of 'you will have it forever,' " he says.

American Don Campbell, coauthor of *Rhythms of Learning:* "Baroque music slows us down. You listen better because you're receiving at your body's speed; you're not revving up. It's the harmonization of mind-body-heart-spirit.

"Music is the highest part of human culture and expression. It allows us to feel connected to something greater. Underneath music is a code of rhythm and sounds that your left brain relates to while the right brain relates to the textures of the sounds."

The Role of Music in Accelerated Learning

You've seen that our Accelerated Learning home study courses teach foreign languages through a twelve-act series of radio plays—complete with lively dialogue and sound effects to enhance their memorability.

After the learner has begun to absorb the vocabulary and sentence structure from these plays, we repeat the same text—but now over a background of classical music, often Mozart. The text is spoken in a dramatic fashion following the basic ups and downs and tempo of the music. We call this the "Active Concert."

The result is very memorable, which, of course, makes it easy to recall vocabulary later. We all know that the words of a song are easy to remember. Words synchronized with music need little conscious effort to learn, quite possibly because they neatly unite left-brain (words) and right-brain (music) activity. We also know that music has a powerful effect on the emotional centers of the limbic system, which is also a gateway to long-term memory (see Chapter 2).

By delivering material in this way our intention is to make the language "emotionally memorable" and therefore easy to lodge in the long-term memory. Certainly our learners confirm it works very well.

Then, in a final version of the radio play, we invite language learners to sit back, relax, even close their eyes, and now listen to yet another version of the same play. Called the "Passive Concert," the text is spoken softly and normally over a background of Baroque music. Each concert ends on a bright, joyful note.

The intention here is somewhat different. It is to capitalize upon the state of relaxed alertness noted by Dr. Lozanov and, as one of our students put it, "float the language into my subconscious." Whatever the reasons for its success the Passive Concert is effective, and learners are always surprised how much material they remember the next day—with little conscious effort.

Putting It to the Test

The music is certainly uplifting—but there's much more to it than that. Scientists have now begun to discover why Plato and Einstein (and more recently Lozanov and others) had it so right—the right kind of music is a potent educational force. New studies show that music actually trains the brain for higher forms of learning.

In a trial at the University of California at Irvine, researchers Gordon Shaw and Frances H. Rauscher split thirty-three children—three- and four-year-olds—into two groups.

> **Music cannot be expressed in words, not because it is vague, but because it is more precise than words.**
>
> **MENDELSSOHN**

Over the course of eight months one group was given a variety of music lessons; the other group none at all.

At the end of the test the music students scored 80 percent higher on object-assembly tasks—putting together pieces of a puzzle as fast as possible. These were tasks that required a child to form a mental image and then orient physical objects to reproduce that image—skills that later translate into complex math and engineering ability.

In other tasks, where the children were given solid objects or drawings to reproduce, and which required no mental imagery, there was no difference between the two groups of children.

The explanation behind this is not fully understood, but it is suspected that when children exercise cortical neurons by listening to classical music, they are also strengthening circuits used for their logical-mathematical intelligence.

The UC Irvine team says that music "excites the inherent brain patterns and enhances their use in complex reasoning tasks."

The Mozart Factor

So does listening to classical music really boost your brainpower? The answer is yes, according to another recent study at UC Irvine's Center for Neurobiology of Learning and Memory.

Researcher Rauscher and colleagues gave a group of thirty-six undergraduate students spatial reasoning tests on a standard IQ test. Before undertaking each test the students: listened to Mozart's Sonata for Two Pianos in D Major, K. 448, for ten minutes before the first, listened to a relaxation tape before the second, spent the time in silence before the third. The results, when translated into the actual spatial IQ scores, were 119, 111, and 110 respectively. By listening to Mozart, students improved their performance on an IQ test by as much as nine points. The IQ gain was seen to fade after about fifteen minutes, but can be duplicated with additional reactivation. More research is obviously needed.

The fact that exposure to music rewires neural circuits has also been discovered through the use of magnetic resonance imaging.

Researchers at the University of Konstanz in Germany reported in 1995 on their examination of the brains of nine string players. They discovered that the amount of somatosensory cortex dedicated to the thumb and fifth finger of the left hand—the fingering digits—was significantly larger than in nonplayers.

What is interesting is that there appeared to be no difference in the cortex based on the number of hours the players practiced each day—but the earlier in their lives they had started to play, the more cortex was apparently devoted to the fingering digits.

Unfortunately schools in America on average have only one music teacher for every five hundred children—according to the National Commission on Music Education—and music is often the first subject targeted when school budgets are cut.

Our culture seems to have been placing a decreasing emphasis on exposing young children to musical skills as well as art and physical education. These three basic skills, so important for improving the quality of life—as well as learning in general—are often considered to be superfluous in the current educational climate.

Even when children *are* taught music, too much emphasis is usually placed on *how* they perform rather than *what* they experience. Parents can help their children to a lifelong appreciation of **how** to interpret music with the following type of activity.

Play some especially evocative music. Ask your child to relax and let images form in her mind. Beethoven's "Pastorale" is a good start because many people do create an image of birds, countryside, and water—and Beethoven's intention was to evoke a stream running through a country scene.

Use these sorts of prompts to encourage your child to interpret music, not just listen to it:

1. What **feelings** did you experience as you listened?
2. What **images** did you see in your mind's eye? These could be scenes, nature, people, shapes, colors.
3. Could you dance or move to this music?
4. What instruments were playing?
5. Can you repeat/hum/sing any tune or melody or pattern that you heard?
6. What was the composer trying to say to you?
7. When would you especially like to play this sort of music? Is it more appropriate for some situations than others?
8. Can you draw a shape, pattern, or even a picture that represents the music for you?

> **Music is the only language in which you cannot say a mean or sarcastic thing.**
>
> **JOHN ERSKINE**

Music (in songs and nursery rhymes) is also an excellent way to introduce children to a foreign language.

In the current debate on the need to raise educational standards, let us not make the mistake of simplistically narrowing down the focus to just English and mathematics. They are vital, but a one-dimensional solution will ignore the role of the arts in building *all* skills *including* language and mathematics. The future requires all-around abilities.

> *And the night shall be filled with music,*
> *And the cares, that infest the day,*
> *Shall fold their tents, like the Arabs,*
> *And as silently steal away.*
> HENRY WADSWORTH LONGFELLOW

Recommended Music

Relaxation

Handel   Concerto for Harp and Lute Larghetto, op. 4, no. 6
Concerto for Harp in F Major Larghetto, op. 4, no. 5
Concerto Grosso in C Major ("Alexander's Feast")

Note-Making the Baroque Way

J. S. Bach	Suite 3 ("Air on a G String")
Vivaldi	"Four Seasons" Spring, Largo
Albinoni	Concerto for Oboe in D Minor, op. 9
J. S. Bach	Concerto in F Minor, second movement
Pachelbel	Canon in D Major
Handel	Concerto for Harp and Lute in B-flat Major
Vivaldi	Concerto in C Major for Piccolo

Concert Review

Mozart	Concerto no. 21 in C Major, K. 467
Beethoven	Piano Concerto no. 5 in E-flat
Vivaldi	Flute Concerto no. 3 in D Major
J. S. Bach	Concerto in D Minor for 2 violins
Mozart	Clarinet Concerto in A Major
Pachelbel	"Canon" from Canon and Gigue

Imagery

Beethoven	Symphony no. 6 ("Pastorale")
Grieg	Peer Gynt Suite
	Prelude, Act 4, Morning

Mahler   Symphony no. 5
Schubert   Octet in F Major, D. 803

The above suggestions have been compiled onto audiotape by Accelerated Learning Systems.

Other suggestions from the work of Georgi Lozanov, taken from "Language Teacher's Suggestopedic Manual" (with Evalina Gateva) and "Suggestology and Outlines of Suggestopedy":

Active Concert

Beethoven   Concerto for Violin and Orchestra in D Major, op. 61

Tchaikovsky Concerto no. 1 in B-flat Minor for Piano and Orchestra

Mozart   Concerto for Violin and Orchestra; Concerto no. 7 in D Major

Haydn   Symphony no. 67 in F Major; Symphony no. 69 in B Major

Beethoven   Concerto no. 5 in E-flat Major for Piano and Orchestra, op. 73 ("Emperor")

Beethoven   Concerto for Piano and Orchestra no. 5 in B-flat Major

Mozart   Symphony in D Major ("Haffner"); and Symphony in D Major ("Prague")

Haydn   Concerto no. 1 in C Major for Violin and Orchestra; Concerto no. 2 in G Major for Violin and Orchestra.

Haydn   Symphony in C Major no. 101 ("L'Horloge"); and Symphony in G Major no. 54

Mozart   Concerto for Violin and Orchestra in A Major no. 5; Symphony in A Major no. 29; Symphony in G Minor no. 40

Brahms   Concerto for Violin and Orchestra in D Major, op. 77.

Passive Concert

Corelli   Concerti Grossi, op. 6, no. 2, 8, 5, 9.
Handel   "Water Music"
J. S. Bach   Fantasy in G Major, Fantasy in C Minor, and Trio in D Minor; Canonic Variations and Toccata
Corelli   Concerti Grossi, op. 4, no. 10, 11, 12.

Vivaldi   Five Concertos for Flute and Chamber Orchestra
Handel   Concerto for Organ and Orchestra in B-flat Major,
               op. 7, no. 6
J. S. Bach   Prelude in G Major ("Dogmatic Chorales")

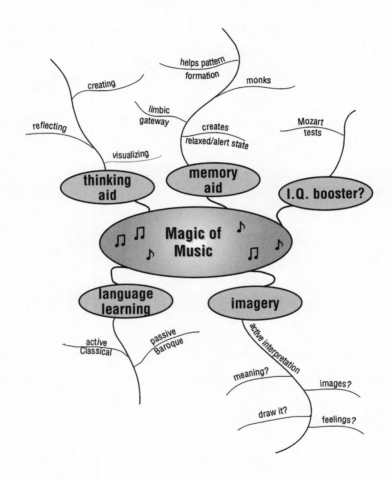

13

Analytical Thinking

You know, it makes a lot of sense if you don't think about it.
DAGWOOD, IN A *BLONDIE* COMIC STRIP

The two pictures above make an important point. The drawing on the left was made by someone who, like most of us, had had no artistic training. The picture on the right was made by the same woman after less than three hours training.

The point is that everyone can draw quite well if he or she follows a few simple rules. In the same way, few of us can think well without some simple rules. These sorts of rules don't restrict us. They liberate by giving us a simple structure that guides us toward a quality result.

We need rules because thinking goes on silently and invisibly in the thinker's head. Unless it is made visible and explicit how can we ever discover and copy what an expert thinker does?

Just as we've developed a simple structure for learning, so we have developed structures for quality thinking. We think structures (or prompts) for thinking are extremely important. At school, with its compartmentalized subjects, we may learn how to solve problems in each subject, but very rarely are we taught how to transfer those specialist problem-solving procedures to other fields. Yet knowing how to solve problems creatively and make rational decisions are skills we need every day of our lives.

We talk about "thinking" but, in fact, there are two main branches of thinking—creative thinking and analytical thinking.

Creative thinking: Thinking for new ideas and products. Seeing a new pattern or a relationship between things that was not obvious before. Finding new ways to express things. Combining existing ideas to produce a new and better one.

Analytical thinking: Submitting a situation, problem, subject, or decision to a logical step-by-step and rigorous examination. Testing statements or evidence or proposals against objective standards. Seeing below the surface to the root cause of situations. Judging and deciding on a logical basis and detecting bias.

These two ways of thinking are not opposites, because they overlap all the time. For example, you need to think creatively to solve problems and you need to think analytically to decide which of several creative possibilities is the best.

You need to be skilled in both types of thought. You need to be a creative-analyst. The children, individuals, corporations, and nations that develop creative-analytical minds shall inherit the 21st century. Thinking plus learning are the new natural resources, the new fountains of wealth.

You have to outlearn, outthink, and outcreate your competitors. Companies have to mobilize every ounce of their collective intelligence by ensuring that quality thinking is spread throughout the organization.

> **You are what you think and not what you think you are.**
>
> **ANONYMOUS**

Who are the giants of history? Creative-analysts like da Vinci, Einstein, Newton, Darwin.

Who are succeeding today? Creative-analysts like Bill Gates, Richard Branson, Stephen Hawking.

Learning to think well as a creative-analyst takes a lot of practice and the discipline not to be impetuous, but to follow some rules. Which is why it's very well paid!

The good news, though, is that the rules themselves are not so complicated. The trick is following them. In this chapter we'll explore analytical learning strategies; creative learning techniques follow in Chapter 14.

Analysis Is Like Good Detective Work.

For most people the idea of learning to think clearly doesn't sound very exciting. That's partly because anything perceived as "intellectual" has, unfortunately, a poor image. Words like *cold fish, nerd, egghead, unworldly,* and *dry* come to mind! And 33 percent of students say it is not popular to get good grades.

It's unfortunate for the people with that attitude—because their jobs are the ones that are disappearing fast. And it's unfortunate for us as a society because the challenges we face are created by poor thinking. They can be overcome only by creative analysis and a widespread understanding of their causes, and by acceptance of the need to apply solutions that may require a short-term sacrifice.

A good way to define something can be to describe its opposite. The opposite of someone who is a good creative-analyst is:

unimaginative	illogical	inconsistent	superficial
pedestrian	unclear	prejudiced	easily manipulated
vague	biased	narrow minded	dull
inaccurate	trivial	unfair	

Not a very desirable set of characteristics, is it?

The one word we didn't use is *emotional,* because, as we've seen, there's emotional content to all thought. And, in fact, analytical thinking turns out to have the emotional satisfaction of high-class detective work.

Quality thinking consists of asking the right series of questions—and remembering to ask them each time.

You use analytical thinking to make a decision, to solve prob-

> **Most people would die sooner than think; in fact they do so.**
>
> **BERTRAND RUSSELL**

lems, and to analyze and judge situations. Let's look at each in turn and use some easily remembered "thinking tools."

The acronym "A FAN DANCE" is a vivid way we have invented to remember how to make rational decisions and solve problems.

Making Decisions

"A FAN" is used to make decisions. It stands for

Assumptions?
For?
Against?
Now what?

In common with all the other analytical tools it ensures you:

- Stop and think—avoiding the trap of impulsively rushing in with the first thought or solution. Reuven Feuerstein, the Israeli thinking-skills expert, advises a deceptively simple first step: "Let's stop and think a minute. Is there more to this than meets the eye?"
- Make sure you start with clearly stated objectives.
- Think about the consequences of your actions.

Assumptions

What exactly am I trying to decide? What have I assumed? What have I taken for granted?

Do I need more information? What are the facts? What's implied here?

It is possible (indeed common) to build an argument that seems completely logical, but from an initial premise that's false. If the starting point (i.e., assumption) is wrong, the result will be wrong. The way to the top may be to climb the ladder of success, but not if it's leaning against the wrong wall.

Example: A man is standing over a corpse with a smoking gun. He owed the dead man a lot of money and was in love with the dead man's wife. It seems reasonable to arrest him. Yet, in fact, he had snatched the gun away just a fraction too late to prevent a suicide. The wrong assumption would lead to the wrong conclusion.

Example: If you assume too much blood is the cause of illness, it's logical to use leeches!

Sometimes the danger is circular logic. Freud suggested every basic motive was sexual. When his patients objected that their motive wasn't sexual, he said that they were victims of suppressed sexuality. You can always be right with circular logic!

$$F = For \qquad and \qquad A = Against$$

This reminds you always to look at a subject from at least two points of view. Your own first belief and the opposing viewpoint.

F = For: What is the evidence for my opinion? Is it good evidence? Is it a fact or a belief? How did I come to believe this? What are the reasons for my belief? How certain can I be this is true?

A = Against: What could be the argument against my point of view? Can I see this another way? What if my starting assumption is wrong? How would an opponent argue this?

N = Now What?: This reminds you that a more careful assessment of the argument may well produce a wiser final decision. It usually does.

Edward de Bono gives a classic example of structured analysis. A class of teenagers were asked if they thought it would be a good idea to be paid to go to school. Twenty-nine out of thirty students immediately gave an enthusiastic yes. He then proposed they use his equivalent thinking tool, which he calls PMI: Plus/Minus/Interesting. It caused them to stop and think (eliminating impetuosity) and look at both sides of the argument.

On reflection, twenty-eight out of thirty students thought it was a bad idea. The search for alternative viewpoints threw up negatives like: possible bullying and cuts in school budgets to finance the payments.

You'll find that A FAN is a valuable structure for "cool" judgment!

Few people think more than two or three times a year; I have made an international reputation for myself by thinking once or twice a week.

GEORGE BERNARD SHAW

Solving Problems

Our acronym DANCE stands for:

D efinition
A lternatives
N arrow Down
C hoose and check the consequences
E ffect—act on it

Let's look at this structure in more detail.

D Is for Definition

"A problem well stated is a problem half solved." It's critical to define exactly what the problem is before you start. It may not be what it appears to be.

There's no point, for example, in finding an imaginative solution to the wrong problem. There's no point in having the most efficient oil rig in history, if you're drilling in the wrong place. Most problems can be defined by asking:

- What's our goal? What are we trying to achieve?
- What do we mean by————? Give an example. How else could we express it?
- Is there anything else we need to know?
- What exactly is the problem? Is it what it appears to be on the surface?

Why? Why? Why? Why? Why?

An excellent example of the need to define the problem correctly is told by Doug Jones in *High Performance Teamwork* published by Nightingale Conant. It also illustrates the power of another thinking tool—"The Five Whys."

A U.S. foundry makes molded iron and steel parts. Their problem was an excessive scrap rate. They asked the line workers why. The answer was, "The tracks are worn, so the molds don't fit correctly. That results in bubbles and rough edges"—i.e., scrap.

So $100,000 was invested in new tracks. But with no improvement. So they asked again.

Why 1: Why are we getting scrap? Answer: "Because the metal is not hot enough." (They also asked, "Why didn't you say so before?" and got the reply "Because you didn't ask!" A lesson here.)

Why 2: Why is the metal not hot enough? Answer: "Because the glow rods are burned out."

Why 3: Why are the glow rods burned out? Answer: "Because there is metal spilled on them."

Why 4: Why is there metal spilled on them? Answer: "Because the cleaning crew spills metal on them."

Why 5: (To the cleaning crew) Why do you spill metal on the glow rods? Answer: "We were not aware we were spilling it—and we didn't realize it was significant if we did. Besides, we are competing with the first-shift crew to see who can clean the most furnaces. There's a bonus on it."

The so simple, but so rarely used, trick is to keep asking, "Why?" until you get to the ultimate reason (which is often five "whys" deep).

In this case a group of people who were not apparently connected with production were having a powerful impact on quality and profits.

The solution was to cross-train the cleaning crews with the line crews so each person understood how the results of his job affected others. And to reward the quality of cleaning, not the speed of work. The overall result was to cut the usage of glow rods down from twenty a week to one a week. At $100 a rod this saved $100,000 a year. It also cut scrap rates down from 10 percent to 2 percent, which saved over $500,000 a year.

The example is a classic because it illustrates:

- The power of what's called Systems Thinking: Looking at a problem not in isolation but as part of the whole. Examining in depth why a problem arises and how it connects to other problems.
- The power of questioning. Questions are like searchlights. They are the tools of truth—which is why quality thinking is based on them.

Just as it's important to define what the real problem is, so it's important to define exactly what the goal is.

If you draw a circle around a target, it's easier to hit. An accurately expressed goal works the same way.

Most goals can be defined accurately by asking:

- What stops this from happening and why?
- What conditions will exist when the problem is resolved, i.e., how will I know when I've reached my goal?
- Can we quantify these conditions, i.e., establish precise criteria for success?

The importance of precision cannot be overstressed. Businesspeople are taught that any action plan must meet the SMART criteria. It must be Specific, Measurable, Attainable, Relevant, and Timetabled. Get SMART whenever you make plans.

A Is for Alternatives

How many ways could I solve the problem, i.e., move toward my goal?

The secret is not to look for a way but several ways to reach the goal. As Nobel laureate Linus Pauling said, "The best way to have a good idea is to have lots of ideas."

This is the point where analytical thinking and creative thinking meet, for you would use your creative thinking tools to generate the possible alternative solutions (see Chapter 14).

N Is for Narrow Down

As we'll see, creativity is best served if you are not trying to judge your ideas at the same time as you are having them. However, having generated a lot of alternative solutions, you now need to start weeding out the least efficient. This is where a clear starting definition is so important—it helps you discard the options that do not fit the criteria you originally set.

A good question to ask is "Which of those possible solutions best meet my original criteria?"

> **All the resources we need are in the mind.**
>
> **THEODORE ROOSEVELT**

C Is for Choose and Check Consequences

Having narrowed down our alternatives we need to choose the ideal option by seeing which solution best meets the criteria you set. You might well test each possibility with the FAN tool, i.e., what's For and what's Against each one.

Then you would check the consequences of the action you propose by asking:

What effect would this have? Will there be any unwanted results from choosing this course of action?

If my conclusion is true—what else must be true?

E Is for Effect

This is a reminder that the purpose of thinking is action—otherwise it's purely an intellectual exercise. As Professor Arnold of Stanford University puts it, "The creative process does not end with an idea—it only starts with an idea." Thinking without action is daydreaming.

Indeed, what marks out the successful creative-analysts is the degree to which they persist in action. It was true of Alexander Graham Bell (whose critics pointed out there was no need for a telephone because no one else has one). It was true of the first Xerox photocopier (which was refused financial support for four years). And Columbus needed fourteen years to persuade the Spanish court to back his voyage—and even then he ended up at a completely different destination!

Rollo May, in the aptly titled book *The Courage to Create,* observed that "commitment is healthiest when it is not without doubt, but in spite of doubt."

That remark highlights the fact that high-quality analytical thinking is not only about rules (though they help), it's also about attitudes.

Those attitudes can best be summed up by asking, "Am I willing to . . . ?"

1. **Persevere.** Writing this chapter took a long time because we read over nine thousand pages of theory and advice on thinking. And then our aim was to summarize it all so it became a series of usable and memorable checklists to help in any circumstances.
2. **Admit doubt.** We can view the world only from our own eyes, colored by our own beliefs and within the limit of our own knowledge. That means few things are certain. Science can

prove few things for certain; it mainly proves what's not true. Admitting there's a limit to our certainty is the start of being fair minded.

3. **Fight for reason.** Since so few people do think skillfully, many base their judgments on emotional beliefs and "gut feelings." Ironically, this is especially common with the major issues. My country right or wrong is a good example.

It takes courage to stand out against peer pressure that is based on prejudice or lack of logic and to look for opinions that can be justified by reason.

It also takes courage to apply the same standards to yourself. Especially when you know that the emotional center of the brain— "the brain of the brain," as Brazilian researcher Luiz Machado calls it—cares little for logic and will be encouraging a snap decision and emotional reaction.

Quality analysis also means developing standards of "intellectual rigor." Any thorough analysis of a subject would need to ask the following eight questions, possibly in the order they are presented.

1. What's the Goal of My Thinking?
Questions to ask are:

- What am I trying to achieve?
- What's the purpose of my thinking?
- What's the problem we are trying to solve?
- What's the precise question we are trying to answer?

2. What's the Big Idea?
We suggested earlier that you need to establish the core idea as you learn. Once you've grasped the essence of the subject, everything else "fits in" and makes sense. It's the same for analytical thinking. Which also underlines the fact that no quality learning occurs without deep thinking.

So, for example, our "big idea" for education is that you need to switch energy and resources into education in the birth-to-thir-

> **For those who do not think, it is best at least to rearrange their prejudices once in a while.**
>
> **LUTHER BURBANK**

teen-year-old age group in order to create self-managed, self-motivated learners who can think clearly. This, in turn, is the key to a big advance in the standard of education of the whole population.

Most fruitless arguments are provoked because the parties haven't agreed on the core idea, the central concept. They are looking for solutions to two different problems. Of course, this is another way of saying you have to start with a clear, specific definition.

3. What Assumptions Are Being Made?

- What are we taking for granted?
- What has been left out?
- What's implied?
- Do we need more information?

4. What Point of View Is Being Used?

Someone's judgment depends on his previous experience and his interpretation of that experience, i.e., his beliefs. There is always some bias in judgment, however small.

So an initiative to improve the quality of a company's products or services will look different to the CEO of that company as opposed to a line operator, because their perspectives are different.

Our beliefs and experience cause us to create snap judgments. We are all too quick to label situations or people. And then the label we apply prevents us from looking deeper.

In other words we prejudge—which is virtually the same word as *prejudice.* Statistically, tall defendants are acquitted more often than short defendants. Overweight people are paid less than "normal" weight people for equivalent jobs. And, of course, racial and religious labeling is the most common form of prejudice. It's completely illogical, of course, but it stems from the instinct to live in groups and the ge-

> **A great many people think they are thinking when they are merely rearranging their prejudices.**
>
> **WILLIAM JAMES**

netic urge to protect "us"—the insiders—at the expense of "them"—the outsiders.

Prejudice originates deep in the primitive instinctual part of the brain. No wonder it's so difficult to deal with, and so urgent to do so. No wonder partisan sports fans can sometimes be so violent.

Understanding our brain is, at least, a starting point.

The fact that all thinking starts from a point of view is crucial to analytical thinking. How can you hope to change people's minds unless you understand their starting point—"where they are coming from"?

For each subject we all carry our own "map of reality" inside our head—our interpretation of what we see—which will always be different from how others see it.

It's a good phrase, because it's clear that a map of France is not France. It's just a representation of France. It's not the reality—it's a version of that reality. And the map is only as good as the mapmaker.

In the early days of cartography, maps were very inaccurate. For example, the cartographers only sailed around Australia. So the first maps were not merely inaccurate, they only showed the edge of Australia. There was no representation of the interior at all. The maps were, literally, superficial. Gradually, through exploration, new perspectives were created and the map of Australia became more accurate.

Now, through the new perspective of satellite pictures, the maps are very accurate. But they are still not the reality of Australia. They are not the sights, the sounds, the smells, the taste, the heat, the humor, the people.

A map is just one perspective. It may be pretty accurate, but it can never be the reality. You can never "live" in someone else's head.

But we can try to make sure that our own map of reality is not superficial. When we hear a different point of view, we need to ask, "What would account for that point of view?" We need to say to ourselves, "I can't just dismiss the opinion. I need to understand it."

To understand someone's point of view helps clarify your own. It switches you from an attitude of "This is how it is" to "This is how I see it." *How I see it* admits the possibility of alternatives.

> The energy of the environmental movement probably stems as much from NASA's pictures of our beautiful blue planet hanging silently, vulnerably, and lonely in space, than from the statistics on how fast our resources are running out.
>
> All of a sudden we could actually see we were one human race, "trapped" on one common home.
>
> It was a new perspective.

Because everything that's said or written is always from the author's point of view, you need to be asking:

- Who wrote this? What does he have to gain?
- Where did the information come from? Is it reliable?
- Is this opinion generalized to masquerade as fact?
- How representative are the examples? Do they collectively favor one point of view? How biased is it? (You know it is biased.)
- What else could explain this?
- What's been left out?

In a sense, everyone is trying to sell you something. The historian, for example, writes history from a perspective. Often he wasn't even there, so his point of view is already constructed from several other points of view, and with their own prejudices.

Sometimes, history is distorted in an obvious way. For example, the old USSR history books deleted all references to the mass killings ordered by Stalin. But often the distortion is very subtle, such as when we talk of other countries as being "isolated." What we really mean is they are isolated from us and our "correct" way of thinking. In fact, most societies have things of importance from which we can learn.

Asking a good question requires students to think harder than giving a good answer.

ROBERT FISHER IN
TEACHING CHILDREN TO LEARN

The existence of explicit and implicit biases bring us to the next question.

5. Is This a Fact or a Belief?

There is nothing wrong with beliefs—we couldn't live without them. But, because they control our actions, we need to examine them. That's not so easy, because beliefs are rarely expressed openly. They exist in our subconscious, often with strong feelings attached, in what seems like midzone between the limbic brain of emotions and the neocortex brain of logic.

You can start to examine your own beliefs or someone else's, by asking:

- What's the evidence for this? Is it credible? Is there enough evidence?
- How did I come to that conclusion?
- How do you know?
- Can I justify and defend this statement?
- Are we certain or do we merely suspect this is true?
- Have you ever tested this opinion?
- How did I come to feel this way?

When you are prepared to ask these kinds of questions of yourself, as well as others, you are being intellectually honest—because you are applying a consistent standard of truth.

The last of the above questions is particularly important because it says that you can separate thoughts from feelings. You may not choose what happens to you—but you can always choose how you respond. This is the essence of free will.

You may lose your job—but you can choose how you react: angry, calm, resourceful, or helpless. Being in control doesn't necessarily mean having the power to order events. It means learning to choose how you react.

That's why reason and emotion are not opposites, they are complementary. Reason is the ability to observe and assess feelings. And what's the point of holding a belief that doesn't stand up to scrutiny?

Of all the things we could teach in school, the ability to understand how beliefs are formed and the willingness to examine them is the most important. Millions of people have been killed by leaders manipulating their beliefs.

6. Is It Clear?

Questions that uncover "woolly" thinking are:

- What do you mean by . . . ?
- Let me see if I understand—I think you mean . . .
- Give me an example or an analogy.
- What would the opposite look like? (We did that to pin down clear thinking).
- How can we measure if we've succeeded?

7. Am I Analyzing This in Depth?

The "Five Whys" technique is an example of thinking in depth. The story of J. Edgar Hoover in the "Searching Out the Meaning" chapter is an example of surface thinking.

Questions to ask are:

- Is this an unjustified generalization?
- Are we oversimplifying the issues?
- Are we merely labeling things and taking them at face value?
- Have we seen how things connect to each other?
- Have I uncovered the real reasons?

8. What Are the Implications of This?

Questions to ask are:

- If this is true, what else follows?
- What are the consequences of this?
- How can I interpret this?

A way to remember this eight-point checklist is:

A — Assumptions
B — Big Idea
C — Clarity
D — Depth
E — Eyes (what's the point of view?)
F — Fact or belief?
G — Goal
I — Implications

Notice we left out *H*. Mnemonics aren't always neat!
Richard Paul of the Institute for Critical Thinking, which pub-

lishes excellent teacher training programs on thinking, makes the profound point that **all** learning is through thinking. Which is why the organization of learning techniques must be linked to thinking techniques. So, for example, he says that to think historically is to:

- Understand the purpose of history
- To answer and frame historical questions
- To gather information about historical events
- To make interpretations about history
- To examine historical assumptions
- To think about historical concepts
- To think about the implications of historical events
- To understand the point of view of the historian

It's a bit different from boning up on a few dates, isn't it?

Richard Paul then poses a further challenge. If the quality of our lives is largely determined by the quality of our thinking, one of the primary purposes of school must be to teach disciplined thinking via the subjects being studied.

All this implies that the structure of analytical thinking is understood and practiced by **all** the teachers and embedded, implicitly and explicitly, in all the lessons. We suggest that this is a vital new perspective for schooling that needs to urgently influence teacher training.

Finally, we encourage the growing interest in philosophy exemplified by Matthew Lippman's excellent *Philosophy for Children* course. Indeed one of the surprise but deserving bestsellers of recent times has been *Sophie's World* by Jostein Gaarder—a history of the main philosophical concepts seen through the eyes of a sixteen-year-old girl.

Clear thinking is not at all automatic because many of the simplistic mental models we build as young children persist into adulthood. These "gut" impressions can override years of fact and training.

Here's an "alert" from a recent TV documentary filmed in the gardens where science graduates from M.I.T. had gathered immediately after their graduation ceremony.

The interviewer pointed to a huge tree and asked, "How did that tree get so big? Where did its bulk come from?"

The science graduates—all from one of America's most prestigious universities—floundered as badly as most of us would. The majority of them thought that the bulk came "from nutrients from the ground." "Why isn't there a big hole in the ground, then?" countered the interviewer. Blank faces.

The answer is that most of the bulk of the tree comes from nitrogen extracted from the air. But this answer—which the science graduates had actually learned—is so counterintuitive that what they had learned was subordinated to the childlike feeling that you can't magic something out of thin air!

The price of rational thinking is indeed eternal vigilance.

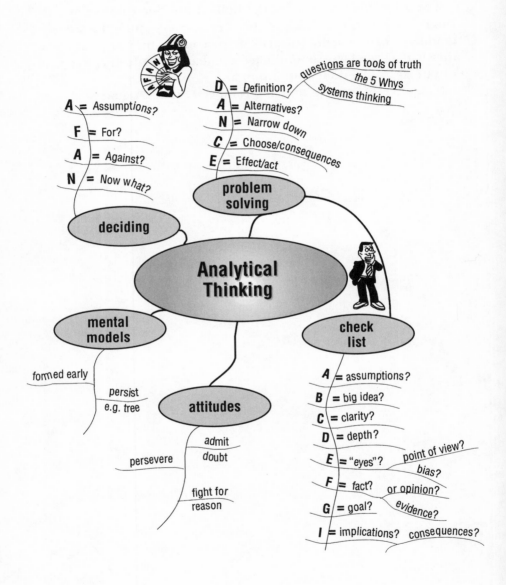

14

Creative Thinking

A foolish consistency is the hobgoblin of small minds.
RALPH WALDO EMERSON

Can you plan to be creative? Absolutely. To be creative is not to sit around waiting for a flash of inspiration. There's always a good deal of hard work and preparation involved.

Beethoven drafted and redrafted his compositions dozens of times. What eventually became masterpieces started as ordinary, sometimes even uninspiring, drafts.

Visit the Picasso museum in Barcelona and what strikes you is the years of practice the great artist spent perfecting the art of conventional draftsmanship. He needed the foundation of technical ability before he could progress toward his innovations. Even then he sketched many versions before creating his final masterpieces.

A survey of authors confirms that the actual creative writing takes up a mere 20 percent of their time while research consumes about 40 percent and revision 40 percent.

In other words, as Edison famously said, "Genius is ninety-nine percent perspiration and one percent inspiration." Of course, motivation helps. When Handel was asked how he could have written a work as glorious as "Messiah" in only twenty-two days, he said it was because he needed the money!

Acquiring detailed background knowledge on the subject is a key to creativity—because almost all new ideas are simply a recombination of existing ideas. The creative person always knows a lot about his subject. The flash of inspiration comes from a background of expert knowledge. "Chance," said Louis Pasteur, "favors the prepared mind."

Isaac Newton, one of the most creative scientists of all time, summed up the importance of wide background knowledge when he said, "If I have seen further than others, it is by standing on the shoulders of giants."

So, the first rule of creative thinking is—do your homework. But facts alone are not enough. The advent of personal computers and the Internet means that there is no shortage of source material on any subject. The creative prizes do not go to the people who can simply acquire facts, but to those who can manipulate those facts and combine them in new ways.

By studying successful creative people it's possible to detect a common pattern in their attitude and work method.

The Creative Attitude

Once you've steeped yourself in the subject, you need a way to look at it from new angles.

Picasso once said, "Every act of creation is first of all an act of destruction." He meant you need to break out of the conventional ways of looking at things.

A work of art is one that gives a new perspective or captures a new trend in society.

So Giotto's fresco cycle illustrating the lives of the Virgin and Christ in the Arena Chapel in Padua (1305 or 1306) is a work of art because it was the first painting to attempt a three-dimensional effect. Albrecht Dürer's painting *The Young Hare* (1502) is a work of art because it was the first time an artist had tried to paint an object exactly as he saw it, correct in every detail. (Although color photography now means such an approach would no longer be considered a work of art.)

It follows that creativity also needs courage. If you are escaping from conventional ways of thinking, you are involved in risk. The fruit of the tree may be out on a limb—but it takes courage to crawl out there and grasp it.

You risk failure and almost certain criticism. Robert Louis Stevenson (who deliberately set out to create the plots of his novels in his dreams) requested, "Give me the young man who has brains enough to make a fool of himself." Rollo May in *The Courage to Create* has a vivid analogy: "The turtle only makes progress when his neck is stuck out."

It's hard to break out of conventional ways of thought, because we need to be on automatic pilot much of the time. Life would simply be too challenging if—each day—we had to work out afresh how to shave, dress, make breakfast, or work. The mind labels activities as routine, and then places all similar events in the same category. But this habit of "labeling" means that, once the label has been applied, thinking becomes rigid—or conventional.

That's why young children are more creative than adults. Their minds are still detecting patterns in behavior and their labels are not yet strong enough to restrict their thinking. Unfortunately, the overemphasis on the single right answer in schools starts to diminish that creativity. As Neil Postman says in *Teaching as a Subversive Activity*, "Children enter school as question marks and leave as periods."

Engineer William Gordon showed how to avoid the rigid thinking caused by "labeling." He was given the job of creating a new way to open cans.

When he briefed his group of engineers, however, he deliberately avoided putting labels in their heads. So he did not use the word *can opener*. Otherwise, they would have had a limiting conventional picture in their heads before they started.

Consequently, they were able to discuss other ways of getting at the inside of things. They looked for analogies and someone suggested that a banana was easy to open because you "unzipped" the skin. The ring pull can was born.

Robert Sternberg of Yale has extensively researched creativity. He sees three stages.

Insight: You define the problem carefully and sift the relevant data from the irrelevant. Like a detective, you need to decide which clues are important.

Combination: You recombine ideas in a new way. When Charles Darwin produced his theory of evolution, all the information

> **The dynamic principle of fantasy is play, which belongs also to the child, and . . . appears to be inconsistent with the principle of serious work. But without this playing with fantasy, no creative work has ever yet come to birth.**
>
> **CARL JUNG**

had been known for years. His talent was to synthesize it into a new concept—a new way of combining old ideas.

Compare old and new: You can't see the value of the new idea unless you compare it to the old, which takes time and patience. So creative people need perseverance too.

All this is very encouraging because it shows that there is a common pattern in all creativity—a structure. It puts creativity within the reach of us all. Follow the plan and you can think creatively. Methodical creativity!

New Combinations of Old Ideas

The common thread in all creativity is the combination of old elements in new ways. A multiplex cinema is a creative idea; so is the Sony Walkman.

Every book written in English is made up of words that are composed from only twenty-six letters. Everything in the world is a recombination of atoms of which there are only about a hundred different types. We humans are made from chemical elements that come from our planet: carbon, oxygen, hydrogen, sodium, calcium, potassium, phosphorus, copper, zinc, etc. In all, about $36 worth of materials—which definitely makes the whole worth more than the sum of its parts.

In turn, as astronomer Carl Sagan points out, our planet is created out of the debris from some long-distant stellar explosion. In essence, we are all made of "star stuff." We are all spacemen and spacewomen.

At the start of this chapter we promised that you can plan to be creative, so let's look at our tools for "methodical creativity." We can say, "It's A FARCE!"

"A FARCE" is our acronym for remembering how to be methodical when being creative. It stands for:

A   Amass—lots of information
F   Four-way thinking—look at it from all angles
A   Alternatives—generate lots of ideas
R   Recombine—look for the best combinations of these ideas
C   Choose—decide on the best combination
E   Effect—put it into action

Let's look at each element.

A Is for Amass

Very few important breakthroughs are made by amateurs. You need to be steeped in the subject. So do your research and get all the facts.

F Is for Four-Way Thinking

The way to break out of rigid thinking is to look at the problem from different directions. We call it four-way thinking:

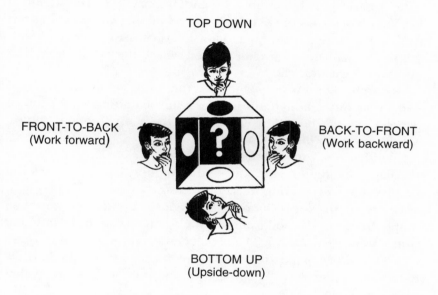

TOP DOWN

FRONT-TO-BACK
(Work forward)

BACK-TO-FRONT
(Work backward)

BOTTOM UP
(Upside-down)

Front-to-Back Thinking

This is our normal approach, which we've examined in detail in the section on analytical thinking. It starts with the problem and works step by step toward a solution. To remind you, the steps are:

D — Define the problem—which must be the starting point of all thinking

A — Generate lots of Alternatives

N — Narrow down the Alternatives

C — Choose one and check for the consequences

E — Effect action

Back-to-Front Thinking

Here you start with the solution and work backward to see how it might have come about.

The legend of Alexander the Great and the Gordian Knot is an example. The town of Gordium had an incredibly tangled knot and the legend held that whoever could untie the knot would conquer what is now the Middle East. No one could. Then Alexander came along and cut it in half with his sword. He started with the solution—which was a disentangled knot.

An American architect provides another example. This architect had supervised the completion of a new building complex that surrounded a large square area. The square was to be seeded with grass. The landscape gardener asked where the paths should be built in the quadrangle.

The architect's answer was to seed the whole area with grass and wait a year. Sure enough, during the year the natural traffic flow of people between buildings marked out the most frequent routes, which were then officially paved.

Good back-to-front questions to ask are:

What is standing in the way of the solution I want? What's the simplest way of removing those obstacles?

The word *simplest* is important. Scientists look for elegant, i.e., simple solutions. A good example of elegant back-to-front thinking comes from pest control. The problem was how to get rid of tsetse flies. Front-to-back thinking would look for ways to kill them. Back-to-front thinking said, "Suppose they didn't exist, how might that have happened?"

The answer is they were never born. And from that insight came a solution. Release insects with a modified gene that causes sterility so that they would gradually die out.

Educational reform needs back-to-front thinking. Currently, the definition of most courses would be something like "a four-year course in French, leading to a specific qualification." The hidden assumption is that the amount of time spent sitting in class determines the learning.

Back-to-front thinking would start with the planned outcome, which might be conversational fluency. Since the method is not now given, you could end up with a completely different answer.

That solution might be to:

1. Take all the hours allocated to French lessons over four years—typically 300 hours.
2. Devote the first 80 hours to self-study (e.g., with a CD-ROM or other home study course), so the learner acquires the basics in his or her own way and at his or her own pace. This would take up a half of all school hours for a month.
3. Then devote 160 continuous hours to total immersion. That would require about twenty-two days of study—about another month, including some homework.
4. Then use the remainder of the time (another sixty hours) to maintain that fluency.

The new result corresponds to what is known about language learning—which is that fluency stems from concentrated, continuous immersion in a language, not from parceling it up into small units, which gives inadequate opportunity to think in the language.

Upside-Down Thinking

This way of thinking asks you to turn the problem upside down. A child sees the world differently when he bends down and peers through his legs.

Edward Jenner had the inspiration to switch from asking why people got smallpox to asking why dairy maids did not get smallpox. In so doing he discovered, of course, that they were exposed to cowpox, a milder disease which immunized them from the more serious smallpox.

So was born the idea that you can protect people from an infectious disease by inoculating them with a weakened strain of that very disease. This triggers the immune system to activate a strong defense against a real attack.

Thinking-skills expert Edward de Bono has an amusing example of reverse or upside-down thinking. There are 120 entrants for a knockout tennis tournament. How many matches must be played to produce the winner including byes (when a player gets a free "pass" into the next round without having to play a match)?

You can work out the answer with logic, but it's time consuming. But if you turn the question upside down, that all-important shift of perspective produces the answer in a second. So, instead of concentrating on the winner, ask instead how many losers are there? If

120 players start, there must be 119 losers. Each loser plays once, including byes. So there must be 119 matches.

Henry Ford employed upside-down thinking when he invented the assembly line and moved the work past the worker, not the worker to the work. Today, we are moving the office to the worker (the electronic cottage), not the worker to the office.

A good question to ask is "How could we express this in a completely different way?"

When "How can we train our people better?" becomes "How can they learn what they need to know?" you shift from top-down corporate training to bottom-up self-directed learning—which is the basis of the Learning Organization.

When you turn the question "How can we cure sickness better?" upside down, and rephrase it as "How can we help people to stay well?" you focus on understanding the common denominators of people who stay healthy into old age. You then start to draw some significant conclusions on the role of nutrition and stress control.

Humor can be a good catalyst to creativity, as in the story of the two shoe salesmen from rival companies who were dispatched to an undeveloped country. One telephoned back, "No opportunity—no one here wears shoes." The other phoned to say, "Fabulous opportunity—no one here wears shoes."

Upside-down thinkers see challenging opportunities. Conventional thinkers see problems.

Top-Down Thinking

Top-down thinking is a way of reminding ourselves of the importance of an overview. It's especially important in resolving problems that involve people. And vital when you are also involved.

> **Genius is seeing what everyone has seen, and thinking what no one has thought.**
>
> ALBERT SZENT-GYÖRGI,
> DISCOVERER OF VITAMIN C

This way of thinking asks you to imagine that you are looking at the situation from above and observing yourself as just one of the participants. All of a sudden you become more objective, a fly on the ceiling, and more willing to see other people's viewpoints.

Chess is a good example of top-down thinking—you cannot

play the game unless you also see your opponent's viewpoint and therefore possible moves.

Top-down thinking is an essential element in any negotiation. If you don't take an overview, you will pursue the deal only from your own perspective, and lose the chance of a win-win solution.

There's an Eastern saying that sums it up: "We can control only those things that we have stood away from." It is part of the art of letting go. When anger or jealousy or regret lives inside us, it has its own existence. It feeds on us, drains our attention and energy.

To overcome destructive emotions requires that we can say, "I am feeling anger at the moment, but I am not controlled by this anger," or "I have failed at this particular task, but I am not a failure."

You cannot learn to understand yourself or others unless you achieve the ability to be detached.

However, to look at yourself and others from outside your emotions doesn't mean you are cold or emotionless. It is a temporary adjustment you need to make to give you a clearer perspective before you then reengage your emotional self. Rather as a painter stands back from her canvas to judge it better. Top-down thinking is most necessary when you feel strongly that you are right!

Good questions to ask would be:

- How would a detached observer see this?
- How does this specific problem connect with the subject as a whole?
- Is this merely a symptom of a bigger problem?

Top-down thinking is to creativity what systems thinking is to analysis. A way to ensure that you don't focus on a detail and miss its relationship to the big picture.

Top-down thinking, therefore, suggests that school must involve a significant element of project work—so students can apply the skills learned from specialist teachers to "real world" problems.

A Is for Alternatives

"The best way to have a good idea is to have lots of ideas." It is so true.

An outcome of our educational system is that we become used to looking for the one correct answer. In the larger world outside of

> **Wealth is the product of man's capacity to think.**
>
> **AYN RAND**

school there are usually several possible answers. If you stop looking—after finding an answer that fits—you will often miss a much better answer.

The question to ask is "How **many** ways could we find to answer this problem? Let's find at least ten."

Robert Olsen, in *The Art of Creative Thinking,* suggests why insisting on quantity works. If you simply ask people to list some birds they will start with obvious examples—sparrows, pigeons, blackbirds, etc.

If, however, you force them to produce a specific quantity—thirty, for example—they eventually start thinking in categories. So thinking of a turkey leads to other domestic birds such as chickens, ducks, guinea fowls, and pheasants. And a seagull leads to albatross, kittiwake, puffin, and skua.

All of a sudden, the obvious starts to become the unusual. By forcing quantity we can lead the brain into new and creative areas.

The other reason that sheer quantity is important is that many ideas are actually not much good! They are still important, though, because they may lead to eventual success. You don't have to be right at each stage in creative thinking—only at the end.

So even apparently silly ideas can be the all-important stepping-stone to a breakthrough. It's like gold mining. On average you have to dig up five tons of ore to produce one ounce of gold, but without the ore there would be no gold.

The best way we know to produce an abundance of alternative ideas is to combine brainstorming with a checklist we call CASPAR.

Brainstorming is a "structured free-for-all," popularized by adman Alex Osborn. Either by yourself or in a group generate many and varied ideas within the following rules, which were partly developed by Osborn and partly by Thomas Bouchard of Minnesota University.

1. Everyone is well briefed on the facts.
2. The more unusual the ideas the better.
3. *Everyone* must have a turn (no one dominates).
4. The more ideas the better.
5. No one may criticize any idea. (This is the key rule. You

need that one—those stepping-stones. If you allow the more analytical left brain to interfere at this stage, you will curb the creative flow. The time to judge or criticize is *after* you've created a large pool of ideas.)

6. Deliberately seek combinations of ideas.
7. Ensure someone monitors the discussion to see that it stays focused and relevant to the problem.

One excellent way to keep track of the ideas would be on a learning map. Because they are all on one visual map, it makes it easier to see how separate ideas could be connected.

CASPAR is not a friendly ghost but a friendly checklist (similar to one developed by Alex Osborn). It reminds you to ask the key what-if questions that trigger alternative ideas.

CASPAR stands for:

C — Cut out—What can we eliminate or replace?
A — Add—What can we add/increase or make longer?
S — Subtract—What can we reduce/decrease or make shorter?
P — Put to another use—What else could we use this for?
A — Adapt—What else is similar? What analogies help?
R — Rearrange—Can we reverse or alter the order?

Let's look at some examples. The point is not to create a finished idea, but to start the process of thought. Remember the key rule for brainstorming is not to criticize any idea right away, but to use what-if thoughts as stepping-stones to the ultimate new idea.

Cut Out

- What if we eliminated income tax and instead paid everyone a minimum wage? But we also increased the sales tax on everything except food, educational material, and children's clothes?
- What if we scrapped conventional grades and concentrated on finished projects as the main form of assessment, and students assessed their own work?
- What if we replaced the habit of routine thinking with the habit of asking, "What if?"

Add

- What if we increased the amount of school time for art, drama, and music (or thinking skills)?
- What if we increased the school year to the same as the business year?
- What if we added parents as active collaborators in education or added grandparents as school assistants? Or added volunteers to reduce the cost of school maintenance?
- What if we added a year of community work to school?
- What if students ran their own bank, "police force," stores, and court? (It's already successfully done in a few schools.)
- What if you knew you would add twenty years to your expected lifespan and live to 110? What difference would it make to how you plan your life?

Subtract

- What if we reduced the number of secondary-school teachers and added more interactive computers?
- What if we reduced primary-class sizes and increased the number of primary-school teachers?
- What if we made schools smaller? Or divided large schools into smaller units?
- What if we reduced prison sentences, but made the guilty parties work directly for the victim?

Put to Another Use

- What if schools became community learning centers and stayed open thirteen hours a day, seven days a week?
- What if school corridors became art galleries for the local community?
- What if retired people became auxiliary teachers or mentors to children?

Adapt

- What if we adapted an oil drill as a domestic tool? (We did, it's called a power drill.)
- What if museums became teachers? (The best have, like the

Exploratorium in San Francisco, which has scores of hands-on, self-discovery exhibits.)

Note: The "adapt" part of the checklist is an excellent place to look for analogies—comparing a familiar situation with the problem you are trying to solve or the subject you are trying to understand.

For example, the flow of electricity along a wire can be compared to the flow of water in a pipe. When you put resistors in an electrical circuit you reduce the strength of the electricity. It's like putting a narrow section in a water pipe—you reduce the flow of the water.

The Wright brothers used analogous thinking to work out how to maneuver a plane. They watched buzzards and noticed how the birds not only dropped a wing to turn but also twisted their wing. The extra pressure leveled the bird off and the analogy produced a wingtip that could be separately maneuvered—an aileron.

Analogies work because they help create a new perspective. In the words of Dr. William Gordon of the Synectics Corporation (who developed the ring pull can), "They help to make the familiar strange." This is necessary, he says, because our inclination is always to oversimplify things to make them familiar. And that inhibits our creativity. Analogies force us to look afresh. We think they are very important in creativity.

A good question to ask is, "What is this like? What can I learn from the comparison?"

Rearrange

- What if students designed their own ideal learning center (school)?
- What if school were open plan, instead of closed classrooms?
- What if classes were composed of students who had reached the same level in the subject—instead of arranging classes by age?
- What if there were much more self-instruction and less whole-class teaching in secondary school?
- What if a three-way team of students, parents, and a specialist educational assessor designed an individual curriculum for each child?

- What if every country's defense department had to be staffed only by women? Would international aggression be reduced?

R Is for Recombine

Creating an armory of alternative ideas rarely produces a breakthrough by itself. Usually you need to combine a number of these new ideas.

Gordon Dryden is a creativity expert and has created an excellent training program to teach creativity that he calls the "Ah-Ha Game."

He defines an idea as "a new combination of old elements." "There's nothing new under the sun," he says, "there are only new combinations of old elements."

Recipes in cookbooks, says Dryden, are merely new combinations of existing ingredients. Every man-made fiber is a new combination of existing atoms. Genetic engineering is a new combination of existing genes.

A fax combines a copying machine and a telephone. The Gutenberg press combined a dye for making coins with a press for making wine.

So once you have generated plenty of alternatives, you then ask yourself, "What can I combine to get a good answer?" (NB: not *the* answer).

So you may add, subtract, eliminate, adapt, and rearrange to get to the final answer—in other words, you'll try numerous combinations.

Learning maps are useful here because the ideas are all on one page, so it's easier to see the potential combinations.

One major tip. Don't brainstorm for alternative ideas and then try to complete the final synthesis all in one day. Study after study of creativity has shown that you are better switching off and letting your subconscious mind work on it.

> **Imagination, not invention, is the supreme master of art, as of life.**
>
> JOSEPH CONRAD

So review your ideas during the evening, focus on the outcome that you want and when you want it. This gives your subconscious a specific goal to work on. Then sleep on it. Beethoven, Wagner, Coleridge, and Robert

Louis Stevenson all deliberately used dreams as a source of creative ideas.

The result, so very often, is a flash of inspiration. But note it comes from a very well-prepared mind indeed. This wasn't a chance flash of inspiration, it came from "methodical creativity."

> **There is no expedient to which a man will not go to avoid the real labor of thinking.**
>
> **Thomas Alva Edison**

The last two elements in our creative thinking plan are **Choose (C)** and **Effect (E).** They are exactly the same as for problem solving because it's here that Creative Thinking gives way to Analytical Thinking, in order to decide on the best course of action.

C Is for Choose and Consequences

Out of all these new ideas, what's the best idea? Which idea best meets the criteria we initially set? What would be the consequence of choosing it?

E Is for Effect

Now put the best idea to work; otherwise it's all impractical day-dreaming.

We believe that the key to the fast-moving and complex world of the 21st century is to learn fast and to become a high-quality creative analyst. **Both talents are learnable.**

Both analysis and creativity need to be methodical. It might, therefore, be a good idea to copy down on four postcards the acronyms we've suggested and commit them to memory. Like M•A•S•T•E•R, they will give you checklists for learning.

A FARCE	for creativity (including CASPAR for alternatives)
A FAN	for decision making
DANCE	for problem solving
A,B,C,D,E,F,G + I	for general analysis

Of course, thinking cannot be done in the abstract. You need a particular subject or problem to work on. So you may memorize the checklists, but you cannot become a good thinker without applying these thinking tools over and over and over, until their use becomes automatic.

The Spark of Genius

Fantasy. Reverie. Intuition. Playfulness. Emotion. Sleep.

What do these have to do with creative genius, or with some of the most monumental milestones in human development? Actually, such elements have made quite an amazing contribution.

Quite often, after years of dogged determination and almost obsessive persistence, a relaxing moment has led to a flash of inspiration and a breakthrough revelation.

Getting away from taxing work seems to refresh a tired mind, just as it rejuvenates tired muscles, thus making it more receptive to intuitive impulses. Unlike computers the mind is capable of doing many things at once. While we are sleeping, walking in the woods, washing dishes, or shaving, important work is being done outside our awareness. The factory of the mind continues to work while the manager is out, assembling diverse raw materials and putting them together in unusual ways to create new products.

Many of the greatest minds have talked freely about the spark that led to the discoveries that have changed the way we think and live.

Einstein, for one, believed you could stimulate ingenious thought by allowing your imagination to float freely, unrestrained by conventional inhibitions. He attributed his discovery of the Theory of Relativity to "daydreaming." As an adolescent he dreamed up a thought experiment, imagining himself astride a light ray.

Later in life he said, "When I examined myself and my methods of thought, I came to the conclusion that the gift of fantasy has meant more to me than my talent for absorbing positive knowledge."

Beethoven, asked where his ideas for composition came from, poetically responded: "They come to me in the silence of the night or in the early morning, stirred into being by moods."

German chemist Friedrich August Kekulé came up with the structure of the benzene molecule, while in a "half sleep" in front of the fire. Kekulé saw fantastic shapes and forms in the flames and later gave this colorful description: "The atoms flitted before my eyes. Long rows . . . all in movement, wriggling and turning like snakes. And see, what was that? One of the snakes seized its own tail and the image whirled scornfully before my eyes. As though from a flash of lightning I awoke."

His unconscious had given him the key to the structure of the benzene molecule. Soon after, in 1865, he announced the molecule to be a closed hexagonal ring formed of six carbon atoms not unlike the snake in his vision.

Sir Isaac Newton talked about his life work this way: "I do not know what I may appear to the world; but to myself I seem to have been only like a boy playing on the seashore and diverting himself and then finding a smoother pebble or a prettier shell than ordinary, while the greater ocean of truth lay all undiscovered before me."

John Maynard Keynes, writing about Newton said: "It was his intuition which was preeminently extraordinary. So happy in his conjectures that he seemed to know more than he could possibly have any hope of proving. The proofs were . . . dressed up afterwards; they were not the instrument of discovery."

Goethe walked in order to get ideas. Rousseau did his best thinking on trips he made alone and on foot. Nietzsche listened to a musical performance in the evening and awoke full of "resolute insights and inspirations."

Sleep is a terrific ideas incubator—"dear mother of fresh thoughts," according to Wordsworth.

A great number of creators like Gauss, Darwin, Hemingway, and Nevelson have preferred to create in the early morning immediately upon waking. Edison slept in his laboratory, sometimes on a table, so that he could start work as soon as he awoke. The reason most give for the morning work schedule was expressed by Balzac, who said he wanted to take advantage of the fact that "my brain works while I sleep."

Asked where he found his melodies, Bach said, "The problem is not finding them, it's—when getting up in the morning and getting out of bed—not stepping on them."

René Descartes, whose name is virtually synonymous with rationalism, was a soldier undecided about his future when he realized in a dream that he should combine mathematics and philoso-

> **Every discovery contains an "irrational element" or a creative intuition.**
>
> **KARL POPPER**

phy into a new discipline. Robert Louis Stevenson dreamed the plot of *Dr. Jekyll and Mr. Hyde.*

Benjamin Franklin wanted to make contact with a thundercloud. No tall tower was available, and predictable ideas such as using spires and long iron rods were futile. Then, while relaxing one day, he drifted into a daydream and the memory of kite-flying crossed his mind. The rest is history.

Says Jonas Salk, famed for his development of the polio vaccine, "It is always with excitement that I wake up in the morning wondering what my intuition will toss up to me, like gifts from the sea. I work with it and rely on it. It's my partner."

For most creative giants it was intuition as well as logic, rhythm combined with structure, daydreaming coupled with careful planning, imagination teamed with evaluation that constituted genius.

The history of thought contains innumerable examples of intuitive discoveries. The most famous is probably Archimedes' fortuitous bath, in which he discovered the principle of water displacement and gave us the term *Eureka!* (I have found it).

Mozart's greatest works came to him at odd times, rather than when sitting consciously at the piano, diligently working at it. He reported: "When I am, as it were, completely myself, entirely alone, and of good cheer—say, traveling in a carriage, or walking after a good meal, or during the night when I cannot sleep; it is on such occasions that ideas flow best and most abundantly. *Whence* and *how* they come, I know not; nor can I force them."

In recent times Nobel laureate Melvin Calvin, while idly sitting in his car waiting for his wife to compete an errand, found the answer to a puzzling inconsistency in his research on photosynthesis.

> **Trusting our intuition can cure us of "psychosclerosis," a hardening of the mind and spirit that stems from overdependence on rationality and analysis.**
>
> HAROLD H. BLOOMFIELD, M.D.
> AUTHOR OF *MAKING PEACE WITH YOUR PARENTS*

Wrote Calvin: "It occurred just like that—quite suddenly—and suddenly also, in a matter of seconds, the path of carbon became apparent to me."

Intuition, of course, doesn't come from nowhere. Dogged rational work in the preparation phase is of extreme importance, particularly in a specialized field.

It supplies the intuitive mind with the incentive and raw material it needs.

Does intuition have any relevance in today's business world? Surely top-flight corporate executives are out-and-out analytical thinkers who make decisions based on a systematic approach? Not at all.

Henry Mintzberg, of the McGill University Faculty of Management, extensively studied corporate executives. He found that the high-ranking manager operating under chaotic and unpredictable conditions is a "holistic thinker . . . constantly relying on hunches to cope with problems far too complex for rational analysis."

Mintzberg concluded that "organizational effectiveness does not lie in that narrow-minded concept called 'rationality'; it lies in a blend of clearheaded logic and powerful intuition."

What lessons are to be learned for the education of our children?

Philip Goldberg, in his excellent book *The Intuitive Edge,* says that students should be encouraged to appreciate their innate capacity for fantasy, visualization, and imagination, all of which aid intuition.

"We would make great progress toward liberating the child's intuitive abilities if we placed more emphasis on personal discovery rather than rote memorization of facts or the mechanical application of rules for problem solving," he says. Students are usually given problems rather than being allowed to find their own. Then they are told the expected answer and how to reach that answer. "It would be far better if, at least on occasion, they were allowed to experience firsthand what we all have to do in adulthood: identify problems concerning matters we care about and find our own ways of solving them," adds Goldberg.

Since we learn by example, an excellent way to start would be to get teachers to display intuitive thinking in the classroom.

Says Goldberg, "Right now, teachers tend to recite facts and display the finished products of their after-hours work. If students could see their teachers make guesses and wild stabs, run up blind alleys and chase after fugitive hunches, their own uncertain intuitions and meandering images would gain legitimacy.

"Of course, this would require teachers who were, in fact, in-

> **The really valuable thing is intuition.**
>
> **ALBERT EINSTEIN**

quisitive and took joy in pursuing knowledge. It would also require teachers who were willing to make mistakes in front of their students. This may be asking a lot, but we nevertheless ought to realize that teachers are not only dispensers of information; they are models for how to use the mind."

These two chapters on the acquisition of thinking skills can be neatly summarized by Henry Ford's observation "Thinking is the hardest work of all. That's why so few people do it."

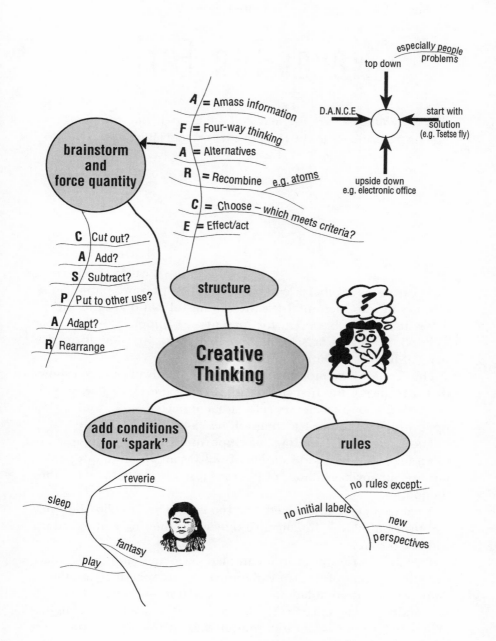

especially people problems

top down

D.A.N.C.E

start with solution (e.g. Tsetse fly)

upside down e.g. electronic office

A = Amass information

F = Four-way thinking

A = Alternatives

R = Recombine   e.g. atoms

C = Choose – which meets criteria?

E = Effect/act

brainstorm and force quantity

C Cut out?

A Add?

S Subtract?

P Put to other use?

A Adapt?

R Rearrange

structure

Creative Thinking

add conditions for "spark"

reverie

sleep

fantasy

play

rules

no rules except:

no initial labels

new perspectives

15

Never Too Early

From the child of five to myself is but a step, but from the newborn baby to the child of five is an appalling distance.
LEO TOLSTOY

Children are born to be smart. In their earliest years they are like sponges, easily absorbing immense volumes of information about the wonderful world around them.

It's tempting, however, for parents to adopt the view that "schooling" begins at school. And that these first few formative years of life are nothing more than "play" years.

They couldn't be more wrong. A growing body of research shows that it is during the first five or six years of life that some 50 percent of the brain's nerve cells are connected—the foundation upon which all future learning will be based.

There are vital "windows of opportunity" during these years when exposure to a wide variety of skills is an absolute essential—because a baby has billions of neurons just waiting to be wired into a mind.

A baby, as we've discovered, has 100 billion brain cells—but they can turn into usable intelligence only when they are connected up with each other.

The circuits for music and math, language and emotion—in fact the entire gamut of human experience—mature at different times. And they need stimulation at the right time—when that young, demanding mind wakes each day eager to discover new delights. When he or she is naturally inquisitive. When there's an overwhelming impulse to be a little explorer, to investigate everything with all of his or her faculties.

Just look at these diagrams and see the difference between a brain that benefits from a wide range of stimulating activities and one that doesn't. It's a telling example of the importance of early learning!

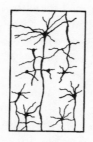 

The brain cell connections of an unstimulated brain

The brain cell connections of a stimulated brain

This example means that:

- parents are the most important teachers
- the home—not the school—is the most significant learning environment
- and it's vital, therefore, to provide a rich, stimulating home life right from the very start.

From the moment of birth you can gently begin to stimulate your child's awareness and ability to learn and make playtime an enriching journey of discovery. The earlier you help your youngster appreciate that learning is a joyful adventure, the more likely he is to achieve his full potential in life.

Says Carla Shatz of the University of California, Berkeley, president of the Society for Neuroscience, "The baby's brain is not a miniature version of an adult . . . the baby's brain is a fabulous learning machine. We're all walking miracles, when you think about how everything is wired up."

Eminent researchers such as Marian Diamond, neuroanatomist at the University of California, Berkeley, and author of *Enriching Heredity*, say that our raw "intelligence"—the complexity of our neural connections—depends not just on what nature bequeaths to us genetically, but also on how positive, nurturing, and stimulating a learning environment we grow up in.

Pediatric neurobiologist Harry Chugani, of Wayne State University, says that early experiences are so overwhelmingly meaningful, "they can completely change the way a person turns out."

Neural connections that don't develop within the child's first five years of life may never develop at all. That's why seizing the "windows of opportunity" when they are open is absolutely critical. As each year goes by, as the child celebrates each new birthday, windows are closing that can never be reopened.

Some experts go so far as to say that when a child enters first grade, the most important learning years have already passed.

"Children who do not receive mental enrichment in the preschool years will start school less able than they might have been and will achieve less that they once had the potential to do," says Joan Beck, author of *How to Raise a Brighter Child*.

The general point was graphically illustrated in studies conducted on vision by the Nobel prize–winning team of American neurobiologist David Hubel at Harvard and his Swedish colleague Tortsen Wiesel.

Longtime collaborators on vision research, they found that sewing shut one eye of a newborn kitten led to permanent blindness in that eye. During the time the eye was closed, vital neuronal connections to the visual cortex were not made—and lost forever. When a similar experiment was performed on an adult cat, its vision was not impaired.

> **When a baby comes into the world her brain is a jumble of neurons, all waiting to be woven into the intricate tapestry of the mind.**
>
> **SHARON BEGLEY IN** *NEWSWEEK* **MAGAZINE**

The obvious conclusion is that there is a brief, early period when circuits connect the retina to the visual cortex. Use it or lose it.

Neurobiologists and other scientists are still working out all of the implications for children, but the "never too early" message is crystal clear. "Connections are not formed willy-nilly but are promoted by activity," says Dale Purves of Duke University.

So don't put your newborn in

a traditional room of pastel colors. Instead, place cards with black and white shapes and face patterns around the crib and on the walls.

Learning Your Native Tongue

Take the acquisition of language, for instance.

Imitation plays a vital role in the development of spoken language. The accent you developed to speak your native tongue was based on the way people around you spoke—particularly your parents—during your first five years of life. It probably stays with you for life. It is very difficult to change later, because it has been implanted on the main pathways of the brain that deal with language. So even though you grow more dendrites as you improve your vocabulary, the way you speak is—by and large—determined by the main branches you developed in those first few years.

> I consider the period from age two to age six or seven a fascinating period of human development . . . it harbors more of the secrets and power of human growth than any other comparable phase of growth.
>
> **HOWARD GARDNER**

The more words a child hears, the faster she learns language. In one study infants whose mothers spoke to them frequently (even using monosyllables) knew 131 more words at the age of twenty months than did babies whose mothers were not so talkative. By the age of twenty-four months the gap had widened to 295 words.

Says Guy McKhann, MD of Johns Hopkins University, "Some two-, three-, four-year-olds are very language deprived. By the time they get to school they're way behind. It's a gap that's very hard to make up."

Learning a Foreign Tongue

If children live in a home where two languages are spoken, they will almost certainly acquire both. If three languages are spoken they will probably be able to speak all three.

Infants learn the basic sounds that comprise their native tongue by the time they are six months old—before they say their first words, according to a study conducted by Dr. Patricia Kuhl of the University of Washington in Seattle.

Dr. Kuhl's research indicates that the language a child hears during those first six months actually alters the perception of speech sounds.

Some linguistic experts say that when a child "babbles," he actually makes all the sounds that occur in all the languages of the world—even though, of course, he's never heard them. And, given the right environment, children can learn to speak a foreign language fluently in the first four years of life.

In fact, it's easier to learn a second language at the same time you're learning your native tongue because at this stage of life the brain circuitry is wired with the ability to easily absorb both. If this doesn't happen, the "undedicated" neurons lose their ability to form connections for the foreign language.

What's worse is that the brain's "perceptual map" of the first language dominates and constrains the learning of a second language. A child taught a second language after he reaches the age of ten is unlikely to become able to speak it like a native. Many Japanese adults, for example, unless they were raised around "proper" English speakers in the first few years of life, have a hard time pronouncing their *l*'s. Instead, their *e* sounds like an *r*.

So why doesn't the education establishment encourage the learning of a foreign language much, much earlier than it does?

> **By the time children reach school they have absorbed a tremendous amount. In fact, they have achieved the greatest feat of learning: essential mastery of a spoken language.**
>
> **WILLIAM A. REINSMITH,**
> **PROFESSOR OF ENGLISH,**
> **PHILADELPHIA COLLEGE OF**
> **PHARMACY AND SCIENCE**

As Professor Chugani is fond of inquiring, "Who's the idiot who decreed that foreign-language instruction not begin until high school? We're not paying attention to biological principles. The time to learn these is in preschool or elementary school."

Martha Denckla, MD, of Johns Hopkins University, agrees: "We should be using the nursery-school years to expose our children to a second, even a third, language. It's a marvelous, enriching, very appropriate thing to do."

Infants who are routinely ex-posed to sounds from foreign languages such as songs and nursery rhymes develop tonal memories that enhance their ability to later learn multiple lan-guages.

Math, Music, and Logic

Does the "Mozart Factor" have a meaningful impact on very young children? Absolutely.

In a study conducted at the University of California at Irvine

> **Children are like seeds planted in the ground. They must be watered daily. With constant care and at-tention, the seed will grow into a plant and eventually flower.**
>
> SHINICHI SUZUKI IN
> *NURTURED BY LOVE*

by Dr. Gordon Shaw, nineteen preschoolers were given piano or singing lessons. Eight months later their spatial reasoning was tested—their ability to draw geometric shapes, copy patterns of two-color blocks, and work mazes. Compared with children who had no musical lessons, their performance "dramatically im-proved."

Researcher Shaw suggests that when the preschoolers exercised their cortical neurons by listening to classical music, they were also strengthening the circuits deployed for mathematics.

PE for the Brain

A daily exercise routine for your child improves your child's ability to read and write.

Dr. Lyelle Palmer, professor of education at Winona State Uni-versity in Minnesota, has extensively tested the mental benefits of physical exercise with five-year-olds.

In the gymnasium the children are encouraged to go through a series of routines including spinning, rope jumping, balancing, somersaulting, climbing, rolling, and walking on balance beams.

In the playground they are encouraged to swing on low "monkey bars," climb, roller-skate, perform somersaults and flips.

In the classroom they play with a variety of games designed to stimulate their sight, hearing and, touch.

Palmer, a former president of the International Alliance for Learning, says that all of the activities "are specifically designed to activate the areas of the brain we know will promote their sense of sight, touch, and hearing—as well as their ability to take in knowledge."

The result: At the end of each year many of the children— mostly from low-income families—take the Metropolitan Readiness Test to measure whether they are ready for first-grade schooling. And pass with flying colors. Most are in the top five percent for the state.

Says Dr. Palmer, "When you ordinarily look at children playing, moving, dancing about, and doing gymnastic activities, we think of muscle development. But the major result of my research is that brain stimulation, that is, the increase of sensory activity to the brain, changes the brain cells. These changes allow for the emergence of higher levels of abilities and skills in children. By *abilities* I mean the sensory abilities, such as seeing and hearing. By *skills* I mean the ability to perform schoolwork.

"The importance of the research is that the brain is plastic. What we have here is an opportunity with children to make a huge difference by being systematic in the way that we supply stimulation. The brain is growing faster at that point than it ever will again in the child's lifetime. We can boost that growth curve by increasing the amount of stimulation by light, sound, touch, movement, and the contents."

One such activity developed by Dr. Palmer is the "helicopter spin." It's for three- to five-year-olds. They simply spin around as fast as possible with their arms held out for fifteen seconds. Then, they stop, stand still for twenty-five seconds with their eyes closed— and stay balanced. This sequence is repeated ten times. It helps build, says Dr. Palmer, the basis for long-term motor skills like sports and holding a pencil.

Former Olympic athlete Jerome Hartigan, who runs preschool brain-exercise classes in New Zealand, agrees: "Developing the physical and muscular system has a huge impact on the development of the brain. The more we can nurture the muscles, the senses, the whole body, the more the brain will develop its ability to learn intellectually later on in life."

So aim to stimulate all of your child's senses; let her walk on balance beams; balance a book on her head; pour water, rice, and sand; roll and catch balls; string macaroni (which leads to finger control and writing ability); play blindfold guessing-games; smell spices; explore tastes. When taking walks, stop to listen carefully to sounds, and when you are at home, sometimes dance with your child in your arms. The more actively you develop all of your child's senses, the more he will be able to use them in later life.

The Venezuelan Initiative

What happens when a country's leadership makes a commitment to boost the intelligence of its entire people? It starts at the beginning! From the moment of birth.

Back in 1979 a new government with that kind of mission created the world's first minister of state for the development of intelligence. It appointed to the prestigious position philosopher and poet Luis Alberto Machado, who quickly assembled a team to seek the best advice from experts around the globe.

What was eventually implemented—called "The Family Project"—began in maternity hospitals, where new mothers were not only given personal training by volunteers (some ten thousand of them) but also benefited from an extensive collection of video programs. The mothers were thereby given the foundation for the fuller development of their children through loving care, proper nutrition, sensory-motor stimulation, and physical exercises. During the first three years of life parents were also given follow-up advice through local community centers.

Machado's program went on to bombard the country with new information on how to develop human capacities. Hospitals, schools, the media, civil service, the military, and industry were all recruited to participate. There were even five-minute television spots broadcast twenty times every day on all four of the country's commercial television channels.

Dee Dickinson, founder of the New Horizons for Learning network, who reviewed the Venezuelan success, referred to it as "an educational Amway." She noted

> I believe that we shall gradually come to take it for granted that children should learn to read, to turn written words into sounds, to write and to spell at home, as naturally as they now learn to hear and speak.
>
> FELICITY HUGHES IN *READING AND WRITING BEFORE SCHOOL*

that in schools five psychologists trained 150 selected teachers, who trained 42,000 other teachers, who subsequently taught creative thinking and problem-solving skills to more than one million children. More recently, a similar "Family Project" has begun in Arlington, Virginia.

The U.S. "School of the 21st Century"

In a 1996 TIME/CNN poll in the U.S., 73 percent of people surveyed were in favor of more of their tax dollars going to programs that benefit the young. Shockingly, however, some 20 percent rated preschool education programs as a "low priority" or even or "no priority" item.

Fortunately, many child advocate groups and educators agree that it's never too early to get children on the right track—and that the way to do it is by working with the whole family and transforming the neighborhood school into a "caring community."

Margot Hornblower, writing about the concept in *Time*, says, "It may sound like a platitude, but it is in fact a revolution, one that is spreading through the country, from inner-city ghettos to prosperous suburbs and rural enclaves, as fast as you can say ABC."

One exemplary program, pioneered by the state of Missouri, has now spread to forty-seven states. In this "Parents as Teachers" program, parenting skills and developmental screening are offered to families with young children. It starts in the third trimester of pregnancy and lasts through the first three years of life. Children's possible learning difficulties are handled at the time when intervention can do the most good.

Some schools are beginning to stretch beyond traditional academic roles and assume responsibility for the emotional and social well-being of the child—even from birth. In a way they are becoming "surrogate parents."

Yale professor Edward Zigler created the "School of the 21st Century," which provides all-day preschool throughout the year—starting at the age of three. The program, which has spread to more than four hundred cam-

> **Nothing is more fundamental to solid educational development than a pure, uncontaminated curiosity.**
>
> BURTON L. WHITE IN
> *THE FIRST THREE YEARS OF LIFE*

puses, also involves taking care of kids before and after school hours. Vacations too.

At some schools teachers "adopt" at-risk children for out-of-school activities.

"School has to be about more than reading, writing, and arithmetic," says Herman Clark, principal of Bowling Park Elementary in Norfolk, Virginia, whose efforts were featured in a major *Time* article. "These kids need so much—and sometimes what they really need is a good hug."

Bowling Park now enjoys higher test scores and a 97 percent attendance rate.

And these lessons are not just for low-income neighborhoods. The concept of making use of school facilities for more hours in the day and more weeks in the year applies equally throughout the system.

"We have fine buildings. Why let them sit vacant fourteen hours a day and three months of the year?" says Independence, Missouri, school superintendent Robert Watkins. "Now we can see a child with a speech impediment at age three and get started on remediation."

In Independence all thirteen elementary schools operate on the 21st Century model and 35 percent of parents take advantage of the state-provided home-visit program for the under-threes.

Will other school districts follow these examples? There are obstacles, of course. "Overcrowded classrooms, pinched budgets, and teachers set in their ways are only a few of the obstacles," says writer Hornblower.

But not to do so will ultimately cost society much more.

Says Julia Denes, assistant director of Yale's Bush Center of Child Development and Social Policy, "We must invest in children at an early age to prevent special needs and delinquency."

Putting It All Together

Fifty percent of brain capacity is built in the first five or six years! Of all the statistics we have come across in twelve years of educational research, this is the one that gave us most pause for thought.

> **Understanding a child's brain and the way it develops is the key to understanding learning.**
>
> JANE M. HEALY IN *YOUR CHILD'S GROWING MIND*

And the more we thought about it, and talked to parents about it, the more we realized that parents instinctively know that an early, rich, thought-provoking environment is the key. But the common question was: "What exactly does it entail? What do I actually do?"

Every parent knows that a child can grow physically to his full potential only when all the elements of complete nutrition are provided. But what are all the elements they must provide to ensure full mental development?

Answering that question has been the inspiration behind a five-year project to devise a complete preschool program designed to do more than help a child to read, write, and do basic arithmetic before formal schooling. Its goal is to nurture other vital attributes including self-esteem, creativity, clear thinking, concentration, persistence, musical sense, and basic values such as responsibility, honesty, and self-control.

In other words, the ultimate goal of the program, which is called *FUNdamentals,* is a happy, well-rounded child.

We see it as a pyramid of building blocks as depicted in the accompanying diagram. These need to be put in place—step by step—in order to reach the top goal.

The *FUNdamentals* program is realistic. It takes into account the fact that in today's fast-paced society no one has unlimited time. So it tackles the need to create that all-important rich and stimulating environment by providing what we call "purposeful play."

We've already mentioned some examples of how to develop senses. Here are some more that show you how to aim for **rounded** growth, to build all the intelligences. Try these kinds of mentally stimulating games and activities with your child:

Building a rich vocabulary. Try an inflatable globe in the bath. Where should we go tonight? Talk briefly about the country and its people. Or play "rhyming words." One person starts, the next tries to think of a word that rhymes.

Or play categories. How many ways of traveling can you think of? How many farm animals can you name? How many things that fly? When you unpack the groceries, see where the items came from and discuss any countries of origin and their customs.

Reading. The *so* simple reason children don't read early is because the size of letters is too small for their developing eyes. So-

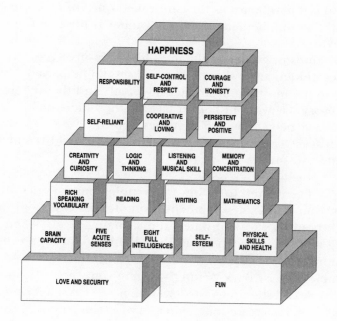

The building blocks in *FUNdamentals*. Each one is developed through a wide variety of stimulating yet fun activities, and each one contributes to a foundation of success and happiness.

lution: Create word cards with "action" words in letters at least two inches (five centimeters) tall. Words such as *jump, run, hop.* Have your child read them, and act them out. Then put noun cards around the room for things he can see and touch—*door, bed, lamp, wall, teddy, leg, arm.* When he has "broken the code" and understands the principle of reading, progress to phonic words on cards or on a blackboard, so he sees how *cat, mat, sat,* etc., all relate. Play "phonic snap" with the word cards you have constructed.

Then progress to games we've developed, like Word Bingo. Here, the 400 most frequently encountered words are printed on individual cards, which the child seeks to match to pre-printed words on a Bingo board as they are called out. Instead of trying to mark off five numbers in a line, the winner is the one to mark off five words.

These kinds of games, and games like Treasure Hunt, with written clues hidden around the house, all should be played as a background to the most important activity of all. And that is being read stories every day without fail. In fact, by the time a child is five he should have been read 1,500 stories (obviously not *all* different ones). It's *not* as many as it sounds and it will build reading skills gradually and surely.

Writing. The secret to writing is simple: build pencil control. Early in your child's development promote hand-eye coordination through pouring rice and water, and stringing beads. Then comes drawing and tracing shapes and then the breakthrough into letter formation.

A simple idea is "Back-Writing"—where you trace a letter on the child's back and she draws the letter on a piece of paper pinned to the wall. It helps create motor memory for the letters.

When she's begun to write, a fun game is Word Jigsaw. You simply split up a word like EL E PHANT into jigsawlike pieces. It helps develop the key spelling strategy of breaking words into their component parts.

Math skills. Counting is the seed from which all math grows. So count everything, every day. Weigh toys, sort laundry and buttons, talk about which things are bigger and smaller. Have shape hunts around the house, where you look for ten round objects, five oblongs, seven squares, four triangles, etc.

Take a pack of playing cards and have a "battle." Each player takes two cards and adds them together. The winner has the highest total. Play lots of games with a stopwatch. How long does it take to sing the "Alphabet Song"? Play Animal Adding. Add the legs of six animals. So a cat and a spider and an ant total 18. (4 + 8 + 6).

Creativity. Mime things—opening a door that doesn't exist, drinking a glass of water, putting on a sweater. Make fingerprints on a piece of paper. What can you turn them into by adding some lines? A flower? A pig? A rocket?

One person starts a story, another takes it in turn to keep adding to the story. Make up new words to an old song.

Play the What If? game. (What if you lived like an Eskimo? Could fly? Were a drop of rain? etc.) Play some music. Draw whatever the music makes you think about.

Memory. Play the Cup Game. You take three cups, put a ball under one and move them around on the table. Where's the ball? It's fun—and it builds concentration.

Or mental hide and seek. Someone chooses a place in the house from memory in which to hide a small object. The game is to ask deductive questions to discover where it is. This activity builds visual memory, which is a key learning skill.

Self-esteem. Try the Effort Coupon. When your child really tries hard at something, give him a coupon for effort. Let him save five coupons for a reward such as a trip to the swimming pool.

In all, the *FUNdamentals* program has almost a thousand ideas like these. They are all fun but all build skills, character, or values. The driving idea is to help develop all of a child's eight intelligences and an inquiring, thoughtful mind.

One of the outcomes of *FUNdamentals* is that a child will almost certainly be able to read before going to school. Some educators question whether this is desirable. We think it's helpful for a child to enter school being able to read, for three reasons.

First, most children who follow the kind of activities we have mentioned find that reading is natural, easy, and fun. If you can read at four, why wait till six?

Second, the child is already beginning to acquire some independence. She's moving from "learning to read" to "reading to learn."

She can start, therefore, to learn for herself, to discover that books are an endless source of fascinating ideas that she can discover by herself. She doesn't have to wait for someone else to do it for her.

Finally, when a child enters school with the ability to read, it's a major confidence boost. His experience is one of success and it gives him a positive early attitude to school.

The same is true of the basic mathematics processes. It's possible to structure games so that addition and subtraction—and even simple division—are well within the grasp of a four-year-old. So again a child can enter school feeling capable and positive and motivated by mathematics.

Our hope is that parents will not just follow the hundreds of games and activities we have developed but use our models to invent and swap ideas of their own in order to create fun and challenging activities for their preschoolers.

The operative word is *challenge*. When children develop an intense curiosity about everything and an enjoyment in puzzling out why things happen the way they do, you have the basis for success.

Children are naturally curious, but they need to be given a lead. One of the most valuable things you can do is ask thought-provoking questions throughout the day, every day. Not just with preschoolers, but even more regularly with primary school–age children.

Questions that arise from everyday situations, such as:

I wonder how they make cornflakes? Maybe we should write and ask.

Where does water go when it runs down the sink?

Why does food go bad?

Why can't we drink pond water?

Why doesn't the grass grow in winter? (After all, there's still daylight and rainwater.)

Who writes and prints the morning newspaper?

Why doesn't electricity leak out the sockets?

Can we invent a new game that involves adding and subtracting?

I wonder where your heart is? Let's draw an outline of you on the back of some old wallpaper and draw in your heart, your liver, your stomach, etc. Let's look it up.

What are your five favorite things? I wonder what Grandma's five favorite things are? Does it help you understand how she feels?

What does *influence* mean? Shall we look it up?

Can you draw something to represent influence? Shall we take a new word each week and think about it like this? How about words like *peace, temporary, justice, anger?*

How much water do we use each week? How could we measure it? Could we make a graph? Is there water in food? What would happen if we only had half the water that we do now?

How much does the food cost that we buy each week?

We say "as brave as a lion." What animal do you think you are like? If you had to be an insect, which would you choose? Why?

Can we write a poem? Here's a fun form of poetry; it's called a CINQUAIN.

> Wind
> Strong, blustery,
> Howling, tugging, rushing,
> I need to shelter,
> Gale.

See how it's made up.

In line 1 you start with a thing (it's called a noun).

In line 2 you use two descriptive words (adjectives).

In line 3 you use three action words (verbs).

In line 4 you make a statement in four words.

In line 5 you use a word that means the same as the thing you first chose.

Shall we make up some cinquains?

A Loving Challenge Pays Off

It's impossible to overstress the importance and effect of loving challenge for children. An English couple we know had a Down syndrome baby. They believed in the power of loving challenge to build brain capacity. They played music to their child each day. They encouraged her to play lots and lots of ordinary but thought-provoking games, and they read extensively to her every day. They even had her sleep on a bed that was at a slight angle so there was a little bit of a challenge to settle down. That child at the age of eight achieved a reading age of seven.

In New Zealand, Choon Tan is a telecommunications engineer.

He believes passionately that because math has a finite number of basic processes, with patient, loving guidance these processes can all be learned by the age of twelve. When one of us saw his youngest, Michael, age eight, he was doing his homework on an ironing board, having come in from a basketball session. A happy, fun-loving, normal boy. Except that he was doing the math work of a sixteen-year-old. Choon Tan's eldest has gotten his Ph.D. in pure math from Cambridge at twenty, and his daughter, at fourteen, was taking a math degree at the local university.

We cite the example of Choon Tan not because there is necessarily merit in an individual child attending an institution along with much older students (social development is as important as intellectual development) but because it illustrates what can be achieved by loving challenge. If for a few, why not for the many? **We seriously underestimate what our children can achieve.**

We make the same point in our seminars for parents as we do in our seminars for business people: The limits to learning are largely self-imposed.

Creating a rich, stimulating, **thought-provoking** environment that will nurture your child's wonder, curiosity, and creativity doesn't cost money. It just costs a little time. And the return for that investment is a child with the basic attitude and thinking skills to succeed in the 21st century.

Isn't that worth the effort? David Morris of Cape Town, South Africa, certainly thinks so. He and his wife have established the first early learning center, the Preschool Learning Alliance, based on the principles of the *FUNdamentals* program.

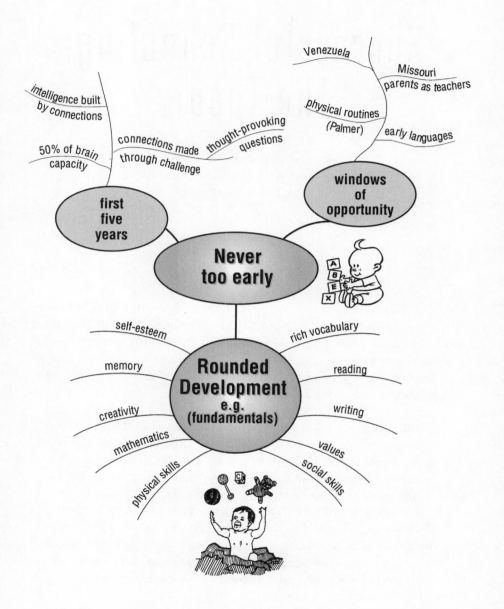

first
five
years

intelligence built
by connections

50% of brain
capacity

connections made
through challenge

thought-provoking
questions

Venezuela

Missouri
parents as teachers

physical routines
(Palmer)

early languages

windows
of
opportunity

Never
too early

self-esteem

memory

creativity

mathematics

physical skills

Rounded
Development
e.g.
(fundamentals)

rich vocabulary

reading

writing

values

social skills

16

Successful Schooling: The Theory

American education is at a turning point.
HOWARD GARDNER IN *MULTIPLE INTELLIGENCES:
THE THEORY IN PRACTICE*

For Sir Winston Churchill they were not the happiest days of his life. The great British Bulldog's time at school was a long succession of clashes with authority—and dismal academic results.

Years later, in typical Churchillian prose, he railed, in particular, against the exam system:

I had scarcely passed my twelfth birthday when I entered the inhospitable regions of examinations, through which, for the next seven years, I was destined to journey. These examinations were a great trial to me. The subjects which were dearest to the examiners were almost invariably those I fancied least.

I would have liked to have been examined in history, poetry, and writing essays. The examiners, on the other hand, were partial to Latin and mathematics. And their will prevailed. Moreover, the questions which they asked on both these subjects were almost invariably those to which I was unable to suggest the satisfactory answer.

I should have liked to be asked to say what I knew. They always tried to ask what I did not know. When I would willingly have displayed my knowledge, they sought to expose my ignorance. This sort of treatment had only one result, I did not do well in examinations.

For all too many children today school is no more enjoyable than it was for Churchill. And the burden of examinations is heavier than ever. As mentioned earlier, a review of forty years of educational reform revealed that testing of students has increased a phenomenal 10 percent to 20 percent *per year.*

Churchill would get plenty of sympathy from innovative educators such as Howard Gardner, who says, "American students are the most tested and least examined students in the world. When things go badly, we just add another test—as if taking the temperature more often would heal the patient."

English professor William A. Reinsmith, author of *Archetypal Forms in Teaching: A Continuum,* agrees: "Tests are a very poor indicator of whether an individual has really learned something. The main reason for this is that, except for disciplines which are extremely abstract and theoretical, tests provide an artificial context for demonstrating one's knowledge. They seldom address the real world."

Corporate educational consultant Myron Tribus points out that in any group of one hundred children, fifty of them will be ranked in the bottom half on any test, no matter how well they do.

"In short, half of each generation is branded 'inferior' and, what is worse, believes it for life," says Tribus. "There is nothing so destructive of the joy of learning than to be told you are a failure, branded for life. It will take years to wipe out the practice in industry. In my experience it will take even longer to remove the grading system from education. It is easier to move graveyards."

Tribus, in an article coauthored with teacher David Langford, who helped pioneer a business approach to teaching in an Alaskan school, adds, "It takes a quality experience in education to create a learner for life. The quality experience varies with the age of the learner. It takes constant engagement to create a quality education.

"What matters is not how students do on examinations. What matters is whether they are hooked on learning; whether they shall be learners for life. The students of today will be living in a world unlike the one in which we grew up. Work and learning have become joined. In the world of tomorrow those who do not wish to study, and who do not know how to learn, will become unemployable."

> **Children are travelers in an unknown land and we are their guides.**
>
> ROBERT FISHER, AUTHOR OF
> *TEACHING CHILDREN TO THINK*

Churchill was by no means the only famous individual to be a failure at school. The most recent Conservative Prime Minister, John Major, was a high school dropout. And biographies and autobiographies of some of the world's most notable figures, time and again, reveal their academic inadequacies.

While at Cambridge in 1663 Isaac Newton failed an exam, owing to his woeful incompetence in geometry. Albert Einstein flunked his admissions exams in science at the Zurich Polytechnic. The renowned mathematician Henri Poincaré, did so poorly on the Binet IQ test that he was judged an imbecile. Prolific inventor Thomas Edison was notoriously slow in school.

Charles Dickens, Mark Twain, and Maxim Gorky did not manage to reach the equivalent of secondary school. Presidents Washington, Lincoln, and Truman never went to college. The list goes on and on.

The exam system, of course, is just one manifestation of an educational system today that does not appear to fulfill the needs of society. Who knows how many geniuses are unhappily scrambling through school today—because they are not in tune with the way they are being taught?

In all too many classrooms, if the student is not in accord with the traditional teaching methods catering to those with strong linguistic and logical-mathematical intelligences, he or she will struggle.

It doesn't have to be that way.

There are innovative educators in many countries who are embracing Accelerated Learning techniques to stimulate the minds of their young charges. Educators who share our philosophy that:

- students should first and foremost "learn how to learn" and learn how to think
- learning should be fun, while building self-esteem
- knowledge should be shared in a multisensory, multimodal approach using a variety of intelligences

- parents—and the community in general—should be fully involved in children's education
- school should be real preparation for the real world and
- Total Quality Management business principles should inspire schooling.

Learning How to Learn

Just think about it. The child going to school for the first time in 1997 could still be in the workforce in the year 2050. It's impossible to imagine the awesome changes that will occur during his scholastic and business life.

The whirlwind technological changes of the last fifty years will pale in comparison. All the more reason that learning how to learn is more important than what is learned. Sadly, the opposite often prevails, says educator Sylvia Farnham-Diggory.

Writing in the Harvard University Press publication *Schooling*, she says, "Each child is *extraordinary*. Nature has equipped every child with learning capabilities that far exceed anyone's ability to describe them. Unfortunately, the education system—based as it is on outdated, incorrect, oversimplified psychological principles—all too often collides catastrophically with children's natural learning skills, teaches them to mistrust and repress those skills, and moves countless numbers of children through fifteen thousand hours of systematic training in learning *not* to learn."

Learning Can Be Fun

A 1996 MORI poll in the UK asked students which word (or words) they associated with learning. Perhaps unsurprisingly, the most frequent comment was *hard work*. That was the first thing that came into the heads of 42 percent of the students.

A close second was *qualifications*. The implication, of course: you have to grit your teeth and endure hard work to get the qualifications necessary to make it in tomorrow's world.

Says Professor Reinsmith of the Philadelphia College of Pharmacy and Science, "Quite often—perhaps far more often than we can afford to admit—the classroom is an inappropriate context for genuine learning. At the very least we should try to make our classrooms vibrate like a crossroads where powerful ideas intersect.

People learn in direct proportion to how much fun they are having.

BOB PIKE,
CREATIVE TRAINING TECHNIQUES

"The more learning is like play, the more absorbing it will be—unless the student has been so corrupted by institutional education that only dull, serious work is equated with learning. It is frightening how hard a teacher must work to convince today's college students that study and learning can be interesting—even joyful—activities."

Learning Through All the Intelligences

Some students need visual and physical representations of concepts. Some students prefer abstract mind-work. Some need ideas expressed verbally in several different ways. Some students benefit when a classmate explains materials. Some work best when given the opportunity to play for a while with materials, as in a science lab, before they discover the key information. Others want to be told the answer directly.

As we've discovered, there are multiple paths to the acquisition of knowledge, and therefore, teachers need to be ready to engage the multiple intelligences that students bring to the classroom.

Thomas Armstrong, author of *7 Kinds of Smart,* emphasizes, (as we do), that children should not be simplistically labeled as an "interpersonal learner" or "visual learner."

He says: "Our goal is to broaden, not limit, each learner's potential. Let children use their special gifts, but also encourage them to explore all of the intelligences. That's the road to discovery. Classroom teachers spend too much time on paper-and-pencil tasks and not enough time on active learning that engages the total individual."

Says Thomas Hoerr, principal of the New City School in St. Louis, Missouri, which has incorporated multiple intelligences into its curriculum, "Over the course of the day all children should be able to bring their unique balance of learning styles into play."

Learning with Parent Power

Parents make a difference. Parents need to be involved. Parents are the resident experts on their children. They know a child's history and way of approaching the world. Good teachers would ask them: 'What is your child really good at? What is important in his life?' Parents should, in any event, make teachers aware of their children's "hidden" talents.

All the research indicates that the amount of parental support and encouragement that the young learner receives—or doesn't receive—is a key factor in her life.

A research team led by Benjamin Bloom supplies vivid evidence. Successful young professionals in a variety of fields were subjected to in-depth interviews about their lives. The most common characteristic they shared: "enthusiastic parent involvement."

Say researchers Raymond J. Wlodkowski and Judith H. Jaynes, "Parents appear to be the primary influence on a child's motivation to learn. Their formative effect on their children's motivation to learn has an impact at every stage of development, lasting through the high school years and beyond."

Quality Management Goes to School

Myron Tribus of Exergy, Inc., is one of the leading practitioners bringing appropriate Total Quality Management (TQM) principles into education. In an excellent series of papers he cites some key principles of TQM that can help toward successful schooling. We have picked out the four we think are the most significant.

1. Concentrate on the Process

TQM aims to continuously raise the quality of the product (in this case, educational outcomes) by involving everyone in improving the **process** by which the "product" is produced.

It follows that not only teachers and administrators but also parents and students need to have input into what is taught and be **directly** involved in **how** it is learned. Students should be encouraged to be "obsessive about improvement," constantly asking, "How can we do this better?"

Myron Tribus provides a good example of how this works. Students made up a flow chart to show the processes that took place between the time a student was given an assignment and when it was completed and marked. They discovered that the difference between good and poor results was mostly due to failure to do homework.

The class then asked why the homework wasn't done (remember the "Five Whys?"). This revealed problems that were mostly outside of the students' control, so time was allocated at school and peer tutors assigned. The failure rate declined swiftly.

As Tribus notes, "By concentrating on the **processes** and not just increasing the pressure on teachers or students, the failure rates were reduced." In other words, they solved the problem instead of just dealing with the symptoms.

Here's a truth that should guide every teacher, every parent, and every politician:

> **Poor school results are symptoms, they are not the problem. Setting goals won't help. Analyzing what caused the result and teaching students how to solve their own problems, *will*.**

The George Westinghouse Technical Vocational School in Brooklyn, New York, offers a similar example. Students plotted the correlation between the number of homework assignments completed and exam scores. They discovered **for themselves** that the higher the number of completions, the higher the scores. It was a more powerful lesson than any amount of external exhortation. It illustrates a simple principle: People believe their own data.

When students are able to analyze their own ways of learning (**the process**), they can then collaborate in producing a quality outcome. When teachers offer to let students evaluate and improve all the processes in the classroom—including their own input—they are really creating the basis for quality education.

> **What we teach in most of our schools does not remotely resemble the realities of the world on the brink of the new millennium, the world of EC and NAFTA and no USSR, the world where Mandarin is the most prevalent language.**
>
> PETER D. RELIC, PRESIDENT OF THE NATIONAL ASSOCIATION OF INDEPENDENT SCHOOLS

2. Quality Is Defined by the Customer

Quality is defined as that which **exceeds** the current needs and expectations of the customer. In this case the "customers" are the students and the parents. A quality education would delight the student and make him addicted to learning.

When the student enjoys learning, extrinsic motivation like grades, prizes, or threats become less powerful than the **in**trinsic motivation of wanting to exceed his own previous best. And when that happens he becomes a self-motivator. That's why Records of Achievement are important—the student can **see** his own progress.

3. Results Are Produced by the Initial Vision

Control isn't exercised by rules and procedures, it is achieved by agreeing on shared values and visions so people know what to do without being told. That's why it's so important that students are involved in setting the rules and values of their class, and why the parents/customers **must** be involved in setting their vision of what education is for. If you don't have a clear vision, you can't expect a quality outcome.

What are the outcomes we should expect of school today? What is the purpose of school in today's circumstances? In other words, what's our vision? Schools should produce:

A. **Knowledge.** You need an ever-expanding body of facts in order to understand what you are currently learning, and from which to synthesize creative solutions.

B. **Skill.** Skill is what puts knowledge to work. It would include learning how to learn, analytical and creative thinking, clear writing, reading, computer skills, communication skills, and the ability to see the interrelationships within systems. Skill enables the student to become a self-managing, self-motivating learner.

C. **Wisdom.** The ability to decide priorities, to allocate time effectively, to interpret and judge, to be flexible and open minded. Wisdom is the ability to analyze experience and act on the conclusions.

D. **Character.** Which is most easily defined by traits such as honesty, self-reliance, cooperativeness, persistence, empathy, the ability to work in teams, to set realistic goals, and integrity. In short—decency.

E. **Emotional maturity.** The ability to recognize, express, and manage one's own moods and emotions and respond sympathetically to others; to delay gratification; to manage stress, anger, and anxiety; to resolve conflicts rationally and be assertive without being aggressive.

Some will say that the development of emotional maturity goes beyond the scope of school. We say that with over 50 percent of marriages ending in divorce, with domestic and social violence increasing, we simply *must* put emotional education on the syllabus.

Although these are the five outcomes we want, it's doubtful that the current school system delivers more than the first and some of the second. And the first outcome is transient anyway because knowledge so quickly becomes out of date. The other outcomes, however, last for life. If that's all true, it's up to you—the parent/consumer—to collaborate with your school to precipitate the changes you want. It's not necessary to know how to achieve them. The first step is to define the outcomes and competencies you want when your child leaves school and the level of competency you expect. For example, do you want your child to be able to think analytically? If so, to what level?

It is then up to the school administration to work out how these competencies can be delivered, involving you and the other "customer" (the student) in the development of the final curriculum.

Be aware also that new outcomes demand new ways of assessment. A multiple-choice questionnaire may go some, albeit limited, way to measuring the retention of knowledge—but it's useless for assessing the other four outcomes we would like to see.

So aim for a parent/student/teacher consensus on how knowledge, skills, wisdom, character, and emotional maturity, can be demonstrated and evaluated. And remember that when we cease to rely so much on external testing and teach students how to check on their own quality, experience shows that the standard of work rises sharply.

Questions to debate about evaluation would be:

- What level of competence do we want in these five outcomes?
- How will the student and the teacher know when that level of competence is achieved?

- How can the student attain it, and how can the teacher help?
- How could the competence be measured independently?

We think that the purpose of school is much more than the acquisition of knowledge. That's why the final chapter contains many more suggestions to modify schools to meet the needs of the 21st century.

4. The Whole System Must Change, Not Just Parts

People working in a system cannot do better than the system allows. If you don't like the outcome, change the system. This implies that a teacher working alone to implement the ideas we present in this book risks frustration and struggle, because he or she may have changed, but the system hasn't.

Of course we urge you to get started anyway, but the big results will come when the system changes, which means all parts of the system collaborating for agreed-upon outcomes—parents, students, teachers, principals, and members of the school board, all working together.

Learning for the Real World

The school years should prepare students for the challenges they will have to face when they leave school.

As Renate Nummela Caine and Geoffrey Caine put it in their book *Making Connections: Teaching and the Human Brain:* "One function of schooling should be to prepare students for the real world. They need to have a sense of what will be expected of them, how they will be challenged, and what they are capable of doing.

"The assumption is that, by and large, schooling as we know it meets those goals. The reality is that it does not. On the contrary, it fosters illusions and obscures the real challenges."

In Britain author Tony Buzan, who has garnered—by any standards—a wealth of academic qualifications, looks back with amazement at what all of his years of schooling failed to cover.

"At school I spent thousands of

> **A child's life is like a piece of paper on which everyone who passes by leaves an impression.**
>
> **CHINESE PROVERB**

hours learning about mathematics. Thousands of hours learning about language and literature. Thousands of hours about the sciences and geography and history," he says. "Then I asked myself: How many hours did I spend learning about how my memory works? How many hours did I spend learning about how my eyes function? How many hours in learning how to learn? How many hours in learning how my brain works? How many hours on the nature of my thought, and how it affects my body?"

The answer: none at all.

"In other words, I hadn't actually been taught how to use my head," says Buzan, whose book, entitled *Use Your Head,* has sold more than a million copies.

One solution, according to many educators, is to place a renewed emphasis on apprenticeships, which, says Howard Gardner, "offer the designer of our educational utopia a new and exciting option."

Gardner and other educational visionaries such as John Abbott spell out the benefits: Aspiring youngsters get to work alongside accomplished professionals, establishing personal bonds as well as a sense of progress as they work together to achieve a goal. The youngsters experience, firsthand, the step-by-step process that leads to a final result. It's highly motivating for them to be involved in the excitement of a real enterprise. And the apprentices experience those moments when centuries of lore about how best to perform a task can be unveiled by their mentors at the precise moment it's needed. In reality—not in theory.

The apprenticeship system is actually alive and thriving—in Germany. Half a million companies provide on-the-job learning opportunities to more than 750,000 students. Ninety-five percent of all apprentices are later offered jobs in the companies where they trained. If Germany can do it, why not the U.S., the UK, and other countries?

Learning the High-Tech Way

The information superhighway potentially delivers the best teachers in the world to everyone's doorway. So every school needs to get wired. As Microsoft's Bill Gates has said, "When teachers do excellent work and prepare wonderful materials now, only their few dozen students benefit each year. The network will enable teachers to share lessons and materials, so that the best educational practices can spread. The interactive network also will allow students to quiz themselves anytime, in a risk-free environment. A self-administered quiz is a form of self-exploration. Testing will become a positive part of the learning process. A mistake won't call forth a reprimand; it will trigger the system to help the student overcome his misunderstanding."

Two professors at George Washington University, Washington, D.C., agree.

William E. Halal, professor of management, and Jay Liebowitz, professor of information services, in an article in *The Futurist*, observe: "Teachers will always play an essential role, but that role is changing to focus on the more complex issues in learning that machines cannot deal with. Distance learning can be viewed as a vast increase in the range of instruction, permitting especially gifted lecturers to reach an almost limitless number of students around the world, while other teachers give the students individual assistance.

"The key to unlocking the new possibilities is to envision modern education as an omnipresent activity. As the technology for acquiring and distributing knowledge permeates home, work, and all other locations, all social functions should be integrated into a seamless web of learning. Everyday living will then take place in an electronic school without walls."

We think it's urgent that we implement these proposals. Many existing PCs are out of date and many, many schools still don't have PCs at all. Says education professor Robert Sylwester, "What's really terrible right now is that more than twenty-five years after the appearance of the word processor, schools are still mostly dependent on pencils—on pencils without spell-checkers that rapidly report errors and so actually improve the writer's spelling. On pencils (with their little pink rubber delete buttons) that punish writers for writing tentative thoughts by forcing them to rewrite an entire page, rather than simply replace a word or a section."

And what about the basic ability to use a computer—mastery of the keyboard? Says Sylwester, "We continue to teach elementary students manuscript and cursive writing, but not touch-typing—at an age when they can easily master it. We may complain that our communities won't fund the hardware, but practically all businesses are now computer driven. Only our schools are still pencil driven."

President Clinton weighed in to the debate. In announcing a

drive to develop computer-savvy teachers, he declared that teachers need to be "as comfortable with computers as with chalkboards."

The initiative, sponsored by a consortium of eleven educational groups, was geared to use the Internet to recruit a hundred thousand computer-literate teachers who in turn would voluntarily mentor five other teachers on the use of technology in the classroom.

Called "21st Century Teachers," the mentors will aim to teach about 15 percent of the nation's three million teachers much-needed computer skills.

One interesting development is Cyberschool, the brainchild of two college teachers, Richard Cook and Richard Hurley, based in Hurstpierpoint, Sussex, England. They got into multimedia very early and started producing CD-ROM materials in 1990.

The two Richards (their company is called RX2) recognized that many teachers and students were becoming proficient not only at using but also creating multimedia products. And as teachers they, of course, knew what needed to be learned and how to make it interesting.

Cyberschool uses the Internet to call for developers who have the ideas and technical ability to create outstanding multimedia programs to teach school subjects.

The Cyberschool experts then assist those developers to produce a polished, finished product. Cyberschool offers high royalties and then markets the resulting programs back via the Internet and through conventional CD-ROM outlets.

> **Fortunately, the information-technology revolution is creating a new form of electronic, interactive education that should blossom into a lifelong learning system that allows almost anyone to learn almost anything from anywhere at anytime.**
>
> **WILLIAM E. HALAL AND JAY LIEBOWITZ IN THE FUTURIST**

This is a great example of electronic-age cooperative publishing. It's equitable for the developers and ideal for students who receive well-constructed, syllabus-relevant self-study programs. In fact, many of the programs are created in conjunction with older students themselves—after all, multimedia is a young person's industry!

A CLASSIC MISSION STATEMENT

A community task force helped the public school system in Edina, Minnesota, devise an overall strategic plan to improve educational performance. Part of its mission statement, reproduced here, is a wonderful encapsulation of the goals to which any school district should aspire.

Mission

The mission of the Edina Public Schools, working in partnership with the family and the community, is to educate responsible, life-long learners to possess the skills, knowledge, creativity, sense of self-worth, and ethical values necessary to survive and flourish in a rapidly changing, culturally diverse, global society.

Beliefs

We believe that:
Every person can learn.
Individuals learn at different rates and in different ways.
Learning is a lifelong process.
Every person wants to do a good job.
Self-esteem affects learning; learning enhances self-esteem.
Success promotes further success.
Education and learning are shared responsibilities among
   students, family, school, community, and society at large.
We cannot be all things to all people.
This community values education and community service.
People are accountable for their own decisions and actions.
Every person has inherent worth.
Appreciation of individuality and diversity is important.
Global awareness and understanding are essential compo-
   nents of education.
Working cooperatively is essential in a competitive world.
Family education and involvement are vital components in
   the education process.
Creativity linked with knowledge is valued in the educa-
   tional process.

Educational progress requires innovation, risk-taking, and the ability to manage change.

Continuous improvement is desirable and possible.

A positive and supportive environment is essential to the educational process.

Physical and mental well-being of people is essential for a healthy school community.

Cultural diversity enhances education.

Survival of our democratic society requires a commitment to fundamental ethical values.

A well-balanced education includes participation in extracurricular and community activities.

Lifelong community service benefits the individual and society.

A healthy organization provides access to information.

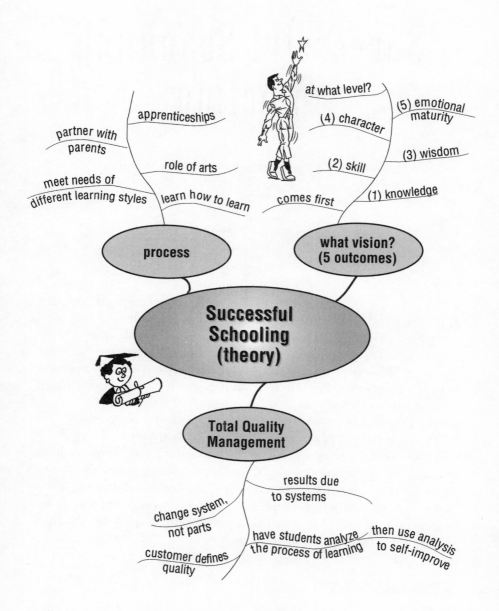

17

Successful Schooling in Action

A school should not be a preparation for life. A school should be life.
ELBERT HUBBARD

The tide of change is swirling throughout the world of education—and it is about time.

Authors Gordon Dryden and Jeannette Vos, in their authoritative book *The Learning Revolution,* are blunt about the need for change: "No one would think of lighting a fire today by rubbing two sticks together. Yet much of what passes for education is based on equally outdated concepts."

No one could accuse the following teachers of "rubbing two sticks together." They are teachers we have discovered whose efforts we wholeheartedly applaud. From kindergarten through high school; from the application of multiple intelligences in various ways to the use of a wider range of Accelerated Learning techniques; from business principles, to the arts, to the joy of a summer camp—it's all teaching that has a meaningful impact on the lives of students, for the rest of their lives.

Spectrum Comes Across

Focused on preschool through the early primary grades, a program called Project Spectrum was established by Howard Gardner, fellow Harvard researcher Mara Krechevsky, and David Feldman of

Tufts University. Its goal: to discover whether preschoolers already exhibit distinctive profiles of intelligence.

To this end the researchers equipped a school with a wide variety of "intelligence fair" materials—the idea being to encourage play across the range of a student's intelligences.

The children are allowed to gravitate naturally to the materials of their choice and reveal—through play activities—their particular combinations of strengths and interests.

Miniature replicas and props are used to motivate children to create a story—thereby employing linguistic intelligence. Household objects are taken apart and reassembled—challenging the children's spatial intelligence. There is a "discovery" area, which houses natural objects such as rocks, bones, and shells. The children use them to conduct small "experiments"—comparisons and classifications—developing their logical abilities. There are also group activities such as biweekly creative-movement sessions providing children the opportunity to regularly exercise their bodily-kinesthetic intelligence.

The teacher monitors the extent to which the child exhibits each intelligence and develops a "spectrum profile." Preliminary results are described as "promising," with teachers reporting "heightened motivation" on the part of students.

Says Gardner, "We confirmed that even students as young as four years old present quite distinctive sets and configurations of intelligences."

Since it started in 1984, Project Spectrum has evolved from a means of assessing strengths into a rounded educational environment. It has been adapted for children ranging in age from four to eight. It has been used with average students, gifted students, handicapped students, and students at risk for school failure.

"At best, the Spectrum approach promises to increase the chances for all children to find their place in the sun," says Mara Krechevsky.

Seven Success Centers

We're impressed by the innovative teaching of one elementary teacher in Washington State, who has truly turned theory into action.

Inspired by Gardner's theory, Bruce Campbell came up with an action plan for working with the third- to fifth-grade classes at Cascade Elementary in Marysville.

Campbell opens the daily learning session with a fifteen- to twenty-minute overview of the specific subject. This is provided by himself or even one of the students. It includes visuals, possibly kinesthetic activities, and the posing of provocative questions.

Then the students split into seven working groups (which presumably will be extended to eight as a result of Gardner's recent introduction of an eighth intelligence.) The "centers" are appropriately named:

William Shakespeare—linguistic
Albert Einstein—logical-mathematical
Pablo Picasso—visual-spatial
Ray Charles—musical
Thomas Edison—bodily-kinesthetic
Mother Teresa—interpersonal/social
Emily Dickinson—intrapersonal

The students move from "center" to "center" spending twenty-five minutes at each, learning about the topic of the day through exercising seven kinds of intelligence. A "flow time" or free-work period provides the opportunity for any unfinished assignments to be completed.

While students are at work in the centers, the teacher spends time with individuals or small groups—helping those struggling with reading or math or giving gifted students assistance with challenging research projects. Or maybe advising a small group in designing a structure or creating a dance.

Time is set aside each day for students to come together and share what they have learned, the daily log they have been keeping, and discuss the relevance of what they have learned. What does it have to do with real life? Where does it lead? What do they want to learn next?

Teacher Campbell says the review is an important part of the learning process because it "brings a meaningful closure to each lesson by reinforcing information for long-term memory and allowing students to demonstrate what they have learned."

Students also work on their personal independent projects, generally unrelated to the main unit being studied. They are expected, after about three weeks of preparation, to make a multimodal presentation to the class through the use of songs, skits, posters, and other forms of artwork or visuals, videotapes, computer-generated information, surveys, class participation activities, raps, constructions, puzzles, and problems.

Says Campbell, "Such a program decentralizes the classroom, empowering students to take a proactive role in their education as well as transforming the teacher's function from director to facilitator."

A typical day under Campbell's tutelage was described in an article on the Internet by Dee Dickinson, founder and president of the international educational network New Horizons for Learning.

The subject under review—in a unit on outer space—was comets.

- In the Shakespeare Center students read books and articles about comets and took notes.
- In the Einstein Center students solved story problems related to the lengths of comets' tails.
- In the Picasso Center they designed—on graph paper—elaborate, colorful, glitter-laden comets.
- In the Charles Center each group came up with a rap song about comets, incorporating some of the facts they had learned.
- In the Edison Center the students constructed model comets using sticks, marshmallows, and ribbons—and then created a dance to illustrate a comet's orbit around the sun.
- In the Mother Teresa Center the pupils worked collaboratively at the computer, creating a database of information related to comets and outer space.
- And in the Dickinson Center they wrote poems about comets on colored paper cut out in the shapes of comets.

At the end of the day everyone's efforts were reviewed together.

Teacher Campbell, reports Dee Dickinson, "has found that his students have demonstrated increased responsibility, self-direction, and independence. All students have improved in cooperative learning skills and interpersonal behavior. Furthermore, the academic achievement of all students has markedly improved, as measured by both classroom and standardized tests. Several students who previously had been unsuccessful in school have become high achievers."

Campbell has words of reassurance for teachers who may feel that constructing such a class environment is a lot of extra work.

"Although initial planning for such diverse activities can be challenging and time consuming, it soon becomes no more difficult than preparing for a more traditional program. It is important to realize that the teacher does not plan seven centers each day. Many activities are continued for more than one day, perhaps for as long as a month," he says.

"Since students themselves are sometimes involved in the planning process, the teacher's role is simplified accordingly. With practice the teacher becomes more skilled at planning in multimodal ways and finds it requires less effort. Finally, whenever teachers work as teams, other teachers can prepare different centers."

Individualized Learning

In the Capistrano unified school district in Orange County, California, teacher Kristen Nelson, as a mentor teacher on multiple intelligences, works with children throughout grades K–6.

"Even the youngest students naturally take to the idea that there are multiple ways of being intelligent," she says.

Ms. Nelson first asks her students what being smart means to them, which usually elicits responses about reading, writing, and math. After discussing the importance of these subjects in school success, she gets them to brainstorm other ways people can be smart.

Writing in *Instructor* magazine, she reported: "With grades 3 to 6, I discuss famous people who performed poorly in school but were smart in other ways. Albert Einstein and Pablo Picasso—who both disliked school rules and dropped out to study under experts—are two good examples to use. With younger students we talk about the fact that not everyone likes school all of the time."

Over an initial seven-day period Ms. Nelson focuses on one intelligence per day. For example, on a spatial-intelligence day with fourth graders you might find them drawing floor plans of the Spanish mission they are studying and practicing the art of picturing numbers in their minds as they do oral math calculations.

On bodily-kinesthetic day they might role-play a scene from a novel they're reading and learn a new sport.

Each day, Ms. Nelson devotes forty-five minutes to exploring the famous people, book characters, and historical figures who are good role models in that particular intelligence.

After this opening week she integrates the Theory of Multiple Intelligences into lessons throughout the year.

"In personalizing each student's education experience I find that an increasing percentage of students discover their own strengths, put more effort into improving their weaker areas, and feel better about themselves."

Panning for Gold——Literally

Maxine Rudoff, a fourth-grade teacher in Los Angeles, who also trains other teachers, gives another example.

The subject: the California Gold Rush.

The learning methodology: students not only wrote about the miners of 1849, they read a variety of facts to each other and received "gold nuggets" (gold-wrapped candy) for good work.

Finally, they actually journeyed four hundred miles to an historic prospecting site and panned for gold!

In Grand Rapids, Michigan, Katy Lux, PhD, director of the Midwest Regional Teaching and Learning Center at Aquinas College, encourages teachers to allow restless (kinesthetic) kids to straddle their chairs if that makes them more comfortable and even to quietly leave their seats from time to time.

"For older kids who are not real auditory, we tell them to tape the lectures, go home, and listen to them on a portable cassette player while they jog," she says. "Truly, it makes a dramatic difference."

At the Guggenheim School in Chicago, an inner city public school with a population of 98 percent black students, all teachers are trained in and use Accelerated Learning techniques. Attendance averages 94 percent, teachers' morale is high, and student achievement is steadily improving.

It's Really a Key School

One of the first (and best known) schools to implement the theory of multiple intelligences was started after a group of public-school teachers in Indianapolis were motivated by Howard Gardner's book *Frames of Mind.*

Eight teachers under the leadership of Patricia Bolanos—who

became the first principal—raised funds, lobbied, and persuaded the local school board to give the green light to the opening of the Key School.

A K–6 elementary "magnet" school, located in downtown Indianapolis, it draws children from all areas of the city and benefits from an advisory board made up of representatives from local business, cultural institutions, and universities as well as parent-advisory committees.

In addition to the regular school curriculum of English, math, and so on, each student participates in an apprenticeshiplike "pod," which children from any grade are free to join. There are a dozen pods in a variety of real-world skills ranging from architecture to gardening, from cooking to "making money."

Once a week an outside specialist (often a parent) visits the school to share his or her skills. An important element is continuing involvement with the community at large, either through the visiting mentor or the local children's museum.

The school's teachers try to give students a diet of activities across all the intelligences every day. The school curriculum is tied together by themes that last nine weeks, at the end of which period the students are expected to present a project associated with the current theme.

Key School projects are based on broad schoolwide themes, such as "Heritage," "Connections," or "The Renaissance: Then and Now."

During "The Renaissance," for example, the art teacher helped students construct life-size paintings of Renaissance-era people. The music teacher encouraged students to learn to play Renaissance music on the recorder or the violin. Classroom teachers discussed the theme not only on an historical basis but also in terms of the current rebuilding of the children's own city.

> As every thinking teacher knows, the trouble with education is that it is too often about teaching and not enough about learning.
>
> PETER EVANS AND
> GEOFF DEEHAN IN
> THE DESCENT OF MIND

At the Key School youngsters work alone or in small groups to create their projects. Much of the actual work is carried on outside of the school, often at home.

Toward the end of the theme

period the children present their projects to their classmates. Their presentations are videotaped for the children's individual "video portfolios." These video recordings represent an attempt by the school to document interests, strengths, and achievements that are not readily captured by standardized tests or other written assessments.

At the end of the school year every child has four projects in his or her video portfolio, building to twenty or thirty by the end of his school career.

300 Percent Improvement

Are Accelerated Learning techniques beneficial for all levels of students?

The six-step M•A•S•T•E•R program (which obviously goes beyond the introduction of multiple intelligences) was put to the test in a secondary school in London—one branded as a "failing school" by the Office for Standards in Education (Ofsted), the national body in the UK charged with assessing the performance of schools. This school's management team—in danger of being axed—was anxious to see improved exam results.

The dramatic result: a 300 percent improvement in students' achievement of grades A to C—according to educational psychologist Ian Millward, who instituted the Accelerated Learning program.

Says Mr. Millward, "It was essential that the workshops were motivating, well-paced, and relevant to the student population of an East London comprehensive school in a multicultural community."

To achieve this goal he played "ambient" music as the groups of sixteen to twenty students entered the classroom. As part of "getting the learners into the right state of mind" he had them "vote with their feet" by standing on a continuum marked out along the length of the room to express their confidence level of being successful in the annual exams.

This combination gained their attention and stimulated their interest. "It also helped to identify the physical learners whose activities could have easily disrupted the workshop," says Millward. "Their physical energy was put to efficient use by recruiting them as 'apprentices' to help with handouts, props, and technical equipment."

Adds Millward, "Before the start of the workshops it was anticipated that a group of East London students with poor exam results and a culture of low academic expectations would be a challenging group to work with. However, they showed great interest in the ideas of Accelerated Learning and demonstrated imagination and maturity in applying them."

In a follow-up survey on a scale of one to five, between 62 percent and 78 percent of students gave positive ratings to the Accelerated Learning course of either four or five. The only consistent complaint was that they had not been given more Accelerated Learning training sooner!

Adds Millward, "The six-stage model has proved to be an invaluable framework for enhancing the speed and motivation of both teachers and students across a wide range of topics, including 'Boosting Student Exam Performance' and 'Understanding How Children Learn in the Classroom.' " The model has now become a standard part of the way lessons are prepared and presented.

In another part of London, schools in the City of Westminster have been testing both learn-how-to-learn programs and foreign language courses using our Accelerated Learning principles.

On all counts students using Accelerated Learning were outperforming those using "traditional" methods, according to Richard Dix-Pincott of the Department of Education.

Says educational consultant Lesley Hossner, who independently reviewed the progress of Accelerated Learning at three Westminster schools, "I received excellent feedback. All the teachers involved are being very positive and achieving success.

"For me the overriding principle of Accelerated Learning is to assume the student has unlimited capabilities: to reduce the focus on teaching and let them learn. It is a course designed to reach all learning styles, not just visual and auditory, and it is important to give this free rein. It is often the children with lower ability who benefit most."

This is borne out by the fact that originally the Accelerated Learning courses were given to the bottom two groups of language students, while the top two groups continued to use conventional materials. Within six months, the "bottom" groups were significantly outperforming the "top" groups. So much so that the teachers of the former top students (from predominantly upper-income areas) made a fact-finding trip to the schools using Accelerated Learning (in predominantly lower income areas). It was, says Hossner, an unheard-of event.

Ms. Hossner stresses that one important element is positive suggestion and enjoyment.

Referring specifically to students learning foreign languages with Accelerated Learning techniques, she says, "The students must be made aware of how well they are doing, even though it seems easy. We find that those using Accelerated Learning learn vocabulary and structures so easily that they are unaware that this is unusual."

> **Give me the young man who has brains enough to make a fool of himself.**
>
> ROBERT LOUIS STEVENSON

At another London school, the John Kelly Boys' Community School in the borough of Brent, a pilot group in Year 11 even returned after school hours for "enrichment" time and subsequently continued using the Accelerated Learning techniques in Year 12.

Says head teacher Alexander Young, "The school remains enthusiastic and convinced of the need to develop Accelerated Learning as a lifelong technique for an evolving 21st century."

Back in the United States, Arizona high-school teacher Ron Reddock strongly believes in creating the right environment. He says, "Take people away from the black and white, from the typewritten notes, and the sterile and silent and nonaffectionate environments. If a person is not comfortable, regardless of what we say or do, they will not learn. My main focus is to create an environment in which students can learn.

"I like to take chairs out of rows and put them in circles so you don't have students looking at other students' backs. I want everyone to see each other. My ideal setting would be to have couches and easy chairs."

Ron Reddock is also a firm believer in using color posters and other visuals as well as classical and modern music and creating his own version of learning maps that he calls "memory art."

It's a Bird . . . It's a Plane . . . No, It's SuperCamp

Thousands of teens and preteens have become high-flyers in their own right after graduating from a summer camp with a difference.

SuperCamp, organized by The Learning Forum of Oceanside, California, uses Accelerated Learning techniques to give the youngsters a vacation they never forget. SuperCamp incorporates a finely orchestrated combination of three cardinal elements: academic skills, physical achievements, and life skills.

Says cofounder Bobbi DePorter, "We believe that the whole person is important—the intellectual, the physical, and the emotional/personal. And we believe that high self-esteem is an essential ingredient in the makeup of healthy, happy learners."

The environment is all-important. The classroom has a warm, safe, comfortable atmosphere, enhanced by plants, art, and music. Outdoors, the students build rapport and emotional bonds through a series of physical challenges. Those challenges include climbing tall trees, walking across a tightrope forty feet high, jumping from a tiny, elevated platform to catch a trapeze, and falling backward from the top of a ladder into the arms of fellow team members.

Many frightened students start the day thinking they won't be able to do it. The "high" that they feel when they are successful—and they all succeed, says DePorter—gets transferred directly into the classroom.

The results are reflected in improved grades. Researcher Jeannette Vos, in a study of more than six thousand SuperCamp graduates between the ages twelve and twenty-two, found that 97 percent of them with a grade point average of 1.9 or less improved their grades by an average of one point. In general, 73 percent of campers improved their grades and 84 percent reported increased self-esteem.

It is not surprising that SuperCamp has expanded beyond the American shores to other parts of the world, including England, Singapore, and even Russia.

Classroom = Boardroom

Why not run a school like a business? Why not prepare students for life in the real world? Why not give them—as students—practical "hands-on" experience that is going to be meaningful to them as adults?

It's actually happening. Not in a community near Harvard or Stanford, Oxford or Cambridge, but in the small Alaskan community of Sitka, where temperatures in the winter fall well below zero.

It's happening at Mt. Edgecumbe High School, a public boarding school with 210 students—mostly Native Americans—and 13 teachers.

In the way it operates, the school has drawn from the business concepts of Total Quality Management and the Continuous Improvement Process (or Kaizen)—both used to transform the Japanese economy into the world force that it is today.

The objectives of the school's pioneering leaders, Superintendent Larrae Rocheleau and teacher David Langford, was to turn the students into successful entrepreneurs so that they could return to their villages and make a difference.

Like most go-ahead companies the school developed a "mission statement" debated and agreed upon between school staff and pupils. The aim was to capture the "hearts and minds" of the students in a consensus vision that would internally motivate them. The vision included such points as:

"The school places high expectations upon students, administrators, and staff."

"Program and curriculum are based upon a conviction that students have a great and often unrealized potential."

"The school prepares students to make the transition to adulthood, helping them to determine what they want to do and develop the skills and self-confidence to accomplish their goals."

The school has identified the customers it needs to service—"internal" customers (students, teachers, administrators, and other staff members) and its "external" customers (higher education institutions, corporations, the military, homes, and society in general).

Teachers and students are all regarded as comanagers. They establish individual and collective goals and even evaluate themselves. There are no "incompletes" and "F" grades, as each task is pursued until it meets agreed-upon high standards of excellence.

The school operates four ninety-minute classes a day rather than seven short periods—because that's what the students (the customers) wanted. The curriculum is ripe with field trips, lab work, hands-on projects, and a variety of teaching styles.

The school makes extensive use of computers. The computer lab, library, and science facilities are all open at night—because that's what the customers asked for. And the school teaches speed-typing first—because that's also what the students asked for.

But where the school really mirrors the real world is in the way it has established four pilot "companies" designed to help the students develop the skills and experience required to run an import-export business aimed at Asian markets.

In math lessons the students calculate dollar-yen exchange rates. In social studies the geography of the Pacific Rim is learned. In art classes promotional brochures and product labels are created. And business and computer students produce spreadsheets just as they would for any business undertaking. Market research trips to Japan and other nations, as well as lessons in Japanese, Chinese, and Russian, round out the learning experience.

Frequently whole classes work unsupervised—just as they would in the adult workplace.

In media studies students teach other students—again as one business colleague would show another how to get a job done.

The result: almost 50 percent of all graduates from Mt. Edgecumbe have gone on to successful college careers—a rate much higher than the national average.

Another school successfully employing Quality Management techniques is the George Westinghouse Technical Vocational High School in Brooklyn, New York.

The school has seen:

- the number of dropouts decrease dramatically to 5.3 percent compared to New York City's average of 17.2 percent.
- sixty-nine percent of the school's graduates enter college, even though many of them are the first in their families to complete high school.
- parent involvement increase from 12 to 211 parents attending PTA meetings—even though dues tripled.

Learning Through the Arts

When schools take time to teach the arts, dramatic improvements are often seen in all other subjects.

> **Education is that which remains after one has forgotten everything he learned in school.**
>
> **ALBERT EINSTEIN**

Schools that incorporate music, art, drama, dance, and creative writing into the basic curriculum have observed improvements by all measures, including test scores, use of higher order thinking skills, student promotion, dropout rates, student and teacher attitudes, disciplinary measures, and parental satisfaction. But less than one tenth of one percent of the U.S. Department of Education's $30 billion budget is devoted to arts education.

It's a strange state of affairs when, according to research conducted by the Center for Arts in Basic Curriculum, "not only do the arts enable students to achieve academically at rates far beyond what might be expected of them (in subjects such as math and science), but other marvelous things happen as well."

Says educator Eric Oddleifson, writing in *Phi Delta Kappan,* "They become motivated to learn. They enjoy coming to school, working hard, and succeeding. Through the arts the whole school 'ecology' changes. High standards become the norm in all subjects. Relationships between students and teachers improve."

Asks Oddleifson, "Could it be that our schools at present allow children to play with only half a deck? Is it possible that the failure of our schools can be attributed to a significant degree to the dismissal of the arts from the curriculum? Those of us at CABC think so. We believe that we need to regain a balance between the rational mind and the perceptive mind. We need to integrate head, heart, and hand. At the moment we concentrate on the head—"the basics"—and our efforts aren't working. We suggest a new paradigm for education in America: arts integrated education, or education in and through the arts."

At the FACE (K–11) school in Montreal, Canada, which places great emphasis on the arts, students achieve higher scores in most academic subjects than at five other local high schools combined. Test scores run an average of 20 percent higher than the scores of other Canadian students, even though the school is not selective.

The Elm Elementary School in Milwaukee progressed from the bottom 10 percent of the district in 1979 to the first out of 103 schools eight years out of ten. St. Augustine Elementary School in the Bronx, composed of 99 percent minority students, has 90 percent of the students reading at grade level.

A project designed to figure out the strengths of junior and high school students in the arts and humanities was actually designed by Howard Gardner's Harvard group in collaboration with the Educational Testing Service and the Pittsburgh Public Schools.

The project, called Arts PROPEL, features sets of exercises and curriculum activities organized around a central specific concept—

such as notation in music, character and dialogue in playwriting, and graphic composition in the visual arts.

The drafts, sketches, and final products generated by these and other curriculum activities are collected in portfolios (sometimes termed "process folios"), which serve as a basis of assessment of growth by both the teacher and the student. The process folio is, in effect, a detailed "cognitive map" showing the student's progress during the learning period.

The Lessons of Home Schooling

The theme throughout this book is that the only meaningful jobs of the future will be for independent, creative, self-motivated, self-directed learners.

The current school system—large classes of children waiting to be taught an imposed curriculum—tends to militate against that objective and is more likely to breed uniformity, dependency, and lack of engagement. The need is for small classes of pupils working on subjects and projects that challenge and engage their minds.

Home schooling takes this to its logical conclusion. A class of one. In the U.S. about 1 million children are being educated at home—compared with 49 million in public and private schools—through the twelfth grade.

> **Teaching, learning, and knowing are three different activities. Knowing—especially knowing how to learn—is one mark of the educated person. Teaching is simply a way to promote that outcome.**
>
> **PROFESSOR CHARLES WRIGHT, UNIVERSITY OF OREGON**

While it is not a practical option for many people, those parents who opt for home schooling are passionate about its benefits. Personal computers, educational compact disks, on-line databases, will make home schooling increasingly effective.

Let's take a look at the results so far, as they give a pointer to what we should do in the educational system of the future. We've drawn on an article by Professor Roland Meighan of the School of Education at England's University of Nottingham, which appeared in *Education Now*.

1. Despite many people's expectations, studies show home schoolers are more mature and better adjusted socially. There are three reasons.

   First, schoolchildren are grouped together in one narrow age band—an "immaturity time capsule," as Professor Meighan puts it. At home they interact with all ages.

   Second, so much conventional classwork is one-way communication—teacher to student. Few questions by the student, most by the teacher. At age five, children are on average asking thirty questions an hour—at age seven it has dropped to two or three. Home-based education reverses the processes—most questions are asked by the student, and that keeps her motivated. She wants to see the answers to her questions.

   Third, although children appear to be learning socially at school, they are not. They are learning "alone together." Humans learn well when they collaborate. At school that's often called cheating.

2. Home-based education works to personalized, flexible educational outcomes, while school imposes a universal curriculum. At home there's instant feedback on how well your child understands. At school the child may be too inhibited to say he doesn't understand.

3. Home schoolers develop more self-discipline and automatically learn to be independent. Children become voracious readers—they have to be. They initiate action to discover what they need to know; they don't wait to be taught. Indeed, their "teachers" (parents) mostly learn *with* them, and that models the need to actively search for information. One parent eloquently described herself as a "learning site manager."

4. Almost all home schoolers use computers extensively for research and to write reports, a direct preparation for future work life. That's still an exception in school.

5. Research over twenty years shows that average academic results of home schoolers exceed those of children in the school system. The typical home schooler is two years ahead of her schooled peer—and peer group pressure is all positive, not negative.

One researcher on home schooling, Alan Thomas, told the British Psychological Society that new studies challenge the almost universally held views that children of school age need to be formally taught if they are to learn.

"The education of these children seems to embody all that teachers strive for but rarely achieve. The quality of learning appears to be markedly improved if children are taught individually," he said.

Our only surprise is that anyone is surprised. How can assembly-line schooling bring out the best in a child? Using a highly directed curriculum to produce creativity and adaptability is a contradiction.

Of course, home schooling is not a realistic option for most families. And it is hardly surprising the results are good. After all, the sample is self-selected—you wouldn't home-school unless you were really concerned to get the best educational outcome for your child. And that determination for excellence will transmit to the child.

But what can we conclude from the benefits of home schooling when seeking to design a better public educational experience?

1. Ensure each child has an individual curriculum and as much scope for personal explanation as possible. We can do that if we properly use the computing technology that's available, and teach children how to learn early.
2. Have them work in small groups in secondary school and in small classes in primary school, so feedback on what is not understood is immediate.
3. Ensure community project work is featured so that pupils interact with people of various ages and backgrounds as they try to solve "real" issues. This means they are learning through experience, not through theory.
4. Involve parents in supervising challenging, fun projects at home—so that learning isn't seen as an isolated activity confined to school but as a seamless home/school/home sequence. A natural part of a child's whole life.
5. Make school a year-round activity. Home schoolers don't take

> **The greatest classrooms of this nation or any nation are not in any school or university. They're around the dinner tables in the homes.**
>
> ASTRONOMER/EDUCATOR
> DR. RICHARD BERENDZEN,
> QUOTED IN *CREATING THE FUTURE*

off fourteen weeks a year—even though they have many more "field trips."

6. Exploit the totally new situation—the arrival of the "information rich society."

Historically, people mostly lived in an information-poor environment, so the teacher was the font of knowledge. Now radios, TV, magazines, museums, libraries, churches, videos, and, above all, the information superhighway dramatically change the balance. But we are not adjusting properly to the new situations. Once children stop waiting to be taught and manage their own learning, following a clear personal learning plan—all these sources become a natural part of their education.

We must stop confusing education with schooling. Teachers should move more and more into a support role. School should be seen as one of many learning resources—albeit a central one. Learning can and should occur anytime, anywhere. "Just-in-time" learning has arrived, to be accessed by students when they need it.

It's not just teachers who must respond. Parents need to be alive to the huge Aladdin's cave of educational resources around them and guide their children toward the videos, TV programs, computer programs, museums, and exhibitions that fire up that lust to learn.

7. Investigate flexible schooling, i.e., part home/part school. If the idea of a LIFE fund were implemented, (see final chapter), schools would have an incentive to tailor their service to the customer's needs.

In London, The Otherwise Club, a group of home-schooling families, combine to create challenging projects. If they can do it, why can't schools?

An adult learner can use a home-study course to gain the basics in a foreign language and then go to night school to gain conversational fluency. Why not a child?

One final telling point. In the UK about 33 percent of parents who home-school are ex-teachers. What does that tell you?

THE UTAH EXPERIENCE

We tested our Accelerated Learning six-step M•A•S•T•E•R plan with students, teachers, and parents in Utah. Here are some of their experiences:

Mrs. J.'s Joy of Teaching

High-school teacher Marilynn J. was at a loss.

Some of the students in her study skills class were, she says, "extremely unmotivated. I was very discouraged with this particular class. I knew I needed to do something to get their attention, but I didn't know what."

Then she was introduced to our *Accelerate Your Learning* program (a learn-how-to-learn program for students).

"It was an answer to my prayers. It had a phenomenal effect on the students. I've attended many workshops on how to teach and I've read everything I could find, but never had anything that really gave me the 'what to do' in the way that Accelerated Learning did," says Mrs. J.

"For me, as a teacher, Accelerated Learning was such a rewarding experience. It was unlike anything that had ever happened in my teaching career before. I saw my children's attitude toward school and learning completely change. I can now be effective with students in a way I never was before."

More important, she says, Accelerated Learning is a tool the students can use throughout their lives—in the real world.

"I had several students come up to me at the end of the school year and express their appreciation because they felt Accelerated Learning would make a difference in their college careers. This was the first time ever that students had made a point of telling me that something I had done for them was going to make a difference in their lives," says Mrs. J.

All in the Family

Outside of the schoolroom Accelerated Learning also made a dramatic difference for Marilynn J.'s family.

She introduced our program to her daughter so she, in turn, could help her son Jeremy, who was struggling with math. In a matter of weeks Jeremy's grades picked up.

"He went from a near failing grade to a B-plus in just a few weeks. The confidence it has given him is amazing," says Mrs. J.

Says her daughter, "I picked out the things that interested me in Accelerated Learning and got Jeremy involved that way. It was fascinating to see the different learning styles preferred by him and my other son, Adam. We discovered that Jeremy's strengths are visual, musical, and interpersonal—not the linguistic and logical way in which he was being taught. His grades went up dramatically from a 2.5 average to a 3.5 the next trimester."

Adds her daughter, "It made us remember that when he was two we taught him our home phone number set to music and people were amazed. And that's still the way he learns today! He used to have the attitude, 'I just can't do math.' Suddenly, he's saying, 'Math is easy.' I used to spend hours trying to explain things to him. It was hopeless until I realized what his personal learning style really was. Accelerated Learning is a great communications tool for a parent to use with a child."

Adds Marilynn, "Education has not kept up with the needs of today. We have to keep up to empower our children. We can't wait for the entire education system to make the changes—but individual parents can do it in their own homes."

A Shot of Self-esteem

One of Marilynn's students, fourteen-year-old Joan, confirms that the introduction of Accelerated Learning techniques into the classroom was a transformation.

"I wasn't very good at taking tests. I knew and my parents knew that I was smarter than what the grades showed. Accelerated Learning helped me study better while taking far less time," she says.

"In English I went from failing to one hundred percent and in psychology I got one of the highest grades in the class. I went from fifty percent to eighty-five to ninety percent—and that was a hard class. I was amazed."

Joan also says she got far more out of Accelerated Learning than better grades: "I learned so much about myself. It didn't just help me in school. I found out who I was. I overcame my shyness. There was a whole different person hiding inside. It made me realize I could accomplish anything I want. Before, I was lost and felt like giving up. Accelerated Learning has helped my self-confidence."

Johnny Makes the Grade——on the Football Squad

Seventeen-year-old Johnny was devastated.

His grades were so poor, he wasn't allowed on the football team. Ashamed and embarrassed, he tried to hide his report card. His ambition was simply to get out of high school and get a job—knowing it would probably be a dead-end job.

Then Johnny's father encouraged him to try our Accelerated Learning program. He did and it worked—almost immediately. Johnny's grade point average went up from 1.7 the first quarter, to 1.9 the second quarter to 3.1 the third quarter and a stunning 3.7 the fourth quarter—and a place on the honor roll.

Says Johnny, "It was fabulous. Accelerated Learning taught me how to learn the way it was best for me. Now I feel I can learn anything I want. I now know there are no limits to what I can accomplish at school."

Johnny's father: "I watched him have a huge struggle in school and become labeled by the teachers as a poor learner and a disturbance in class. We took him from the public school and put him in a private school and there was only a slight improvement.

"He went back to the public school because he wanted to play football—he's a great athlete—but his grades were not good enough. He needed a 2.0 or better."

Johnny's father began looking for a learning method to help—and discovered Accelerated Learning.

At first Johnny was not impressed: "When my father introduced me to it I felt awkward and offended, like he didn't believe in me. But I knew I had to do something. I wasn't pulling the grades I should have. I was putting in the hours but it wasn't happening.

"The improvement happened almost overnight. I was immediately hooked. It became apparent to me that I was a physical learner, and that made all the difference. It was really neat."

> **I have never let my schooling interfere with my education.**
>
> **MARK TWAIN**

A "Problem Child" No More

Eight-year-old Peter was diagnosed with Attention Deficit Disorder. Doctors had prescribed Ritalin.

"It was frustrating to me as a parent. It was hard for me to accept that he had this problem," says his father, "I tried to help him with some learning strategies from the business world but nothing seemed to help. When I came across Accelerated Learning I explored it for myself first and saw a potential key to unlock his problem."

The improvement was dramatic.

"There was an immediate change. Accelerated Learning gave him the tools that he needed. The response was amazing. We found he liked to learn with the aid of music and rhythm. He was a failing student—now he's a C student. He's not 'damaged goods' or a problem child," says his father. "It's been a real touching thing for me to see the change in my son. There was an awakening. I saw a light of hope, a twinkle in his eye that he could make it, a realization that he has the same abilities as the other children."

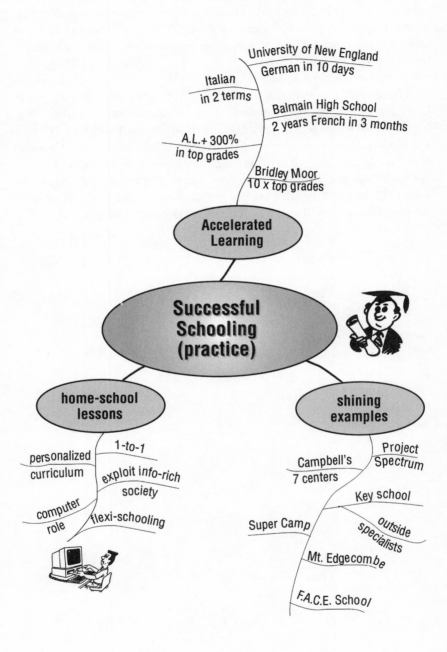

18

Accelerated Teaching
(Essential Reading for Parents Too)

I touch the future; I teach.
CHRISTA MCAULIFFE, TEACHER/NASA ASTRONAUT

Teachers are among the most valuable members of any society. Of greatest value are those teachers who elect to guide rather than lecture their young charges and teachers who are designers of thought-provoking experiences and relevant problems to solve.

Through the application of Accelerated Learning techniques in the classroom, children—even those labeled as poor learners—have been seen to blossom.

Although this chapter focuses on providing teachers with basic "get-started" Accelerated Learning strategies, it is essential reading for every parent. Not only do you have a right—and a need—to know what is going on in your child's classroom, you will want to encourage the kind of teaching and learning that is focused on developing the whole child.

You will also find that many of the recommended strategies can be implemented by yourself—at home.

Corporate trainers will also benefit from this chapter, as many of the ideas can be applied equally as well in an adult environment.

GETTING IN THE RIGHT STATE OF MIND

Research shows that students rate the quality of their relationship with their teacher as the number-one factor in whether or not they enjoy learning. So it's critical to spend time building rapport and ensuring students are in a receptive, stress-free, and resourceful state of mind. You will find that all of the following examples are tremendous ways to develop a motivated learner:

Explain to Students How Their Brain Works and About Learning Styles

When students have an insight into their brain capacity, they legitimately feel optimistic.

Explain that the key is to find and use the learning techniques that match their learning style. When they do that, learning becomes more comfortable and more successful. Students come to realize everyone **can** learn—the only difference is that in some subjects, some people will take longer than others.

Seeing the Relevance

In the first period of a new academic year, debate with the students why it's worth spending the next year studying your subject. Let them brainstorm all the advantages of learning the subject and the negative consequences of not knowing it.

Perhaps you could get some adults to attend the session and explain how the subject has become absolutely vital to them in their jobs. Remember WII-FM? What's In It For Me?

Math becomes alive and important when students see it being used in real life, say in insurance or engineering. Students who see learning a foreign language as a chore get excited when they use it in real situations.

Students have to see the relevance of what they are learning to be committed to it. Arousal of interest precedes learning.

Visualizing a Quality Outcome

Have a class discussion about what constitutes work deserving of an A grade. Show examples. Bring in A students from the previous year to talk about what they did. Many students have never been given an A. They don't know what one looks like! So the first step is to show them exactly what it takes to get there, and how attainable it really is.

The next step is to actually give them an A—before they've even done any work. There's a big psychological difference between feeling that you will never be able to achieve an A and actually having one and not wanting to lose it. Once they have it—they'll want to hang on to it.

And then: Tell them they are going to mark their own work before handing it in. You have now firmly placed the responsibility where it belongs—in the hands of the learner.

Teach the students how to work in pairs to edit and grade each others work. There are tremendous benefits to this idea, not just in terms of attitude but for creating the kind of collaborative and thinking skills they will need later in life. Repeat and demonstrate in everything you do that you expect high standards and low failure rates.

Give Students a Sense of Control

The aim is a self-managed learner. A confident **independent** learner.

Let the class debate the rules they want to establish to achieve a happy class and effective learning. When **they** help set the rules, discipline problems are reduced, because peer pressure is exercised to enforce **our** rules. Rules can cover homework, talking, behavior. They should be signed by the whole class and displayed on the wall.

One teacher we know explains that if someone doesn't understand something it's up to both her and the student to find out how to reach an understanding. Notice the hidden message: learning is certain, the only question is the time it will take. The teacher gives each student a red card. If anyone is "lost," he or she can silently raise the "warning" card. A forest of red cards is powerful feedback for the teacher, and students feel in control.

People feel really committed only when they have participated in a decision, not when it's imposed. When we taught one class about TQM (Total Quality Man-

> **The mind is not a vessel to be filled, but a fire to be ignited.**
>
> **PLUTARCH**

agement) and then asked what level of mistakes they thought acceptable, the students as a group decided they should aim for zero "defects"—i.e., 100 percent. They cooperated in testing **and tutoring** each other to try to achieve perfect work. That class had learned lifetime skills.

When you give responsibility—you get more responsible behavior.

Create a Class Motto

Have the students themselves discuss and decide what they want their class motto to be. It gives them a sense of group identity. A simple motto might be: I can do it.

Environment

Have one child (or one group) responsible each week for turning the classroom into a bright, pleasant learning environment with the addition of flowers and wall posters bearing upbeat and inspiring messages.

Music is a highly effective way to create a positive state of mind. Thirty seconds of upbeat music—or calming music after PE—works wonders in giving a message that this is a different, **enjoyable** class. If possible seat children in blocks of four—not theater style. It suggests a collaborative class.

Involve the Parents!

Give parents an overview of the curriculum and seek their active input. Let them know what projects, activities, or visits will help and what books to read. Let them know what topics for home discussion will complement schoolwork.

> **You cannot teach people anything. You can only help them discover it within themselves.**
>
> **GALILEO**

Parents **want** to help, but they don't always know how. Learning is more effective when it's an active three-way collaboration between students, teachers, and parents. And it greatly improves the child's motivation.

Teach Students the Value of Positive "Self-Talk"

We are all too familiar with negative self-talk. "I knew I couldn't do this." "What a stupid mistake!" "I'm no good at math." We accept this as human nature—but it reinforces negative expectations.

Instead, reinforce a culture of success. Encouraging yourself ("Come on, Helen, you can do it.") and using affirmations **does** work. Students need to learn the skill. They need to learn to manage their own motivation.

Enjoyment

If the **process** of learning is enjoyable, motivation will be high. That's why the environment is important and why teachers should display their enthusiasm—it becomes infectious.

When possible use pair-learning techniques and Cooperative Learning. We're social animals and solo work is less enjoyable. And use group activities and games to reinforce and test (see, for example, the power of Challenge Match later in this chapter).

Use One-Minute Breaks

Short breaks every twenty minutes actually increase attention and memory. They also enliven the mood. You can simultaneously reinforce what's being learned during the break by throwing a bean bag or a koosh ball (today's modern equivalent) from student to student while you ask factual questions.

Give Time to Self-Esteem

High self-esteem correlates with academic success. Time spent on building self-esteem repays itself many times over. Some examples:

(a) Headteacher Murray White, who now runs Esteem Workshops in the UK schools, developed "Circle Time":

The class sits on the floor in a circle and the teacher gives an incomplete sentence and an example to finish it off, e.g., "Today I'm feeling . . ." The first child repeats the phrase with her own ending to it, and so it goes around the circle.

The activity not only establishes group rapport, but allows a sensitive teacher to pick up concerns to deal with (e.g., "Today I'm feeling anxious"). Other partial sentences: "My favorite thing is . . ." "I wish I could . . ." "I'm good at . . ."

(b) Twice a term (and on his birthday) every child is "Special Child for the day." He gets to wear an "I'm Special" badge and the class discusses what they can say that's nice about him (volunteers make their individual contributions).

Comments are phrased, "I think you are . . ." or "I believe you are . . ." so the Special Child accepts them as opinion. Afterward the recipient says which comments meant the most to him and then volunteers one thing he's pleased with about himself.

Rules: Everyone can have fun. No one can spoil anyone else's fun.

Make It Safe to Make Mistakes

A key characteristic of a successful classroom is that mistakes are seen as feedback. A good teacher will say things like: "That's not actually what I was thinking of, but how did you come up with that answer?" In other words, it's more important to focus on the *process* of the student's thought than on the answer—because it's more important to get the *approach* right rather than one particular answer right.

It's also important to stress that most of the time you are looking for *an* answer, not *the* answer. In real life there's rarely only one answer.

Smart teachers encourage students to analyze their own mistakes to see if there's a trend—they may be making one **type** of mistake that is leading to many similar errors. Correct that and the students' grades may zoom up.

The Power of Suggestion

We are all familiar with a hypnotist's ability to make his subjects believe and act according to his suggestions. Hypnotism is only an extreme form of suggestion.

We nod in agreement at Henry Ford's aphorism Whether you think you can, or whether you think you can't—you are probably right! We know that a student's expectations are a big factor in determining her educational outcomes. Yet do we act on the knowledge?

An important early influence on Accelerated Learning was the work of the Bulgarian Georgi Lozanov. A qualified medical hypnotist, he reasoned that everything in the classroom needed to suggest success.

Negative limiting expectations needed to be broken down and positive expectations needed to be built up. That's why an Accelerated Learning classroom uses music, art posters, and interactive games. They suggest warmth, playfulness, and enjoyment. That's why we present much of the foreign language in our language programs through radio plays, concert readings, and role play. They suggest you're capable of a lot, and the structure or mental model of the language is worked out through the language, not taught in the abstract.

We don't state in advance that you'll learn two or three hundred words today—that would seem against the "norm" and raise doubts. We simply involve everyone in a challenging, playful environment and point out at the end how much they have learned. You've overcome negative expectations and created positive ones.

Parents and teachers should be constantly planting positive suggestions of success and avoiding any conscious or unconscious suggestion of limited expectations. It is so important for students to understand that learning is itself a process they can become better and better at. No one has a fixed ability. We can all achieve remarkable success when we master the techniques that suit our learning style.

That's why Dr. Cecilia Pollock, Professor Emeritus at Lehman College, the Bronx, New York, and a dyslexia specialist, says, "Accelerated Learning is a profoundly humanistic system of education for all. It helps children overcome their school-related fears. Dropouts become remotivated, tensions and anxieties relax and disappear."

Fostering a "Culture of Success"

Ideas to orchestrate that all-important challenging "culture of success" in the classroom **or home:**

1. Photographs on the wall of successful graduates of the school. Peer pressure unfortunately can all too often level down; it's vital that it should level up. So create role models from academic success as well as, for example, sports success. They did it—so can we.

2. No put-downs *ever.* Look for every opportunity to show how everyone is smart, albeit in different ways.
3. Analyze examples of quality work as a class, note what went into it, and display it with the notes. Let the class propose the standards they want and let peer pressure now work positively to achieve them. People surpass standards they set themselves.
4. Teach students to encourage each other. When you are comfortable with achievement, it's natural to do your best. Look for ways they can work as a team so everyone's success matters to the others.
5. Explain to the students that success *does* breed success. What do they suggest that will make the class exciting and will create high expectations and challenge? How can we become the best we can be?

Faster learning is also gentler learning.

A student's state of mind is such a powerful determiner of her success. If she's confident, motivated, and enjoying herself you have a potentially successful learner and a potentially successful member of society. **Learners need high challenge/low threat.**

ACQUIRING THE INFORMATION

Teachers (and public speakers) should take special note: when you have presented a significant amount of new information, it is natural for the audience to start to process that information internally.

Listeners with a visual preference will generally start to look up in order to sort out the information visually. Listeners with an auditory preference will tend to turn their heads and look sideways (or down). Listeners with a kinesthetic (physical) preference will tend to look down and perhaps fidget.

To the presenter all this can seem like inattention. Many teachers will instinctively react by increasing the pace and volume

> **If he is indeed wise [the teacher] does not bid you enter the house of his wisdom, but rather leads you to the threshold of your own mind.**
>
> **KAHLIL GIBRAN IN *THE PROPHET***

of their talk in an attempt to force attention and "hammer the point home." The result is to irritate the class and reduce their level of understanding.

An effective strategy would be to reduce the pace or, better still, stop and encourage a couple of minutes' discussion with a neighbor. This allows the internal processing to take place and time for a "recap"—and a respite from the lecturer!

Perhaps this would be a good time to look for a way to physically represent the subject—to use kinesthetic modeling.

A teacher who comes to recognize that she is primarily a visual communicator will find a much better rapport if she deliberately adds auditory and kinesthetic elements to her teaching. Clashes in learning styles versus teaching styles often explain why a child can do poorly one year and then bloom the following year in the same subject—but with a new teacher.

The Core Idea

As we have previously stated, every subject has a core idea. Once a student has grasped the core idea, everything else begins "to make sense," and adds to this centrally understood concept. Present this core idea to students at the start. It's a key to Accelerating Learning.

Next, ask the students to create a group learning map of what they already know. It is reassuring and encouraging for them to see the amount of knowledge they already have. It also indicates the gaps of knowledge you, as a teacher, need to focus on.

From the students' own group learning map create a "big picture" of the subject with the core idea in the center. Then start to fill in all the main subheads. Create this overview or big picture by asking the students what they need to know in order to really understand the subject. If they provide the questions they will be more inclined to listen for the answers, or find them out for themselves.

Now that you've created the all-important overview *with the students' involvement,* you can begin to present the new information they need. Take care to involve all three main senses—visual, auditory, and kinesthetic, i.e., you implement the VAK attack!

(**V**) For visual appeal: create learning maps, wall posters, charts, graphs, diagrams, and pictures—and color-code the material. Use imagery. You could have students imagine what it would be like to be inside a piece of equipment so small they could never climb into it—a computer, for example.

(A) For the benefit of auditory learners, allow time for frequent discussions between the students, either in pairs or small groups, to enable them to summarize to each other what they have learned so far.

The very fact that they have had to put their thoughts together and speak out loud serves as a memory device. Remember, you recall better the thing you have said yourself, and putting it in your own words ensures you have understood it and not just parroted the original words.

You'll find that the energy and enthusiasm in the room rise when the students are given the opportunity to "talk among themselves."

The teacher should continuously change both the speed at which she speaks and the tone of voice. There's nothing worse than delivering information in a monotone! Think of the way great orators can keep an audience spellbound—and can inspire!

(K) For kinesthetic learners: look for concrete examples and analogies and opportunities to role-play.

One excellent example is to have a student pretend to be a reporter for a famous newspaper. He interviews another student who is the expert on the subject that has been studied. The "reporter" spends time preparing quality questions and the "expert" spends time preparing for the interview.

Look, too, for ways of physically representing information. For instance, let's imagine you were trying to get students to understand how chromosomes from the mother and father mix together to form a new identity, to bring a new life into the world.

You could put different characteristics on Ping-Pong balls and have the students draw them out of two buckets—one to represent the father, one the mother. The Ping-Pong balls are then put into a third group, which represents the baby. Then the students would find out whether the new baby had blue or brown eyes, black or brown hair, straight or wavy hair, etc.

You might role-play the function of parts of speech in a sentence. Where do the noun, verb, subject, object go?

Experiential learning is the most powerful—for adults as well as children. What's more powerful—talking about what it's like to be disabled, or sitting in a chair with oil smeared over a pair of glasses to simulate limited vision, cotton wool stuffed in your ears to simulate poor hearing, and wearing rubber gloves to simulate a poor sense of touch?

The chromosome example also introduces an absolutely key element in Accelerated Learning—Cooperative Learning.

Let's Work Together

One of the most valued skills in life is the ability to work effectively in informal teams. The best classrooms teach that skill through cooperative learning. This is **not** children simply talking together—it needs careful structuring, as the leading experts on cooperative learning, David and Roger Johnson, emphasize in their book *Learning Together and Alone*. Here's one good way.

1. Set up small groups—four students in each is ideal.
2. Each student is responsible for learning about one quarter of the material to be learned.
3. They each then learn their parts.
4. Afterward each student teaches his other three teammates, and tests them to see that they understand the material. (At this point there has been individual learning and group learning.)
5. Then there's a classwide tournament set up to test understanding (teams compete).
6. Next, the teacher gives each group a project to which they all contribute, working together—that is, it's a collaborative piece of work based on what they've learned before.
7. The teacher now grades the finished group project **AND** tests each pupil individually. Marks are allocated according to:
   (a) How each student performed individually,
   (b) with a bonus awarded based on the average performance of the group
   (c) and a further bonus based on how all the group collaborated, i.e., on the *process* of cooperation.

See how powerful the concept is. Learning is individual, group, and competitive. There has been individual accountability, interdependence, and collaboration. Just like real life!

In the process students build interpersonal skills; they learn to work for a common good; they see other points of view; they learn how to present information so they understand (mindful of other

> **The authority of teachers comes not to rest on a "store" of permanent knowledge, but an awareness of how knowledge is changing. This has to be among the essential transmitted attitudes.**
>
> DAVID BRADSHAW, *THE LEARNING SOCIETY EXCHANGE, ROYAL SOCIETY OF ARTS*

people's learning styles!); they learn how to rely on others' work and to ask politely when they are not clear. And they learn the power of articulating what they **think** they understood.

They finally begin to reflect and discuss how to make their group function better. Above all, they haven't been taught collaboration skills in theory—they have learned them through experience.

Of course, the teacher can then use the experience to suggest ways of listening effectively, communicating well, the value of using praise and encouragement, how to give and receive criticism objectively, how to negotiate, and how to resolve conflicts constructively. The students will be ready for such advice because it is now important and relevant to what they are doing. They have discovered that they succeed or fail *together.*

The whole experience for students is positive and involving. They see the importance of trust, clear communication, and support in team situations. Add a suggestion at the end that they debate within the group how to cooperate better next time, and you've built in the skill of reflection too.

SEARCHING OUT THE MEANING

It cannot be stressed enough: The aim isn't just to transfer knowledge, it is to get students to create their own meaning, to truly understand the subject.

Involving a spectrum of the intelligences gives your students a multiple chance to "get it." All the strategies we recommended earlier for individual learners will work equally well in a class—especially if you give the class a choice of strategies to use in groups. In addition, try these ways to encourage real depth of thought.

The aim is to create a cycle of activities over a period of time that involves as many learning styles and intelligences as is appropriate and possible.

Get Them to Look for Analogies

Analogies help you understand unfamiliar ideas by comparing them with familiar concepts.

For example, Accelerated Learning teacher Glen Capelli has good metaphors for the three human brains.

a. The primitive brain is like an engine room. Capelli sucks in his breath and beats out a rhythm to represent breathing and heart rate.
b. The limbic system is like a chemical factory, all swirling emotions.
c. The neocortex is represented by two rooms: 1.) the cool, blue, calm room (the logical left brain); 2.) the kaleidoscopic art room representing the more artistic, intuitive right brain.

Help Them to Create a Visual Framework for Their Thoughts

Children rarely lack ideas, but often they do lack an organized structure to express those ideas properly. For example, a simple structure for an essay is:

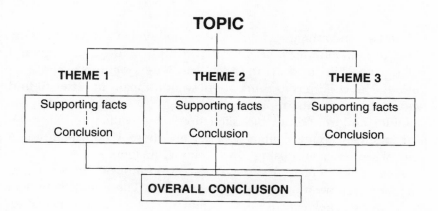

The structure works well because now the facts, conclusions, and arguments can be marshaled in a logical—not haphazard—way. And it is easy for students to retain this mental model of an essay at exam time.

The more we use visual models, the easier it is to understand and remember, because we're using the largest part of the human brain, the part devoted to visual processing.

Can your class make a flow chart to illustrate the subject better, or a diagram or graph, in order to see how it "all fits together"?

So use visuals for cycles and processes such as the weather, hormonal rhythms, or even thinking:

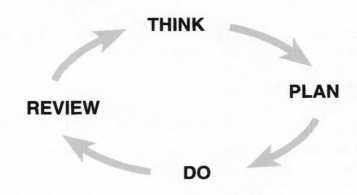

You can encourage a child's ability to visualize and, at the same time, to better understand a topic by simply taking a concept and asking the child to draw the idea—no letters or numbers are allowed! The child has to think about what it means in order to find an appropriate visual representation.

Older children could be asked how they would prepare a TV documentary about a subject. (They are thereby both planning a logical sequence and using lots of mental imagery.)

Suggest they create a storyboard—an outline of the documentary in a step-by-step sequence of drawings. There are no budget restrictions! They can use extravagant sets, star names, special effects, and a huge cast if they want, because it's all imaginary. How will they make the opening interesting? How will they keep your interest and make the subject relevant? What will the commentary say?

You could have an Academy Award ceremony at the end. Notice the students are now using imagination, logic, linguistic skills, and must think about how other people may see things. It's a powerful multisensory, multiintelligence project. Suggest they form teams of four, and you have added interpersonal collaborative skills too.

Deep Thinking

If the subject involves a problem, challenge the students not simply to solve the problem but always to ask why the problem arises in the first place. Students then begin to go beneath the surface to look at situations and problems—not as isolated incidents, but as a whole system.

Let's use an example of interest to teenagers! An acne cream might get rid of spots, but it is more productive to probe *why* the spots are arising.

Is it poor diet? If it is poor diet, what's behind that? Maybe a poor lifestyle? What's the cause of the poor lifestyle?

You see the point. The students begin to see how apparently unconnected events or problems may be part of a pattern that leads back to a faulty system. It's the skill called "Systems Thinking," which we referred to in Chapter 13. It's a vital way of deeper thinking.

How Can You Involve Bodily-Kinesthetic Intelligence?

Here is an activity we call "Sequence Shuffle." Each student makes a card with a different part of a math, biology, or science process on it.

Say it's a chemical equation. The student with the card representing the beginning of the sequence goes to the front and describes the significance of the card he's holding. The student with the next step in the process stands next to him and describes how his part of the process fits into the preceding one. And so on. The last student will be describing the whole sequence of the system.

It's an outstanding way to physically, logically, and linguistically represent processes—even a complicated one like the linking of atoms to form complex molecules.

You can review what's been learned by sitting in a circle and asking each student, in turn, to describe the next step of the sequence.

Ask your students themselves to find a way to physically represent the problem or subject. (Just thinking about it is a way to deepen their understanding). For example, some of the students we have met in classes where we were consulting have suggested they could:

- Role-play the spread of a contagious disease.
- Act out the math concept of dividing or "borrowing."
- Team up with other students and make an isosceles triangle.
- Each take a part of speech (noun, verb, adjective, pronoun, adverb, etc.) and position themselves in a line to represent a sentence in a foreign language. It's a dynamic way to register different word orders in a foreign language.
- Represent the orbit of the planets around the sun, using the correct spin and distance relationships (you'll need to be in the playing field!).
- Role-play historical figures or fictional characters—how they felt, what their motives were, what they would have said.

Guided Imagery

Guided imagery works well because it combines visual and physical intelligence. Young students could learn **about** growth and photosynthesis. Or they could experience it by becoming a seed in their imagination, splitting open as the temperature warms up. Feeling the growth of their stem. Feeling leaves unfurling. Feeling sunlight fall upon them.

Challenging Questions

Japanese teachers are taught not to ask questions that can be immediately answered—because if they can be immediately answered, they obviously did not require much depth of thought.

Challenge is the key to academic success and to sustaining a student's interest. Questions that challenge thought—the Socratic method—focus not so much on fact but on prompting the student to analyze, evaluate, rate, judge, and solve problems.

The sort of questions you might pose could be:

- If you ruled the world what laws would you pass?
- How could we become educated if school didn't exist?
- What would you change about school?
- Why does that happen? (of a physics or chemistry reaction)
- Which is the most important part?
- How do you know that is true?

How about resolving to have a challenging question of the week? One that requires some research, some analysis and some creativity.

And when you do ask challenging questions, use the three *P's*—Pause, Prompt, Praise.

Pause because waiting increases the quality of thought.

Prompt because first answers are usually obvious examples. So keep asking for better and fuller explanations.

Praise because we get the behavior we reward. If we praise depth of thought, we get depth of thought: "That was thoughtful, Susan, you didn't stop at the obvious first answer. The more you thought, the better your solution."

Educator Reuven Feuerstein likes to check impulsive and simplistic answers with a stock phrase: "Let's stop and think about this." It's important, too, to establish a habit of looking for good answers, not *the* single right answer.

Interpersonal Learning

Interpersonal skills are one of the key determinants of success in life, so anything we do to build these skills in our students is important. Nice guys finish first. We examined the power of structured cooperative learning earlier. Most of the above ideas can be executed in small groups as cooperative learning (four people is ideal).

> Since the world now changes more in a decade than it once did in millennia, the most important concept to get across in schools is that much of whatever is taught will soon probably become obsolete. That rate of change is, if anything, increasing; therefore adapting to change must be the center of any new kind of teaching.
>
> **ROBERT ORNSTEIN AND PAUL ERLICH IN NEW WORLD•NEW MIND**

304 ■ ACCELERATED LEARNING FOR THE 21ST CENTURY

There are other, less formal ways of involving and developing your students' interpersonal intelligence.

- Ask them to teach what they know to a brother, sister, or grandparent.
- Ask them to invent math problems for each other—and have a math contest.
- Set up a "panel" where students take the role of a famous historical character. Then ask them to solve a problem using the approach that their persona would use.
- At the end of a lesson **always** allow two minutes for students to compare notes. What they learned, what they concluded. Such a simple activity is extraordinarily powerful because the students are always surprised at what the other person heard or concluded that they didn't and vice versa. It's a dramatic illustration of two heads being better than one.
- Set up mentors—where older students are assigned to help younger students. It's not just a question of putting them together—again you need a little structure.

  1. The older students should record the strengths and experience they have that they think would help—not just for academic subjects but perhaps in sports, art, or social activities. Very often a student who has overcome initial difficulties himself, makes an excellent mentor.
  2. The mentor and the younger pupil agree to meet out of class to work through problems and discuss procedures.
  3. A group of mentors and teachers gets together once every two weeks to discuss progress and problems and propose ways to make the idea work better.
  4. The younger students also meet with their teacher to discuss the effectiveness of the process.

We have successfully used mentoring in our learning-how-to-learn program. An older child is introduced to the program and then teaches the basics to younger students. A variation on the mentor system is peer tutoring—when a competent child is given the responsibility to coach a fellow student who is having some difficulties. It is well researched and works particularly well for subjects like reading skills.

One good focus for mentors is to concentrate on **how** the person being mentored is carrying out the task, i.e., solving the problem. This highlights the fact that knowing the best procedure to solve future problems is more important than getting the correct answer in any one test. Correct procedures lead to correct answers because the learner understands the process of thought. It is "systems thinking" in action.

Group problem-solving is quite simply more motivating than solo work. And when senior students design learning experiences for younger students, you build leadership skills too.

The way we have designed schooling gives too little weight to the fact that man's brain has been stimulated to evolve to its current level *because* we have created complex social groups that set us complex tasks. We have become successful by collaborating—not by competing. The time to reinforce our natural inclination to collaborate is in the impressionable school years.

Helping to Develop Intrapersonal Intelligence

Although we can see the world only from our own perspective, there are few opportunities to develop intrapersonal intelligence at school. One way to encourage students to become more reflective is through sentence-completion exercises—thought-provoking phrases the students have to complete.

Here are some that can reveal a lot:

ME AT THE MOMENT

1. Three words that describe me are . . .
2. The subject I like best at school is . . .
3. I'm good at . . .
4. I'd like to be better at . . .
5. What I like doing outside school is . . .
6. I wonder quite a lot about . . .
7. If only I could . . .
8. I learn best when . . .
9. I find it difficult when . . .
10. The subject that worries me is . . .
11. I really enjoy learning when . . .
12. One day I would like to . . .

Another good way to develop intrapersonal intelligence is a Daily Learning Journal. It might include:

- What did I learn today of importance?
- What did I do well?
- Did I ask a good question?
- What could be improved?
- What/who could help me get better?
- What hindered me that I could eliminate?
- What mistakes will I avoid in future?
- What did I achieve that moves me toward my goals?

Ask students to consider how they would be different if they had been raised in another culture. It helps them to learn to see other perspectives.

Personal Projects That Involve Lots of Subjects

The trouble with the factory model of school is that subjects get taught in discrete divisions. Math separate from history, separate from art, separate from literature, separate from geography. But real life is not like that. It is gloriously complex and messy. In other words: challenging. You can easily create four challenging projects a year for your students—or for your own child.

Let them choose the projects—although you may have to suggest some alternatives. Good projects often involve seeing how some aspect of the community works. Explain that it will need some research—from the library, or the Internet, or by asking an expert. Tell the students they should be ready to present the project to the whole class in, say, six weeks' time. If they understand about multiple intelligences and learning styles, suggest they think how best to explain it (VAK it?).

You should do a sample project first for the entire class so they have a model to follow. Give highly positive but constructive feedback on their presentations, e.g., "I loved it when you explained it by . . . Do you think that it was more effective when you . . . ?" Let them discover what works best for them as individuals to communicate ideas.

If you are explicit about how you rated the project and presentation, the student will learn what's important, e.g., how well was it planned, researched, interpreted, and presented.

Here's an example on earthquakes:

Rent a video and make notes. Either one with factual newsreel material or the movie *Earthquake.*

Get a book(s) from the library. Survivor reports, descriptions, facts.

Pull down material—from the Internet, old newspaper reports, university materials, etc.

This was the stage of Fact Finding. Now what does it all mean? Here's how you can involve the whole curriculum:

What causes an earthquake? (Science)

How does the Richter scale work? Who devised it? (Math)

What materials and design for buildings work best in earthquake zones? (Design Technology)

Can you construct a model building and test it with a simulation? (Physics)

Can you map out the main earthquake zones and assess the probabilities of an earthquake at various world locations? Tokyo, Los Angeles, Manila, Turkey, etc. (Geography/Math)

How would you test the water supply to see if it was drinkable after an earthquake? How do you purify it? How do you test for gas leaks? What do you do about sewage from broken pipes? (Chemistry)

Assume the rescue is taking place in a Mexican city. What phrases will you need? How can you translate the injureds' needs? Make up a "phrase vocabulary" book. (Foreign Languages)

How would you deal with shock, broken bones, and resuscitation? (First Aid)

Food is limited. What's the best source of balanced nutrition? Design a simple stove. Design a survival menu for a week. What's it like to live on such a menu? Try it! (Home Economics)

Which are the major earthquakes from the past? Plot them on a time line. Any conclusions? (History)

Have there been any drawings or art or poems or literature on the subject? (Art/Literature)

How did early man explain catastrophes? Should we blame God? (Religion/Philosophy)

Write up your findings and present them to the class. Compose a first-person account (or a poem) from a survivor to her parents and include it. What conclusions do you draw about town planning or building regulations in earthquake areas? Why do people live on earthquake fault lines? (Language/Art)

There's much more you can build into such a project. We include it as an example of how—with a little thought—we can challenge children's minds and inspire them for self-discovered learn-

> **School can be a tool of torture or an instrument of inspiration.**
>
> DAVID HIGGINS AND
> GALINA DOLYA
> UK EDUCATORS

ing. If you're a parent doing this exercise with your children, it is highly likely that you won't know the answers for most of the projects. That's great. It's a powerful demonstration that you can both learn together.

We think project learning is so important as a way in which parents and children can learn together that one more informal example is warranted. The example shows how almost **any** starting point can produce solid learning—given only a willingness to keep asking questions and keep the debate going over a worthwhile period.

You might start with the TV. How does it work? (A stream of electrons is shot across a special screen.) This leads to investigating electrons, and the makeup of atoms.

You may then get into the light spectrum and extend into the spectrum of electromagnetic waves, radio waves, television signals.

How are TV signals originated? How does a TV studio operate? How is the news gathered? How do we know the news is not biased? What is truth? In what different ways do philosophers, painters, and sculptors try to portray truth? Why do modern painters differ so much in the way they express their views from painters in previous centuries?

You get the message. From almost any starting point any parent can create an ever-expanding intellectually challenging environment. The only resource you need is the willingness to ask questions, look things up, and to devote time to exploration. The dividend is an alert, questioning child.

TRIGGERING THE MEMORY

We've seen that a review cycle is extremely important, so always include one in your lesson planning, for example:

- Get students to review the main points quickly at the end of each lesson.
- Ask them to review key points each evening at home.

- Review key points quickly at the start of the **next** lesson.
- Review all key points from the whole week's learning once a week and try using a "concert review"—a four-minute review of all the main points of the week over a background of classical music (see chapter 11).
- Allocate a whole lesson once a month to reviewing key points. Get the students—as a group—to construct a memory map. It's lively and you model the use of these memory aids. Better still, get students individually to draw them too.
- Allocate a whole day every six months to review **all** the preceding six months' material. Ideally, use memory maps and flash cards to review the material. Once they have reviewed the material, get each student to make reminder notes or memory maps of what they can remember without reference to notes.

EXHIBITING WHAT YOU KNOW

Students obviously need to assess what they have learned and how well their learning strategies are working.

When "tests" are seen, not as win/lose but as **feedback,** the student comes to see them as helpful guidance, for their own good—not an imposed means of catching them out. The benefit of evaluations is reinforced when the teacher acknowledges that they measure how well she's done her job too!

The best time to test is when you expect success. Any mistakes then indicate where to put more effort. It follows that evaluations should be frequent and in a form that *does* provide feedback for action.

It's because we want students to see tests in a positive light and as helpful guidance that we start by group evaluation activities, both of which add fun to the process.

Challenge Match

Divide the class into two teams. Team A's job is to devise ten questions designed to stump Team B—and vice versa. They can use their textbooks as references.

All of a sudden that "boring" old textbook becomes a treasure house of potential winning material! And devising questions is, of course, review in itself. Give a fun prize to the winning team, e.g., a fireman's hat for the "hottest" team.

Swap Shop

This great activity can be adapted for a multitude of uses. Let's say you were leading our own learn-to-learn course which we call *Accelerate Your Learning*. It's got a multitude of learning strategies in it. You now want students to think about the most useful ideas and techniques they've learned. Here's the Swap Shop game.

1. Give out three blank index cards to each student.
2. Ask them to write down the three best or most usable learning techniques, one on each card.
3. Now say they must get up out of their chairs and swap one card with someone else, i.e., negotiate to give up their third favorite for a card that might "improve their hand."
4. Now have them get into groups of five and—from the total of fifteen ideas—get them to agree on the best three.
5. Finally, have each group present and rationalize its best three to the whole class.

The result of this exercise is that learners are active, thoughtful, rating, choosing, negotiating, talking, and reviewing—all in one high-energy activity.

These two activities show that evaluation and review **can** be lots of fun. And both can be used in later life.

Individual Assessments

Nothing concentrates a student's mind more than asking her to grade her own work before handing it in. Of course, such self-evaluation needs some training, but it's a key element in developing a self-managed learner.

When students come to want to continuously improve against their **own** previous best (not against that of others) they are becoming intrinsically motivated by excellence, not externally motivated by grades.

In addition, you might ask students to graph or chart their performance on each subject and teach students how to assess one another's work and make suggestions on how to edit or improve their work.

Encourage students to create their own problems to solve either alone, in pairs, or in teams. Now testing and evaluation becomes fun.

Records of Achievement

Increasingly, schools are ensuring that pupils assemble files over the years to show what they can do. They are called Records of Achievement. They include examples of work and an assessment by both teacher and student of the student's achievement. The files include outside achievements, too, and are updated every three weeks or so.

Howard Gardner proposes "process folios"—files, including videotapes, that include work in progress, i.e., that concentrate on how well the student is mastering the **process** of learning each subject. This is valuable because each subject demands a special way of thinking that characterizes a successful practitioner. Moreover, it's best to improve as you go along, not to wait for a final result before you change.

Grades

Tests, SATs, and grades are a fact of life. Whether they always—or even sometimes—measure the most important aspects of school or not, they are part of the rules of the game. If the reaction to such results is "What do I learn from them about *how* I'm learning?" they are positive and helpful.

The point is for students—or your children—to be ever conscious of the process of their own learning. Not to passively accept a grade but to ask, "What can I do to make my learning more effective? How can I get a better mark next time?" And, of course, the teacher's task is to help them find the answers.

Which brings us again to the last step in our M•A•S•T•E•R learning plan—Reflecting on how you've learned.

REFLECTING ON HOW YOU'VE LEARNED

The essence of a truly independent learner is that she is concerned about constantly improving the quality of her own learning. And she can't do that without thinking about it.

Discussing the Record of Achievement, of course, is an ideal trigger to talk about learning strategies that are working and what other activities to try.

A Daily Learning Journal is a good way for a student to establish the habit of reflecting on how he learns. It can be very simple, with prompts such as:

- What did you most/least enjoy about today's lessons. Why?
- What, if anything, did you not understand?
- What could you do to ensure it is understood? Ask a study buddy?
- What was your biggest success today? (Make sure you take time to feel good about it.)
- What learning techniques are working best for you?

David Perkins of Harvard believes that the development of what he terms Reflective Intelligence should be a main outcome of school—"The ability to become aware of one's own mental habits and transcend limited patterns of thinking." In other words, the ability to think about your thinking. It's an outcome that demands much more time and attention than it usually gets.

Since we are all learners as well as teachers, an important reflection for teachers to ask themselves is:

- Did I orchestrate a resourceful state of mind in the class?
- Could I improve the way I presented the material?
- Did I allow adequate time and broad enough exploration across enough intelligences?
- Was a period of memorization appropriate? Adequate?
- Was there provision for students to demonstrate their own understanding to themselves or to me?
- Did the class progress in their understanding of the process of their own learning?

Implementing the above suggestions will give any teacher a good start to introducing Accelerated Learning techniques into the classroom. But, of course, it is only a start. We have had space to give you only a taste of Accelerated Teaching. More resources are listed at the end of this book.

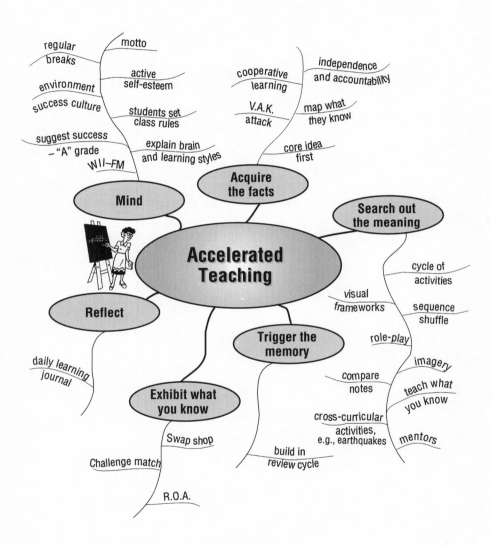

19

Corporate Learning

The rate at which organizations learn may become the only sustainable source of competitive advantage.
SLOAN MANAGEMENT REVIEW

This quote goes to the heart of one of the hottest new management concepts of the last few years—the creation of a Learning Organization. Building a company that is continuously learning and transforming itself to take advantage of new opportunities.

The interest was largely sparked when MIT's Peter Senge published his landmark book *The Fifth Discipline* in 1990. Since then many other books have been written trying to define a blueprint for building this elusive but desirable creature.

The speed of change and complexity of modern business is such that a company won't survive unless it is a learning organization. The CEO of one of America's biggest companies got it exactly right: "If the rate of change outside of you is greater than the rate of change inside you—the end is nigh!"

It happened to the dinosaurs, of course. And it's happened to hundreds of thousands of dinosaur companies that simply didn't foresee changes and trends in their markets and react fast enough.

One third of *Fortune* 500 companies vanish every fifteen years! That's a 33 percent fallout rate of the biggest companies. At the opposite end of the business spectrum nine out of ten start-ups fail within three years. Like the discards of natural selection it's all a failure to learn.

What's new about a Learning Organization is the realization that today companies can't be run by one "superbrain" at the top. Instead, you need to achieve what we call a "culture of success," where everyone so clearly understands and is so committed to the company's objectives that he or she takes on the responsibility for acquiring the skills and knowledge that will contribute to the successful achievement of those objectives. You need to "mobilize every ounce of intelligence."

In other words, "top-down training," where management decides what is to be learned, is replaced by "bottom-up learning" by all of the employees, at all levels.

Since everyone has "bought into" the objectives of the business, they also become highly sensitive to internal or external factors that may prevent or deliver success. Everyone becomes a gatherer of information. Ideas are transmitted rapidly in all directions for immediate action to be taken at all levels.

This fits with the worldwide trend for companies to be reengineered into smaller, more flexible operating units, each empowered to take high-quality decisions about fast-changing circumstances, with minimal reference to the top. Structurally that makes sense, but only if those individual units have the knowledge and skill to act effectively. And only if they have objectives that parallel the whole—like the cells of an animal that each have the same DNA code to ensure that they collectively function as one.

This biological metaphor can be extended. A healthy young body has a well-functioning immune system quietly and automatically dealing with threats to its survival, while the whole grows in stature.

The company as an organism raises a question: Can a company (and that includes public service organizations) learn like a person? And if so, can we usefully apply our six-step model of learning as an action plan?

We think so—because it's not enough to simply become a Learning Organization; a company needs to become a Faster Learning Organization. In fact it needs to do more: it needs to **outlearn, outthink, and outcreate** its competitors. These are the criteria for corporate success in the 21st century.

Some of the following ideas

> **How can a team of committed managers with individual IQs above 120 have a collective IQ of 63?**
>
> PETER SENGE, AUTHOR OF
> *THE FIFTH DISCIPLINE*

are expanded greatly in a program we have produced jointly with Sir Christopher Ball, director of learning for the Royal Society of Arts. It's all about developing what we call a **M•A•S•T•E•R** Organization. The title picks up on our individual six-step model of learning and sees how it might be applied to building an organization where personal development and personal mastery lead to corporate mastery.

The premise is that a true **M•A•S•T•E•R** Organization, by definition, thinks for itself. So, although you need an initial vision at the top to kick-start the process, any attempt to impose a fixed blueprint on a company is bound to fail. Which is why so many top-down initiatives fail and why the didactic model of teaching fails. They do not engage the hearts and minds of the people involved.

> **The era of womb-to-tomb employment is over. The message for the smart worker is to learn as much as you can, about as much as you can, as fast as you can, and increase your value to your employer, as well as your own career marketability.**
>
> **BUD CARTER,**
> **THE EXECUTIVE COMMITTEE**
> **BUSINESS THINK TANK**

Our approach to a **M•A•S•T•E•R** Organization, therefore, is the same as our approach to education. Build the skills from the ground floor up—encourage every single company member to see the relevance of what they are learning and to be enthused by the objectives of the company. And to look to themselves to solve problems.

Here, in outline, is how the six-step master plan can work in enabling a **M•A•S•T•E•R** Organization to evolve. Because we want the members of the company to think and act for themselves, we've posed a series of questions. Some of them are listed below. For each question there is a corollary ". . . and what shall we do about it?"

M = Get in the right state of Mind

- What's the benefit to me, of our becoming a **M•A•S•T•E•R** Organization?
- What will I learn to enhance my own employability?
- What are the values we want in this company?

- Is the physical environment conducive to learning and learning faster?
- What rules do we want to see? (e.g., no discrimination, family life must not be harmed by company hours)
- How do we react to risk-taking and mistakes? Do we fix the blame or fix the problem?
- Is there a healthy restlessness about doing things the same way?
- Do we value novelty and excitement?
- Is learning recognized, celebrated, and valued?

A = Acquire the information

- Can we be explicit about the business we are in? (Publishers who define themselves as "in the information business" have a different future from those who define themselves as "in the book business.")
- How do we rate vis-à-vis the competition?
- Is everyone good at feeding back information on customers' needs? Are the mechanisms in place for intelligence-gathering about the market? Who should know what has been discovered and how do we tell them?
- What am I here for? How does what I do contribute to our overall objectives?
- What's my main responsibility?
- What's the consequence of doing my job badly or outstandingly well?
- What could other people do to make it easier for me to do my job well? Is there a simpler way to do my job?

S = Search out the meaning

- What vision for ourselves can we all agree on? What would inspire us to work here?
- What's the gap between where we are now and where we want to be?
- How can we close it? What skills and knowledge will we need? Who's got them? Can they teach those who need them? What other learning resources will we need?
- What will I learn? When? How? (That becomes a Personal Development Plan).

- How can we make each product or service better? Faster? More cost effective?
- How can we please the customer more?
- Does everyone know how to learn and how to become a creative-analyst?
- What stops us from achieving our goal? How can we remove these obstacles?

T = Trigger the memory

- How do we ensure that what we learn gets captured and is available for reference, so we don't have to repeat the mistakes of history?
- One of an organization's most valuable assets is the expertise of its talented members. Why not routinely ask these people to analyze and record (perhaps on video) the processes they use to achieve the results they get?
- This way you ensure that the expertise can be transferred throughout the organization. You also ensure that the expertise endures even if the individual leaves the company. Training programs don't have to be given by outside consultants; often the most valuable training is given by insiders.

E = Exhibit what you know

- How do we spread information fast and memorably and in such a way that it triggers action?
- Are we getting better at forecasting and anticipation?
- How will we know when we've succeeded?
- How can we reward learning and innovation? Should we reward people for highlighting problems? (You can't find solutions until you realize there is a problem.)
- Can we measure the "intellectual assets" of the company?
- What's the return on investment of being a M•A•S•T•E•R Learning Organization? Is it all worth it?

R = Reflect on the process

- How do we maintain the enthusiasm and impetus of these first few months?
- Do we have a sense of urgency?
- How can we best ensure that the organization's goals, my personal goals, and my family goals are each met?

- How can we go farther? How can the concept of a M•A•S•T•E•R Organization be adapted to our families, to our local communities?
- How can we create a new style of organization that deliberately blurs the world of work and leisure?
- Is there a culture of innovation, excitement and risk-taking?

These are only some of the questions we invite members of the company to consider and debate within a cooperative learning structure—a format that we have found works extremely well.

Of course, some CEOs will complain that these are the sorts of questions that only top management should answer—in which case they've missed the need for swift responsiveness at all levels of the organization.

Other managers will, with more justification, say that some of their staff don't have the ability or educational background to enter into this type and level of debate. If that's true, it only underlines the urgent need for our educational system to make it possible for everyone to contribute at a thinking level.

We trust people to manage their own families, why not trust them to contribute to the running of their company?

If corporations can and do learn like people, can the principles of Accelerated Learning be used to ensure that the individual members of that organization learn better and faster? In other words, can Accelerated Learning be used for corporate training?

> **For you the essence of management is getting the ideas out of the heads of the bosses and into the hands of labor . . . for us the core of management is the art of mobilizing and putting together the intellectual resources of all employees in the service of the firm.**
>
> Konosuke Matsushita in
> Why the West Will Lose

The Sweet Smell of Success—from the Skunk Works

Many large companies have already switched to using Accelerated Learning techniques with great success.

A classic example is the Bell Atlantic Telephone Company, which not only dramatically reduced the costs of two training courses—by 42 percent and 57 percent respectively—but also significantly improved employee performance.

In some instances supervisors said that 100 percent of the employees who went through an Accelerated Learning course performed better in categories such as problem solving and the ability to work without supervision. In general 72 percent of the employees performed a wide variety of tasks better after Accelerated-Learning training, which was initiated by leading consultant David Meier and Bell's managing director of training, Mary Jane Gill.

How did they do it?

Initially, Bell Atlantic had the training department test the techniques on an historically unsuccessful twelve-day technical course. Most participants had complained that the course was complex, confusing, and tedious.

Completely redone in an Accelerated Learning mode, the results were overwhelming: training time was more than cut in half, trainers and trainees were happier, and the trainees learned more.

Needless to say the company was sufficiently impressed to extend the learning program to some of their larger, longer, and more costly courses. They selected two courses for customer service representatives and put together a team to completely rewrite them.

The team worked in a think-tank environment it quaintly called the Skunk Works. Far removed from the team members' normal offices, life in the Skunk Works was deliberately informal, playful, and creative—an energetic atmosphere to stimulate everyone's imagination.

The room was colorful. Fresh flowers were on display. Relaxing music played in the background. Plenty of nourishing snacks were at hand. The team created "mind maps" and used mental imagery.

Their marching orders were to create a course in which the trainees were proactive rather than passive, taking charge of their own learning. The motto was collaboration rather than competition, with the participants encouraged to help one another in any way they could.

Says Mary Jane Gill, "Of course, different accelerators

> **When they tell you to grow up, they mean stop growing.**
>
> **PABLO PICASSO**

work better for different people. The environment has a lot of diversity, and people can pick from a smorgasbord of options and choose learning methods and materials that work best for them."

Compared to graduates of standard courses, the Accelerated Learning graduates—according to their supervisors—exhibit greater confidence, problem-solving ability, and team spirit. They can work better without supervision, provide customers with more accurate information, produce better sales results, and work more speedily with reference materials. And the dropout rate from the original courses declined from 20 percent to 5.5 percent.

The results, published by the American Society for Training and Development, showed that Accelerated Learning enabled the trainees to learn more in half the time, at half the cost, and with twice the satisfaction. "Accelerated Learning has proven to be an instructional technology whose time has come" was the magazine's verdict.

Ms. Gill, who was responsible for the introduction of the Accelerated Learning methodology, says that it "is a powerful ally in meeting today's challenge to do more with less."

Subsequently, Mary Jane Gill has collaborated with us to produce a program that shows managers how to use the six-step Accelerated Learning plan to train their staff.

Why did we produce a "Train the Manager as a Trainer" program? Because in today's flatter organizations it is, and should be, the managers who do the training. Training shouldn't be separated from the people who know the details and skills of the day-to-day operations—they are the best people to transfer skills. On the other hand, they do not often have any formal teaching skills. The Training and Development program is designed to solve that dilemma.

We are not recommending the elimination of Training Departments. Rather we believe their function should change. We feel their staffs should become internal learning consultants, advising learners (and trainer/managers) using the best materials, courses, and teaching and learning techniques. In this way training ceases to be imposed from the top down, but becomes bottom-up learning, instead.

This is also why we have introduced the idea of Learning Action Circles (LAC) in many of the companies with which we have consulted. This is a powerful but simple idea, mentioned in the "Exhibiting What You Know" chapter and sufficiently powerful to repeat in a commercial context.

From the original series of debates on values, vision, and necessary future skills, staff see for themselves where there are gaps in the organization's knowledge—or skills that are in short supply. They, therefore, understand the urgency of closing those gaps. A Learning Action Circle is an informal group that decides for itself what it needs to learn, e.g., "We need to become more proficient in customer satisfaction."

Each member of the group then volunteers to read a book, or take a course on the subject and return in a month's time with a distillation of the ideas. A group of ten people can, therefore, assimilate ten different books on the subject and discuss how those ideas can be adapted to their own circumstances much, much faster than if they had tried to do it as individuals. And it's all self-managed learning.

Our Training and Development program is different from most training programs. It's a 180-degree change from a linear step-by-step presentation of materials by the trainer.

Instead, to give just a few examples:

- Each participant receives a welcome letter and an advance briefing, often on audiotape, plus a learning map giving him "the big picture" and a fair amount of detail.
- When participants arrive, the room is welcoming. Colorful posters on the walls; some with relevant facts and figures; some with motivational messages. There's music playing and delegates sit at round tables with flowers on them.
- They start by debating the importance of learning the subject—the WII-FM (What's In It For Me?).
- There's a group exercise that ensures that what they already know about the subject is captured at the start on a giant learning map. Trainees are therefore immediately thrust into an active role.

> **The primary challenge of leadership in the 1990s is to encourage the new, better-educated worker to be more entrepreneurial, self-managing, and oriented toward lifelong learning.**
>
> **JOHN NAISBITT AND PATRICIA ABURDENE IN MEGATRENDS 2000**

Conventional trainers often object strongly to this idea—feeling that it threatens their carefully planned day. "Supposing," they argue, "that the group already knows what I'm planning to spend the next six hours presenting? I'll lose control!"

Our reply is twofold.

First, if you plow ahead to present what the group already knows, you'll only bore them. Secondly, by finding out what the group doesn't know and wants to know, you have an attentive group ready to fully participate.

The training program then follows the six-step M•A•S•T•E•R plan to ensure that the subject is fully explored in a multisensory, multiintelligence way and techniques are used to lock it all down. In the process we use a lot of pair and group activities and games.

From Australia to South Africa

But does such a different way of training really deliver the results? Take heart from some of these comments from successful trainers across the globe.

> **The whole work force must be trained and it must be continuous training, not a little splat here and there, like an injection. . . . The old idea was that the schools cooked you until you were done, and then you went to work. Now, you've got to be constantly cooking.**
>
> SUE E. BERRYMAN, SENIOR
> EDUCATION SPECIALIST,
> WORLD BANK

In Australia, Jule Fuller, training and development manager for DFS Australia, Ltd., which manages duty-free shops, used our program to reduce a five-day management training program to two days.

Says Jule, after conducting fourteen workshops, "I never cease to be amazed with the depth and knowledge the participants have acquired. I have been involved in teaching and training since 1980, and this has to be the most professional, easiest program I've ever worked with."

Adds Jule Fuller, "On average, back on the job, they are using seventy percent to ninety-five percent of the techniques taught at the training session. One participant told me that not only had the course made a huge difference to her working life, but it had changed her personal life dramatically, as well."

OPTUS is Australia's fastest-growing telecommunications company. Says manager of corporate training and development George Abramowicz, "Our staff actually looks forward to attending the training sessions. It does remarkable things for their self-esteem and confidence. It boosts their motivation and makes them so much more effective at work.

"From the corporate standpoint we have found it is the easiest way to design and deliver training—and it is very economical. Times and costs are reduced and outcomes are improved."

Says John Warley, of the human resources department of the Metropolitan Life Company of South Africa, "Having embarked on offering training to adults in the workplace on a self-learning, self-paced basis, we encountered the problem that adults did not know how to learn. Similarly, most organizations offer loans to employees to study further, but very few employees succeed in completing the courses they register for."

The solution for John Warley was to combine our learning-to-learn program with our learning-to-train program. The result was that learners and trainers became a team—each had an insight into how the other was working, and they collaborated to ensure that the task was completed as enjoyably and as quickly as possible.

In Britain a major car group also saw the importance of creating learning skills as a preamble to extensive retraining.

Rover Revs Up

In the late 1980s the British car manufacturer, Rover, was a troubled company losing more than $100 million a year, the quality of its product was questionable, the

> A century ago, a high-school education was thought to be superfluous for factory workers and a college degree was the mark of an academic or a lawyer. Now for the first time in history, a majority of all new jobs will require post-secondary education.
>
> **WILLIAM B. JOHNSTON AND ARNOLD H. PACKER IN WORKFORCE 2000**

union-management relationship was bad, employee morale was bad—and getting worse.

Today, the company has made big improvements in productivity, performance, and profit records. Worldwide sales are in excess of $8 billion, and the company made a $56 million profit in 1994.

The transformation stems from the leadership of Sir Graham Day, who took over as chairman in the late 1980s and in May 1990 launched Rover Learning Business (RLB)—a separate entity within the Rover Group.

Rover made a massive commitment to learning at all levels. Every employee has a Personal Development Plan, a written commitment that he or she will learn to foster personal growth and corporate success. The Personal Development Plan is reviewed regularly with the employee's manager and a mentor—who may be outside the company.

Rover contributes up to £100 a year ($150) to a learning project of the employee's choice. It doesn't have to be work related, but it does have to challenge and extend the individual.

Rover invited us to create a learning-how-to-learn program for them because they saw that so many of their factory-floor workers had a negative attitude toward learning. School had left them with feelings of failure. Yet those same people were having to go back to training rooms and learn how to cope with training manuals, sophisticated computer-controlled automation, and statistically based TQM initiatives.

We developed, with the company, a simple but motivating pack with a Personal Learning Style test, and tools and techniques for learning to match that personal preference. The format was a liberally illustrated ninety-six-page book with audiotape. It was called *Personal Learning Pays*. It was inexpensive, effective, and was requested by over six thousand people in the first two months. Note: it had to be requested. We felt it should be free, but that the employee should at least make the minimum commitment to ask for it.

Author Michael J. Marquardt, writing extensively about the Rover turnaround in his excellent book *Building the Learning Organization*, says, "At Rover every employee is responsible for his or her learning as well as for long-term employability within Rover. This was a successful and crucial mental paradigm shift for the people of Rover."

Marquardt, a professor at George Washington University, home of the Academy for Applied Research in Organizational Learning, says that true learning organizations utilize Accelerated Learning techniques to help individuals learn more in less time—and retain the information long-term.

"Accelerated Learning techniques engage all parts of the brain in the learning process in conjunction with both conscious and subconscious mental functions," he says. "Accelerated Learning has also proved to be very effective in building innovation, imagination, and creativity into the learning process."

Our firsthand experience from the thousands of companies that have used our Training and Development Program is that Accelerated Learning works just as well for adults in corporations as for children at school. It works for *Fortune* 500 companies like American Express, Boeing, Chevron, Esso, Kellogg's, Procter & Gamble, Xerox, and Woolworth, and it works also for small and medium-sized companies.

It works because it specifically recognizes the importance of emotion in learning, of multiple-intelligence exploration for meaning, and of the need to enthuse learners not just about the subject but about the process of learning itself. Why shouldn't learning be fun? As corporate trainer Bob Pike puts it so well, "Adults are just children with big bodies."

In fact, some of the biggest successes of Accelerated Learning in industry have been in the high-tech industries where you might expect learning to be "serious" and "purely intellectual." Thus, it's been used for training in computer companies, financial service corporations, banks, pharmaceutical firms, and for accountancy training in one of the big audit companies.

"A Way of Life"

"I'm not exaggerating. I see Accelerated Learning as a way of life," says New York financial consultant Christine Salter. A consultant for twenty years, Christine says, "I now communicate much better with people. I can get points over to them by identifying their preferred learning style. It's made me much better at what I do, and it's made me enjoy life more.

"Learning had always been a frustrating experience and I didn't understand why. I've always had to put in a lot more effort to learn. All through my college years I managed to get good grades, but I studied five or six times longer than the others.

"I used to spend hours making notes, outlining them, rewriting, summarizing until I was sick of the information. Learning maps make me focus on what's important to remember. My books are dirty, colored, and have marks all over them—but they're very personal to me.

"Learning has now become fun. I can do it with ease, no effort, no struggle. Accelerated Learning has given me the information and the skills to take control of my learning and adapt to the changes taking place every day in our world. It is one of the best experiences I've ever been through."

Christine Salter's comments are important. She performs better at work because she has experienced personal growth.

Bill O'Brien, former president of Hanover Insurance, pinpoints the mindshift: "When the Industrial Age began, people worked six days a week to earn enough for food and shelter. Today, most of us have these handled by Tuesday afternoon. Our traditional hierarchical organizations are not designed to provide for people's higher-order needs—self-respect and self-actualization. The ferment in management will continue until organizations begin to address these needs, for all employees."

We concur. In our view a leader's job is to create a sense of community via a shared vision to which his colleagues can become passionately committed and to create conditions that bring out the extraordinary abilities that lie in ordinary people.

Bleeding-heart stuff? Well, in thirty years a Japanese company Kyocera has gone from zero to $2 billion in sales and well-above-average profits through exactly that philosophy.

Says Aldo Adriaan, education manager for a major Silicon Valley corporation, "There's just so much to learn. The Information Age is causing us a lot of problems. Technology is coming at us faster than we can possibly absorb it. Accelerated Learning gives you the confidence to attack things and get through them quickly.

"I've looked at many educational systems and they just don't overcome the stress of learning or help you retain the information. And they're certainly not fun," he says.

"Accelerated Learning has a lot of applications in business today, giving people the techniques they need to use their brains in a more powerful fashion and achieve whatever learning their company wants. Our people can also take it into their homes and help their families achieve a new level of learning."

This last comment is vitally important. A true **M•A•S•T•E•R** Organization must actively seek to help its employees transfer the learning and personal-development skills they are acquiring at work, to their homes and families. And when training courses are positioned as being of dual benefit to the person as both a worker and a family member, the motivation to learn and the sense of loyalty to the company are much higher. That translates into lower staff turnover. In the U.S.A. it's 4 percent a month; in Japan it's 3.5 percent *a year.*

> **Brainpower is becoming a company's most vital asset.**
>
> MICHAEL J. MARQUARDT IN
> *BUILDING THE LEARNING
> ORGANIZATION*

We need to break down the hard-edge distinction between work, home, and leisure. Too many people see their personal fulfillment as obtainable only outside of work, because the goal of work is measured purely in corporate financial success.

Such financial success is obviously vital—which is why we must continue to use technology to its fullest. But the rewards of that technology in lower costs must be shared with the staff in order that companies can pursue another goal in parallel—the fullest personal development of the members. The evidence is that those members will then repay that commitment in loyalty and that their higher levels of creativity, clarity of thought, and skill will contribute to further financial success. And a virtuous upward spiral is created.

Some of the most successful companies are recognizing this work/family learning connection. Companies like:

- Motorola, which has created a Motorola University, which spends 3.6 percent of its payroll on training—some $120 million a year—and which has made preschool learning a focus of corporate interest.
- Saturn Corporation, with its emphasis on debating shared values, cooperative decision making, teamwork, and an expectation that every employee should undertake one hundred hours a year of formal education.
- Arthur Anderson, which spends 6.5 percent of revenues on ensuring every member is retrained every four to five years and which even welcomes back ex-employees as alumni.
- General Electric, which has put thirteen thousand employees on a two-day thinking-skills/problem-solving course.

- Fel Pro, which reimburses tuition costs for employees, pays bonuses to people who earn degrees, and specifically helps in the tutoring and education of employees' children.
- The Arup Partnership, which budgets to allow 10 percent of all employee time to be devoted to continuing education.
- Canadian Imperial Bank of Commerce (CIBC), which is so passionate about learning that it is beginning to quantify its intellectual assets on its balance sheet.

CIBC, whose $107 billion worth of assets make it the seventh largest bank in North America, began to look into the subject after the savings-and-loan debacle and the collapse of real estate values in the late 1980s. It came to the conclusion that "soft" assets such as the programming know-how of a computer giant could be a better credit risk than "hard" assets like the office skyscraper.

Recognizing the need to "walk its talk," the bank places great emphasis in valuing its own intellectual assets—and setting up a brand-new approach to employee training.

Leading the entire operation is Hubert Saint-Onge, a recognized authority in the field, who rejoices in the title of vice president, learning organization and leadership development. Saint-Onge and his team operate out of CIBC's Leadership Centre, a facility one hour north of Toronto, which includes a 125-room residential campus.

Says Saint-Onge, "Most companies can't tell you how much they spend on training. It took us six months to decipher—$30 million a year. And only one penny out of a hundred hits the mark."

To ensure their investment is better spent CIBC has switched the responsibility for training—putting it firmly into the hands of the employees themselves. The company makes it easy for them and has made our learn-to-learn materials available to its employees. There are branch "learning rooms" where the workers can use books and software. They are encouraged to shadow other colleagues to acquire new skills. And, of course, they can take regular courses.

Major corporations in the vanguard of the intellectual capital "movement" include the Skandia Group, the biggest financial services company in Scandinavia, which releases an annual report on its knowledge assets, and Dow Chemical, which created a new job in 1993—director of intellectual asset management.

Too many company brochures have nice phrases about their staff being their biggest asset—but don't put their money where their mouth is. We don't think a company can truly claim to be a Learning or **M•A•S•T•E•R** Organization unless it:

- Commits itself to jointly decided values, rules, and objectives.
- Commits itself to making the long-term personal development of its people a specific goal of equal importance to its short-term profit targets.

> **Lifelong learning and training is essential if U.S. industry is to remain world-class.**
>
> **RICHARD L. LESHER,**
> **PRESIDENT OF THE U.S.**
> **CHAMBER OF COMMERCE**

- Switches to bottom-up learning by everyone, which we think should include learning-to-learn and analytical-creative thinking programs and Learning Action Circles as a way of life.
- Actively seeks to support employees in the education of their families, not just financially, but by opening up certain courses—like communication skills, computer courses, teamwork skills, and language classes—to family members too.

If we really are going to turn the perceived threat of disappearing jobs into the actual opportunity of a better lifestyle, we need to deliberately blur the distinction between what goes on at work and what goes on at home.

We run a company ourselves and we know that the first priority of any company is to survive and make a profit. But that cannot be achieved without the enthusiasm and focused effort of everyone. So the continuous upgrading of everyone's skills is in the firm's self-interest as well as the employees'.

A **M•A•S•T•E•R** Organization, however, also performs a vital social function. For even if we make the effort to teach our entire school population how to learn and how to think at a high level—what about the adults already in the workplace? Without an upgrade in their skills all too many will be doomed to a low-wage future.

Where will they learn these skills except at work?

A PROPOSED NEW RELATIONSHIP BETWEEN EMPLOYEE AND EMPLOYER

The changed circumstances of the new millennium will, we believe, necessitate a new relationship between employer and employee. One in which learning has the central role.

We suggest that, as an employee, there are five obligations you have to your employer, and there are five parallel obligations your employer has to you. Note: they are obligations, not rights.

As an employee you must:

1. Add Value
An organization can make a profit only if the combined output of its employees exceeds its costs. Of course, wage costs are only a part of total costs. Other costs like raw materials, rent, light, advertising and promotion, transport, and borrowings (including shareholder investments) are big factors too. But the cost you directly influence is your own.

The first rule of employability is to contribute to your company more than you cost. That contribution isn't measured in the hours you put in, or how busy you are, or how long you've been with the company—though all of these factors matter. In the end it can only be measured by whether you put in more than you take out.

So individuals also make an annual profit or loss—but only companies officially report them.

That's why it is in your self-interest to constantly look for ways to reduce expenses and increase customer satisfaction and sales in your organization. The higher the added value per employee in your company, the more secure your own job and earnings.

For example, the **average** added value per worker in the UK electronics industry in 1996 was £53,000 ($82,000). This means that the average worker added £53,000 **more** than he or she cost in salary + benefits + health insurance, etc.

In the top 10 percent of electronics companies, the average value added was double—£108,000. People working in those top 10 percent have better income security. At least they do as long as everyone in their company **keeps** outthinking, outcreating, and outlearning the competition.

2. Act Like a "Self-Employed" Contractor

Think of yourself as the CEO of your own one-man or -woman consultancy company—John Jones, Inc., or Jane Jones, Inc. Your company has a "contract" to do a job for your current employer.

That means you must continuously invest in the skills of your "company," so its value as a subcontractor keeps increasing. That's the way to ensure that the value of the service you provide does indeed exceed its costs.

That's the essence of lifelong learning—investing in your own Research & Development Department.

If you are not continuously learning, you will be underinvesting in your R & D Department. And falling back.

If you are investing in your own R & D, you'll be employable anywhere—whatever happens to your present "client," i.e., employer. So make sure you know what your organization's goals are and learn the skills to help it achieve them. It's in your own interest. Satisfied customers pay the bills.

Don't wait to be trained—teach yourself; form a Learning Action circle. You'll help your organization succeed and keep improving your employability at the same time. And if you should find yourself outside formal full-time employment, you will have already developed the mind-set and experience to cope.

3. Focus on Quality Service

To view yourself as self-employed—contracting out your own services—has profound implications. It makes you ask questions like "How can I service my customer better?" "How can I help them achieve their objectives?"

Customers aren't only outside the company you work for. Think of the people **inside** your company as also being clients for your services. Do you give them quality service? Do you provide value for money?

Of course, they must approach their jobs the same way—looking for ways to help you do a better and better job.

Acting as if you were self-employed has another important implication. If something is wrong—fix it. Self-employed people don't waste time moaning about their company—they **are** the company. So they look for solutions and move on.

4. Look for Continuous Improvement

The one word of Japanese you need to understand is *kaizen*—the habit of mind that looks for continuous improvement. A daily quest to get better. That's how you add value.

Sometimes a single heroic breakthrough, a new product or new way of doing things, produces a big improvement. The typical Japanese company, however, constantly searches for hundreds, even thousands, of small improvements. Each one may seem insignificant, but cumulatively they add up to the difference between success and failure.

A group of Japanese managers from a Yokohama steel mill was visiting a UK steel mill. Both mills had similar equipment of similar age, but the UK mill was losing money; the Japanese was making money.

At the end of the visit the CEO of the UK steel mill turned to his visitors and said, "We have a lot to learn from you. What's the big difference? Why are you making money and we're not?"

Politely, the head of the Japanese delegation said tentatively, "Well, there isn't one big difference, but we do have one or two suggestions. . . ." He then proceeded to list 124 ways the UK mill could improve! Typical was that, when the three-foot blast-furnace doors opened to let a steel ingot roll out, the Japanese doors opened two inches less than the UK doors, so less heat was lost. It wasn't much, but over a year the saving on energy was appreciable. Added to the other 123 small differences, it was enough to turn a loss into a profit.

So the questions to ask every day are "How can we do this better?" "How can we do this faster?" "How can we do this cheaper?"

These days we compete not just with organizations within our own country but on a global scale. And all companies are asking the same questions.

That's why your organization is asking more of you as an employee—it simply has no choice. And that's why you have to ask more of yourself—because you are ultimately your own employer.

By the way, the Japanese didn't invent *kaizen*. Most of the ideas came originally from the American management expert W. Edwards Deming. But the Japanese added lots of small improvements to his original ideas!

5. Embrace Change

The stability of the past is gone. The only constant is accelerating change—in work practices, markets, and technology.

The organization for which you work simply has to keep up. It has to move fast, because its global competitors move fast. And it can't go fast if its members go slow.

So there's no future in resisting change, just because change is uncomfortable. If efficiencies can be made, they will be made—by someone. If it's not your company, it will be another. And that other company will ultimately offer the best job prospects.

The answer to change is not to resist it, but to learn to adapt to it. Better still, forecast it. Even better, precipitate it yourself. All of which is exactly why you need to be an Accelerated Learner and a creative-analyst.

These five obligations are tough. They call for a lot of self-reliance. But you aren't on your own. Your employer has obligations too!

In fact, we believe that the five obligations of the 21st century employer are **exactly** the same as for the employee.

As an employer you must:

1. Add Value
If your employees are working to add value and embracing new technology to increase efficiency, which often means reduced labor input, you must also add value to them.

Some of the rewards from automation need to be returned to your workforce in the form of shorter hours for the same pay, job sharing, flexi-hours, and perhaps a new form of semiretirement, where older employees work part-time from a younger age. And some of the rewards must be reinvested in education and retraining so that people can function at the new higher-skill levels that the new jobs demand.

Notice we said "some of the rewards." We realize global competition means that organizations need to automate to compete and that not all savings translate into extra profit. Some translate into lower prices or higher R & D, and of course, shareholders deserve a return too.

Nevertheless, a company is not just a vehicle for increasing capital value for its shareholders. As the French name for a company (société) implies, a company is also a social grouping with social responsibilities.

2. Treat Employees as Partners
If your employees act like independent contractors and take the initiative to learn the skills needed to create a common success,

they need to participate directly in creating the values, roles, and objectives of the company.

The high level of self-motivation and self-management needed in the modern company has to be matched by a high level of self-determination. People only commit wholeheartedly to decisions in which they are involved.

3. Quality Service

If every employee is focused on quality service, employers need to be focused on quality conditions.

What ambitions do each of the members have? How can the company help him or her fulfill those objectives? What will make the workplace pleasant and fulfilling? We know people learn and create best in a low-threat, high-energy environment. How can we create one?

4. Continuous Improvement

If employees are focused on continuous improvement to make the organization succeed, the organization has to focus on helping them continuously develop as people. *Kaizen* goes both ways.

How can everyone develop more of their potential? How can we assist their learning? How can we **directly** help to promote quality learning in our employees' homes? Can we buy self-study educational materials wholesale and pass on the benefits? Can we set up self-development courses that families can attend too?

Since no one can predict the skills we will need in the future, having employees with breadth and flexibility makes sense for employer and employee alike.

Technology usually displaces the jobs of the least educated first. Have we **genuinely** explored the possibility of educating those people to be able to contribute in the future? Firing people is an easier option than helping them raise their skills. If we take the easy option, we dump the problem on society in the form of unemployment. Is that morally defensible?

5. Embrace Change

The changes we are asking of employees are profound. Changes that once literally took centuries are happening in months. Hence the sense of uncertainty.

The sort of responsibilities we've proposed for companies are new too. Yet if we want the benefits of a high-tech society, everyone will have to modify his or her role. Companies will have to broaden their objectives to include some semisocial roles, not necessarily out of altruism but out of self-preservation. They should open their doors to involve the children and partners of their employees in self-development courses. They should try to educate before they fire.

If you look back on the five obligations of both employee and employer, they remind you of the obligations that are willingly taken on by the partners in a well-functioning family. We don't think it's a coincidence.

Essentially, these five parallel responsibilities begin to redefine the role of work, broadening its function from pure wealth creation to include personal fulfillment. That's why we would like to see the implications of these new obligations debated as children leave school, as well as within existing organizations.

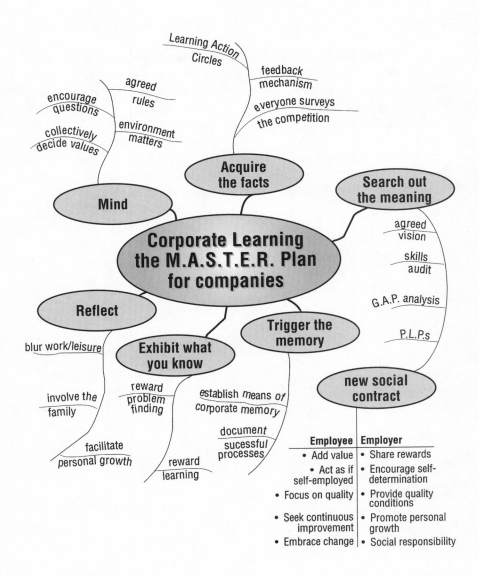

Learning Action Circles

feedback mechanism

everyone surveys the competition

agreed rules

encourage questions

environment matters

collectively decide values

Acquire the facts

Mind

Search out the meaning

agreed vision

skills audit

Corporate Learning the M.A.S.T.E.R. Plan for companies

G.A.P. analysis

P.L.P.s

Reflect

Trigger the memory

blur work/leisure

Exhibit what you know

involve the family

reward problem finding

establish means of corporate memory

new social contract

facilitate personal growth

reward learning

document sucessful processes

Employee	Employer
• Add value	• Share rewards
• Act as if self-employed	• Encourage self-determination
• Focus on quality	• Provide quality conditions
• Seek continuous improvement	• Promote personal growth
• Embrace change	• Social responsibility

20

The Vision

Where there is no vision the people perish.
PROVERBS 29:18

We are at a crossroads. Educators, government leaders, business executives, parents—and even students themselves—are openly expressing alarm.

The problem: When students make the transition from the classroom into the workforce they are—by and large—simply not equipped to handle the challenges they face. They have not acquired the real-world skills they need to thrive—not just survive—in today's laser-fast, high-tech, globally competitive environment.

A recent Hudson Institute study conducted on behalf of the U.S. Department of Labor highlighted the "skill gap." It found that some 41 percent of the jobs in the year 2000 will be in higher skilled occupations, compared with 24 percent in 1984. And these jobs are not only higher skilled, they are different—and they keep changing.

"As we approach the 21st century, a larger part of the population will require adult education—not only to improve basic skills or to receive job training, but also to help face a future that is more volatile, competitive, and complex than ever before," say Fred Best and Ray Eberhard, writing in *The Futurist*. "Education . . . must now do more to make lifelong learning a reality for adults."

President Bill Clinton takes up the refrain, emphasizing, "We must promote lifetime learning for every American, investing in our people at every stage."

The last three words are key: *at every stage*.

Our research and work on four continents, with talented teachers, corporate trainers, academics, concerned government officials, and others, has led to a firmly held vision of a way forward to create a nation of lifelong learners.

Learning needs to be engaged at every stage, from the tiny toddler taking his first steps to the farsighted boardroom executive. Learning is a community endeavor.

The cornerstone of a prosperous nation is its intellectual capital. Its true wealth is the treasure of the collective minds of its populace.

Our vision for the much discussed but poorly specified society of lifelong learners is:

> **A society of continuous learners and creative-analysts with the skills to be economically independent. A society where productivity gains are fairly shared to enable both work and leisure to become the means of fulfilling maximum personal potential.**

Implementation of the following 16 suggestions would go a long way toward creating the ideal of a true learning society for the 21st century.

1. Commitment to Learning-How-to-Learn and Becoming a Creative-Analyst

Make a commitment that **everyone** has access to a course on learning-how-to-learn and becoming a creative-analyst. Make learning-how-to-learn the first course children are taught as they enter secondary school, and embed the principles in every lesson. Embed analytical and critical thinking in the curriculum and make it all part of teacher training. Make the idea of becoming a self-managed, clear-thinking learner explicit and a prime aim of school. Every single child can—and must—function at a high level.

Encourage every organization to offer such courses to every employee. They are surely the foundation skills of any faster-learning organization.

Make such a course available on TV as a "part work" through educational channels such as the Mind Extension University in the U.S. or the Open University in the UK. It was the Open University that pioneered the university-on-the-air concept, making college degrees available to at-home students ranging in age from eighteen to eighty.

> **Education should start at the moment of conception, with parents acting as teachers.**
>
> LUIS ALBERTO MACHADO, PHD, IN *CREATING THE FUTURE*

(In 1987 the Mind Extension University became the first U.S. institution offering college education courses via cable TV. In 1992 it broadcast courses taught at twenty-one universities reaching 18 million homes. The figure is now in excess of 50 million homes.

The Public Broadcasting Service (PBS) now enrolls 350,000 students in distance learning courses—up from 55,000 a decade ago. PBS has a partnership with sixty community colleges around the U.S., enabling students to earn degrees using instruction from twenty PBS stations.)

Encourage everyone to develop a Personal Learning Action Plan (PLAP). This is a central recommendation of a visionary initiative launched in the UK in 1996 by the Royal Society of Arts and headed by Sir Christopher Ball.

Essentially, a PLAP is an invitation to think through, write down, and plan a continuous improvement of your own skills and knowledge. It invites each of us to plan and complete a major learning project each year—learning to draw or paint, acquiring a language, pursuing a new sport, understanding the elements of accounting, becoming fully computer- and Internet-literate. It also proposes you need a mentor to guide and encourage you.

Lifelong learning isn't platitudes—it's specifics.

Only a huge upgrading of the whole population's ability to think with clarity, depth, and breadth can equip us as individuals and as a nation with the skills to match the challenges and solve the problems of the 21st century.

As thinking skills expert Richard Paul says: "The quality of our lives can only become more and more obviously the product of the quality of the thinking we use to create them."

Every school and every company must have a creative-analyst training program.

2. Get Serious about Preschool Education

We need every parent to know how to create a rich and stimulating home environment and we need nursery-school provision for all.

Every parent wants the best for her child, but few of us ever get any guidance on how to create that essential environment to encourage all-around early abilities.

We're piloting an interesting combination of these ideas with a large UK educational authority. It starts with parents receiving the *FUNdamentals* program we described in Chapter 15. This ensures that parents have a practical program that will not simply develop basic reading and numeracy readiness, but will teach them how to encourage and assist in the development of their child's full spectrum of intelligences.

Parents, therefore, become knowledgeable partners with the nursery school, and both home and school combine to develop the child's natural curiosity and excitement to learn. Instead of using the TV as an electronic baby-sitter, parents use time productively, playing games that excite their children to create and think.

The evidence that nursery schooling can raise standards throughout a child's life is overwhelming.

Research in the U.S. shows that for every $1,000 spent providing a child with a preschool education, $4,000 is later saved in public spending.

This research reveals that youngsters who have had preschool education are:

- more likely to own their own home
- less likely to end up in prison
- more likely to have a job
- less likely to take drugs.

Some countries clearly recognize the benefits of schooling at such a young age. In France, Italy, and Germany, for instance, more than 90 percent of three- and four-year-olds are provided with a nursery place. In Israel there is a nationwide parent-education program called HIPPY, and in Missouri the Parents as Teachers program has been a success despite underfunding.

Bottom of the class in Europe—when it comes to providing nursery places—is the United Kingdom, according to the country's respected Royal Society of Arts. In a report calling for compulsory nursery education, the society says fewer than 50 percent of preschoolers in Britain are being provided with places.

Former head of the UK Department of Education Sir Geoffrey Holland agrees that nursery education should be made available to all three- and four-year-olds whose parents want them to have it.

He says, "The first five years of a child's development are crucial—and those kids who haven't had the benefits of nursery education often arrive at school two years behind in reading standards compared to those who have."

Craig T. Ramey, professor of psychology, pediatrics, public health science, and sociology, at the University of Alabama, has shown that positive mentally stimulating experiences in early childhood can permanently boost IQ by twenty points or more.

Indeed, that's what we are aiming at with our *FUNdamentals* initiative. But if positive stimulation can build brain power, how can we blind ourselves to the likelihood that the wrong kind of stimulation will have an equally powerful effect?

We find it difficult to believe that the increase in crimes of violence is unconnected with the equally huge increase in TV and movie violence. Brains respond to stimulation—good or bad.

3. Small Classes, Big Challenges

When children get to primary school the class size should be a **maximum** of fifteen children.

A thoughtful and imaginative early-years teacher, Sally Featherstone, puts it succinctly. "Why do you think we teachers give out so much routine paper-and-pencil work in class? Simple. If I'm concentrating on explaining something to one child, I have to keep the other twenty-nine children occupied with *something!* Far too much primary-class time is taken up with low-grade, low-challenge paperwork because there's simply nothing else we can do."

Large primary-class sizes slow down children's natural progression, because half the time—or even more—they are learning little of value.

If your primary-age child is being taught in a class of thirty, he's being educationally cheated. Why else do parents pay for private education? There is little evidence that the teachers or the curricula are better in private than in public schools. It's the individual attention that's being bought.

If we have any sense of what equal opportunity actually means, we will **demand,** loudly, that class sizes be slashed now.

Can we afford it? Financially, yes—if we reallocate resources as will be recommended later. The real question, however, is can we afford **not** to do it?

It's well known that the roots of our education system go back to the early Industrial Revolution. The demand then was for large numbers of workers who would mind machines and neither complain nor question.

The model for that system was—literally—the Prussian army. The driving thought behind the education and training of the Prussian army was that 20 percent of the recruits would turn out to be officers and 80 percent would be troops (or cannon fodder!) So a factory-model system of education was produced—large classes designed for basic skills. The education of the many sacrificed to the needs of the few.

It's an absolute scandal that we are passively acquiescing in the elitist mind-set of the 19th century as we enter the 21st century. The system is still too dependent on an out-of-date view of how humans learn, for a society that no longer exists.

The hard evidence for small classes confirms what every parent instinctively knows and what results from home schooling conclusively prove. Small is beautiful—and successful.

Researchers followed seven thousand children, between the ages of five and twelve, in the state of Tennessee (the Star Project). Those from smaller classes did better in EVERY SUBJECT.

The reason is obvious. With personal attention misunderstandings can be quickly cleared up and the teacher can be more sensitive to different learning styles. The result is that children read earlier and acquire basic skills faster. This means they can engage in more challenging, thought-provoking projects and begin the journey to self-managed learning at an earlier age.

Young children in large classes take far longer to achieve the basic competencies, which has a domino effect. Too many, therefore, reach secondary school with inadequate basic skills, and there's either too much time spent in remedial work at the ages of twelve and thirteen—or those children never recover and go on to swell the ranks of the structurally unemployed.

Large primary-school classes are a key factor in the tragedy. We must not let them continue.

We applaud an initiative taken by the state of California in 1996.

Faced with the problem of soaring enrollment and overcrowded classes, the state launched a major incentive to reduce the size of elementary classes.

It offered a $650-a-head bonus if classes were reduced from thirty to twenty students. The result: a massive recruiting drive for 20,000 new teachers with schools making room for the extra classes by turning cafeterias, kitchens, and auditoriums into classrooms or having two different classes operate out of one room at the same time.

In the teachers' opinion, such inconvenience was worth it—because of the extra personal attention they were able to give the kids.

4. Primary Parent Power

In addition to reducing class sizes, schools need to invite parents to actively collaborate with the teacher in producing quality education.

Too many parents feel that their educational responsibilities are discharged when their child goes to primary school. They aren't—for the simple reason that a child spends about 1,300 hours a year at school, but 2,500 waking hours a year at home.

In the seven years from age six to twelve—the most formative years for the basic skills—schools will claim about one third of a child's waking life. Home, however, will influence two thirds of his waking life. This time—all 17,500 hours of it—can be filled with fun, inquiry, exploration, and learning. Or it can be squandered.

Of course, there's a vital role for playing with friends and simply relaxing with the family. But home also provides a fabulous opportunity to learn important skills. We're involved in a joint venture in the UK with the Northamptonshire Inspectorate and Advisory Service (NIAS), which capitalizes on that opportunity.

George Gyte, the inspirational head of NIAS, has a vivid way of describing the normal balance between teacher, student, and parent in the average educational administrator's mind, as shown in the following diagram.

The relative size of the circles on the left indicates the usual importance ascribed to each participant. Only the equal balance, says Gyte, will produce the breakthrough we need.

The aim of the collaboration is simple enough. We have produced a series of thought-provoking and challenging projects.

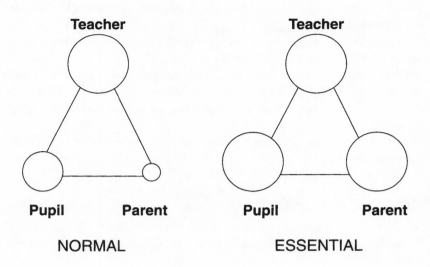

Teacher

Pupil   **Parent**

NORMAL

Teacher

Pupil   **Parent**

ESSENTIAL

They are issued regularly from the school to the parent and are designed to be done by the child at home, with some parental guidance.

These projects certainly are **not** more of the same, i.e., more homework or an extension of school. These are projects that children **want** to experience because they are fun. Children are challenged to solve problems that they see are relevant and interesting. In doing so they **indirectly** build up reading, number, and information technology skills, plus they learn to think logically and look for imaginative answers. Often the projects encourage children to collaborate in small teams. The parents are shown how to be an unobtrusive resource to their sons and daughters.

Almost all parents want to help. The aim of this initiative, called PLANS (Parent Learning Action Networks), is to show them how. Because the work

> **A positive and emotionally rich environment is not a luxury but actually a necessity for better education in the coming 21st century.**
>
> DR. NOBORU KOBAYASHI IN
> *CREATING THE FUTURE*

complements the school curriculum, parents know that the projects their children are doing (and they are supervising) will contribute directly to their child's success. Meanwhile, the children are building their confidence by learning informally on their own or in groups of two or three.

We also think the extension of flexi-schooling should be on the agenda—offering a mix between home schooling and full-time schooling. The customer for education is the student. The system should serve him or her, not the other way around.

President Clinton, in one of his many challenges thrown down in his 1996 State of the Union address, said: "I challenge parents to be their children's first teachers. Turn off the TV. See that the homework gets done. Visit your children's classrooms."

The average American family spends twenty-seven hours a week watching television. That's a lot of time lost from bonding and intellectually challenging pursuits. Diverting just five hours to thought-provoking discussions and projects could transform a child's future. Let's create a new slogan—"Just one hour a day."

Howard Gardner comments, "Our society makes it very difficult for even well-intentioned and well-educated teachers to accomplish their goals. The responsibility for turning around our education system, and educational systems elsewhere in the world, is *everyone's* responsibility."

There's a long way to go. One recent report indicated that half of fathers spend less than five minutes a day in solo contact with their sons.

5. Secondary Student Power

The real value of the six-step M•A•S•T•E•R model of learning is that students come to realize that learning is not something that's done to you—only you can do it. It develops learning classrooms rather than teaching classrooms.

When learners and teachers

> . . . we too rarely realize that today we know far more about the stunningly complex processes of learning than we did ninety years ago, but the template of American secondary education struck then is still very much in place [today].
>
> TED SIZER,
> CHAIRMAN OF THE COALITION
> OF ESSENTIAL SCHOOLS,
> IN *HORACE'S SCHOOL*

both have the same clear framework for efficient learning, they collaborate in the learning process. And that's one key reason why learning is accelerated. The "guide on the side" as opposed to the "sage on the stage."

When a twelve-year-old has the confidence to politely tell her teacher that she doesn't understand and then may turn to a *classmate* for an explanation, you're a long way toward a true learning classroom.

The big payoff from a learn-to-learn program, however, isn't just motivated, independent students. It's that we can begin to use technology properly.

6. Exploit the New Technology

Today's developments in technology are just as profound as when Gutenberg's printing press and Bible broke the church's monopoly on what was taught and by whom. We are currently merely skirting the edge of a true revolution in learning. A really well-constructed CD-ROM, for example, can take a subject and present it in a colorful, entertaining, and dramatic way.

What's more, it can present the subject in a variety of ways so that individual learners can explore the subject in the manner that suits them best.

The format may use text, graphics, animation, 3D, virtual reality, video, sound, and music. It can measure understanding through games and activities. It can create challenges with points awards.

It is infinitely patient, allowing each learner to learn at his or her own pace. It can store records of time spent, and grades achieved, for each individual learner. It allows the user to

> We have allowed a paper-and-pencil technology to expand to fill up the hours. We know that pupils can write faster and more accurately with the use of word processors . . . but that would change the system. People would not know how to cope if pupils achieved their intellectual objectives more quickly.
>
> SEYMOUR PAPERT,
> AUTHOR OF *MINDSTORMS*

experience history with virtual reality, "visit" geographical sites, or interact within a Shakespearean play.

It's the one-to-one tutor you thought you couldn't afford.

That's what it can do.

The downside is that by no means do all current CD-ROM programs exploit the medium as they might. Some current programs are nothing more than talking books, preexisting pictures, illustrations, and text owned by the publisher, to which sound has been added, rushed into production to catch the market.

But this is an inevitable initial stage of any new technology. The next stage is, however, already happening. CD-ROM publishers are already liaising with educational authorities and working on a jointly agreed brief. For example, we are producing "English as a Foreign Language" CD-ROM programs for schools with students who are difficult to teach because their native language is a non-English tongue.

Our CD-ROM program uses virtual reality, so that learners actually go shopping and visit the country whose language they are learning. They literally play with the language to discover for themselves how the grammar works. There is much "peripheral" learning taking place as they engage in over two hundred games that require them to actively use the target language in order to play.

We don't envision students staring at computer screens all day. We do envision two to three hours a day of computer-based self-learning. Followed by time spent creating personal notes on the computer or utilizing learning maps.

We see some time each day in structured group discussions as well as peer teaching—when students teach other students. When students know they will have to teach what they've learned to other students, they are much more careful to make sure they really understand the subject and present it logically and in a carefully written form.

And the teacher? She's working with individuals and small groups. She's answering questions. She's helping the student to find out where to get his own answers. Of course she's also teaching the entire class too. But the balance of time has shifted. Now the "low tech" whole-class paper and pencil exercises are gone—replaced by much more individual tuition; some computer or interactive-TV generated, some teacher led.

The truth is that we haven't even begun to adapt to the fundamental point made by Roland Meigan, the flexi-school protagonist, that we are now an information-rich society. Let's be grateful that there is no longer a single location for education, because "flexible systems produce flexible people."

Through the power of the computer all of the knowledge that teachers currently try to impart in school with such difficulty, with very little true success, and at great expense will instead be readily absorbed by a child as a normal part of growing up—without the limits and structure imposed by the school system.

We don't foresee the death of school, but we do see a big change. We see computers liberating the teacher to have the time to lead joint explorations of the new curriculum as previously stated, and promote the desired outcomes: skill, wisdom, character, and emotional maturity.

At present the UK, the U.S., and Canada boast about one computer for every eight secondary school students, which is actually far better than most other countries but still leaves "room for improvement." In 1994 in the UK, for instance, just one percent of school budgets was spent on technology; 75 percent on teachers. Such a ratio between technology and salaries cannot be sustained.

You don't necessarily need one computer per student, but you probably need one per two students—allowing for time in whole-class and in-group discussions and working on major projects. Of course, this means a huge increase in the number of school computers and on-line facilities. So where does the money come from?

Long term it comes from recruiting fewer secondary-school teachers, because their role will change. They will be more like learning advisers than instructors. Some of the savings will be switched into the primary schools, where we do need to recruit **more** teachers.

The numbers stack up because teaching costs for secondary-school students are almost double the cost of teaching primary-school children. So a 15-percent reduction in secondary-school teachers could fund a 30-percent increase in primary-school teachers. Add in the impact of auxiliary teachers, community volunteers, and mentors and we could achieve that all-important increase in primary school teachers—and reduction in primary school class sizes—without major problems in secondary schools, especially when you take into account the full impact of computers.

Where does the up-front capital come from? When we are faced with external threats (e.g., war) we find the money. We now face an internal threat (social disruption) if we don't massively increase the number of **highly** educated citizens. We *must* find the money. Here's how.

We should issue shares in new tax-exempt educational trusts. Let's say ten giant trusts to start with. The trusts purchase the hardware (they should get great terms for such a colossal order) and compete among themselves to offer schools the best deals. The equipment is leased to individual schools on terms that bring a return to shareholders. Then show parents how to collaborate in order to finance the software for their schools. It's their children—and we all know the price of private education.

Result? Schools get the computers when they need them—*now.* And they pay for them over a period of time, perhaps six years.

At the same time, of course, we need to connect every school to the information superhighway.

These last three recommendations—to increase the number of primary school teachers, to reduce recruitment of secondary school teachers, and to use technology more widely and more efficiently—go to the heart of a belief we share with many other observers. We don't necessarily need a huge increase in educational budgets, but we do need to invest our money more wisely.

This is highlighted by the fact that 80 percent of the educational budget in the UK is spent on teachers and support staff, with just three percent on resources such as books and one percent on computers. That's surely the wrong balance if you are trying to create self-directed learners and if you are trying to utilize technology properly.

Far too often education funding supports a bloated bureaucracy—especially in the U.S.

Says Howard Gardner, "Our school system is top heavy with administrators who do not improve the quality of education in the classrooms. In some cities there is one nonclass employee for every classroom employee."

And in the UK, Sir Geoffrey Holland puts it even more bluntly. He says that if education were a business it would be bankrupt because of all the failures in the system.

7. Improve Teachers' Conditions and Expect More

It's time to acknowledge that teachers do a difficult and vital job, one that requires great skill. And the skill requirement will get greater as secondary teachers assume more of the role of a university-type tutor; that is, as mentor and adviser as well as teacher. They will (or should) also be taking on the responsibility to teach more challenging subjects, including critical thinking skills, communications skills, and emotional maturity.

If we expect more we should pay more—but demand more too. Additional "productivity" in the sense of more students per teacher will occur in secondary school with the impact of technology. But there's no reason why good teachers whose students get good results shouldn't be paid more. And, equally, teachers whose students get poor results should be paid less, be retrained, or asked to leave. Our children deserve the best.

Unfortunately, in the U.S. seniority sometimes counts more than competence, with a "last-hired, first-fired" union-bargained policy. Unions have barred teachers from being paid on the basis of their performance. Instead, they are paid strictly on the basis of years of experience and the number of college courses completed.

To keep their jobs veteran teachers voluntarily accept assignments teaching subjects in which they have no training. The U.S. Department of Education reports that a third of high school math teachers, nearly a quarter of high school English teachers, and nearly a fifth of high school science teachers don't have a college major or minor in their subjects.

President Clinton has made it plain he feels that states should find a fair way to reward good teachers and get rid of bad ones.

Forward-looking teachers' leaders such as Albert Shanker, president of the American Federation of Teachers, are recognizing the need for change. Shanker, who is drafting a variety of teacher-quality reforms, warns, "Unless we restore the public's faith in what we do, public education is going to collapse."

Shanker wants higher entrance standards, performance pay, and a streamlining of due-process protections.

In the UK teachers' leaders have also begun to accept the inevitability of performance-related pay and the idea of a "super-teacher" pay grade. The government's chief school inspector, Chris Woodhead, claims there is evidence that overall standards of pupil achievement need to be raised in approximately half of primary and two fifths of secondary schools in the country. And he provocatively asks the question: "Is the job security of that small minority of teachers who are in the wrong profession more important than the interests of the children?" We believe it isn't.

Teachers have a right to job satisfaction. Our criticisms are rarely of teachers themselves—they are criticisms of the system. Most good teachers want to see the implementation of the kind of reforms we are recommending in this chapter. They also have a right to a reasonable, balanced working life. They work too many hours a day during the semester, but not enough weeks of the year.

Teachers are also called upon to deal with the results of family breakdown—violence, bullying, disruption—a task for which they have not been trained. We should let them get on with high quality teaching and provide specialists to deal with society's problems.

> . . . a national vision of good schools is needed which will require a shift in thinking and approach. The teacher as a dispenser of information will become a coach and guide. Drill, practice, and rote memorization will be replaced by authentic problem-solving, higher-order thinking, decision-making, and cooperative learning. . . .
>
> **THE EDITORS OF**
> **EDUCATION WEEK**

8. Put Brain-Based Schooling to Work

In Chapter 16 we made many recommendations as to how we can take the latest findings about learning and use them in the classroom. Among the most important are for students to be involved in setting their own rules of behavior, values, and quality standards; for cooperative learning to be a norm; and for students to work on cross-curricular real-world problems (often local community problems). But there are many, many others.

These suggestions are not just meant to be read by teachers. We hope parents will read, and reread, these notes. If they make sense, talk to your principal and school board. Do we implement this sort of thing in our classes? Can we adopt these ideas?

We *need* a revolution in education, and revolutions never start from the top down, they spread from the bottom up.

If you are a parent—or student—you're the consumer. You get

the quality you demand. Learning can be fun, challenging, and motivating when a student controls his own learning and constructs his own meaning. It's boring when she gets taught from a curriculum in which she has no say.

At heart we're talking about a change in mind-set:

FROM	TO
Teacher led	Student exploration
Separate subjects	Interdisciplinary projects
Memorization	Creativity
External motivation (grades)	Intrinsic motivation (students trying to exceed standards that they set)
Grouped by age	Grouped by readiness
Whole-class learning	Independent study opportunities
Individual competition	Cooperation
Dependent	Interdependent
Autocratic rules	Rules set by all the participants
Drudgery	Enjoyment
School as separate from real life	School integrated into the community
Treating all students equally	Creating an individualized program that recognizes different learning styles and learning speeds.

We think parents can begin to gauge a good school by the position of the school principal on this checklist. And don't be fooled by the phase *back to basics*. *Back to basics* is an emotionally charged phrase often used to justify a controlling type of teaching in the attempt to achieve a higher standard of education. We're all for *back to basics* as meaning a higher basic standard of the 3 *R*'s. But that doesn't automatically mean it can be achieved by a return to "chalk n' talk." The objective and the means are **not** joined. It's like sex and violence. There's no automatic connection between the two, but if you repeat such pairings often enough, they get joined in the public's mind. Of course an analytical thinker wouldn't get caught in that trap!

9. Extend the School Year

The current school year of about thirty-nine weeks was created over two hundred years ago, principally to meet the needs of an agrarian society—so that the children of farmers could help in the fields.

It made sense when 40 percent of the population was involved in agriculture, but not today when the number is less than two percent. It's nonsensical to have school resources lying idle for so long. Modern parents often have difficulty coping with long holidays, and oftentimes the children's education suffers.

If the school year were increased by just six weeks a year, by the time a child reaches sixteen she would have received eighteen months of additional education. We complain about the outcome of education yet ignore simple steps to put it right.

Of course we'd need to compensate teachers for the extra weeks. We should couple the increased weeks with a reduction in the hours they currently spend at home preparing lesson plans and grading papers. We can also make much more use of community resources. Which leads to recommendation number 10.

10. Involve Members of the Community

Teaching is a highly responsible job that requires skill and training. But there are aspects of teaching that can be covered or assisted by other members of the community. Many retired people complain they have too little to challenge them, many other people want flexible-time jobs, and we know there's going to be a big reduction in the work week of the future. These are resources we should harness.

Some subjects—music, sports, crafts, art, even foreign languages, for example, lend themselves to the use of classroom assistants. Assistants are not as

> In addition to support from family members and other mentoring adults, such institutions as business, the professions, and especially museums need to be involved much more intimately in the educational process.
>
> HOWARD GARDNER IN
> MULTIPLE INTELLIGENCES:
> THE THEORY IN PRACTICE

extensively trained as teachers, but nevertheless work effectively under the direction of the class teacher. Why not make more use of community resources and free teachers up for core skills?

11. Modernize the Curriculum

What's the outcome we want from schools in the 21st century? In Chapter 16 we proposed five key outcomes—knowledge, skill, wisdom, character and emotional maturity. What other specific skills will our children need?

A group consisting of business, educational and social leaders, convened by the Oxford and Cambridge Examination Board in the UK, has debated the same question.

So did Daniel Goleman in his excellent book *Emotional Intelligence*. Drawing these sources together we propose that a 21st century secondary curriculum, should, in addition to the core learning-how-to-learn and thinking skills, incorporate (a) Emotional Education, (b) Citizenship Skills, and (c) one year of community service (a strong recommendation of our own) Let's briefly look at each.

(a) Emotional Education
We recognize the importance of PE (Physical Education) in the development of a physically healthy student. Why haven't we recognized the parallel importance of EE (Emotional Education) for the development of a mentally healthy student? It's time to do something about positive emotional education.

We propose that students should know how to:

- recognize, label, and express their own feelings and be aware of the intensity of those feelings
- manage emotions and feelings, control impulsive behavior, and know how to delay gratification when it's appropriate
- manage and reduce stress
- set realistic, yet challenging, goals for themselves
- assert their own point of view without aggression and be willing to explore other points of view objectively
- recognize and understand other people's emotions and feelings and that differences are normal
- distinguish between feelings and logical thinking and apply that skill to subjects like sex and drugs

- be a responsible parent
- manage fears and anxieties
- adhere to ethics, values
- be able to listen skillfully for feelings as well as facts in other people's conversations
- be able to forestall conflicts by looking for the optimum possible mutually beneficial outcome.

A child who has learned the above skills will be more responsible, empathetic, and well adjusted, both personally and socially. We suggest that an emotional-education program would improve classroom behavior in the short term and social and workplace success in the long term. Surely a highly valuable outcome of school?

In a perfect world children would always learn such skills at home—at the age when we know social concepts and empathy are formed in the prefrontal lobes. But if they're not acquiring these skills at home, school needs to step in. Even if they are learning them at home—because they are social skills—they need to be experienced in a group environment such as a class.

Of course, most teachers themselves have no training in helping children develop these skills. But in most communities there are people with such skills. We must make time for a subject that will have vastly more impact on a student's subsequent success in life than a lot of what is currently being taught in school.

(b) A one-year community project for every student
Skills such as problem-solving and decision-making are often better learned in a real-life context.

John Abbott is an educational visionary. Formerly a successful headmaster, he has founded a trust in the UK called Education 2000, which explores ways in which the community can be centrally integrated in education. He is now temporarily working in the U.S. "on loan" to the Johnson Wingspread Foundation.

Abbott's case is that in the days before the Industrial Revolution, schooling was largely within a work environment. Students were apprenticed to a craft and had no difficulty seeing the relevance of what they were learning. This was how one was going to earn a living and make a contribution to society, which was a geographically compact and comprehensible unit. Learning, the community, and work were all directly interrelated. Therefore, the motivation to learn was high.

John Abbott goes on to say that we need to get the community back in the educational process. We do.

What better way than for students to participate in projects that involve service to the community? We recommend making the completion of a one-year community project of choice a standard part of late secondary-school education. Let students therefore experience thinking and decision-making skills and prework skills through community service.

Not only will they learn through practical projects, but they will encounter adult role models in a way they can't through school. School tends to isolate them from society in same-age groups, rather than integrate them into multiage environments.

You feel part of a society only when you contribute to the society, which is why this idea is so powerful. And why unemployment is so destructive. Unemployment creates not just financial insecurity but a disengagement from structured society. An experience of voluntary community service, however, demonstrates how you can still be a contributor to society, even if you should be out of formal employment for a time in the future. In one imaginative project in Eastboune, England, students wrote, designed, and supervised the production of a local town brochure funded by local businesses. Perhaps the most important concept we should teach our children before they reach the workforce is the concept of employability. This would provide opportunities in which they might effectively be president of their own company—Jane Jones, Inc.—as discussed in Chapter 19.

Now Jane Jones may contract her services out directly to an employer sometimes (i.e., when she "works" for a corporation). But she can't take that relationship for granted. Only by continuously investing in the intellectual capital of Jane Jones, Inc. (i.e., constantly upgrading her own knowledge and skills) will her one-woman corporation thrive.

This concept—that everyone effectively works for him- or herself and must offer a cost-effective and high-quality service that is in demand—is in tune with a 21st-century reality. Increasingly, most corporations will enter short-term contracts with highly skilled specialists. We can expect to see the Internet (or its successor) become a huge market for jobs and services as well as a vast global marketplace for goods and services.

Not only is this the work style of the future but the concept of self-employment goes a long way to defuse the fear of downsizing and unemployment. If you expect jobs to be of limited duration, it's not so traumatic when you lose one!

So the best preparation we can give our children for the work world of the future is to teach them:

1. They are responsible for staying highly employable
2. The essence of employability is learning fast, making rational decisions, thinking creatively, and adding value.

(c) Citizenship skills

Polls tell us that we're highly cynical about politicians. They are thought to avoid straight answers, gloss over difficult issues, and substitute simplistic sound bites for proper debate.

Yet, who is really to blame? If most voters have little knowledge of economics or the law and little patience with "serious issues," what's the incentive for politicians to explore complex subjects in an informed way? Knowledge is our best protection against exploitation.

We suggest that the minimum citizen skills curriculum includes:

1. How to read a balance sheet and profit-and-loss statement. (The best companies tell their employees how they are doing right down to branch level.)
2. How to set up a business. This is especially important. In some areas male unemployment runs at 30 to 40 percent. The response from students tends to be "Learning? For what?" At least one answer is so you can start your own business. But that needs at least an acquaintance with entrepreneurial skills. It can happen. Eighty percent of companies in the UK employ less than ten people.
3. The economics of health care and personal preventative health care maintenance.
4. What is truth?
5. Environmental issues.
6. Basic elements of the law and justice systems.
7. How to interpret statistics, graphs, trends, and assess probabilities.
8. Time management.
9. Money management. Creating and controlling personal budgets and wealth.

10. Principles of Total Quality Management that can be applied to all aspects of one's life.
11. Writing a curriculum vitae and developing successful interview skills.

The above proposals on a new style of curriculum go to the heart of "What is school for?" What is an educated person and is our educational system geared to produce him or her? At the same time we think it is up to the parents and schools at the local level to decide curricula. These ideas are merely to provoke thought.

Who would teach such skills? Community members and local company employees on assignment.

12. Modify the Exam System

On both sides of the Atlantic there are calls for a dramatic reevaluation of when and how students are assessed.

Howard Gardner again: "We need an entirely new approach to assessment. Assessment needs to be built directly into the curriculum, into the day-to-day running of the school. Feedback must be provided when it is useful, not at the end of the year. And the assessment needs to occur locally, in the classroom, with face-to-face feedback, and not generated from some remote spot, scored by machine, and returned with a score, bereft of suggestions about what to do."

Charles Handy, visiting professor at London Business School, makes an interesting analogy to which most of us can relate: "If our driving tests were required to be taken once, and once only, at seventeen, and only the better half passed, we would have fewer, better drivers, safer roads, and lower hospital costs. But half of the population would be deprived of a full access to society, the economy would be seriously impaired, and we would rightly judge it an infringement of our civil liberty.

"Instead, we allow everyone to take their test when they think they are ready for it, and to retake it as often as they like. It would be fairer and better to do the same for the more crucial tests we take at school. Rationing intelligence makes no more sense than rationing driving licenses."

We don't expect testing to disappear—too many people are too wedded to it. But we have made many recommendations in previous chapters as to how school evaluations might involve more self-assessment, "process folios," and exhibitions of work to members of the school board and parents.

To that we add: a key assessment should be how well students plan and carry out their one-year community project. Now, that **is** a preparation for real life.

13. Do Your First Degree in Half the Time

University is about more than acquiring a degree. Nevertheless if we, once again, used existing technology properly and the available time less wastefully, students could achieve a B.A. or B.S. in two years.

This efficiency is important because society needs many more students to benefit from tertiary education as more and more people are opting for university and college programs. The problem in the UK, for instance, is that while governments trumpet their desire for 60 to 70 percent of students to enter university, they are not providing the funds. Reducing the first degree timetable to two years enables us to expand opportunities to more people with less of a budget crisis. In the U.S., if schools could be persuaded to adopt this approach, a two-year course would be less of a strain for students and their parents' finances.

In addition, the information superhighway can become a University of the Wire, with students taking modular courses designed to suit their exact requirements.

In the UK it costs £20,000 ($30,000) a year to educate an Oxford undergraduate. It costs £2,000 ($3,000) for an Open University graduate who learns at home with "downloaded" (i.e., video recorded) lessons. We need the quality of an Oxford University experience, but we also need the sheer economic efficiency of the Open University–type education.

In the U.S., traditionally, public higher education has not been completely free but has cost a nominal amount. The general understanding was that the charge to a student was about 10 percent of the actual cost.

In the last decade, however,

> **To keep the excitement of learning and creativity alive at all ages is the ultimate challenge, giving life meaningful color.**
>
> **MARIAN DIAMOND, PhD, IN**
> **CREATING THE FUTURE**

costs of going to a university have steadily increased. Between 1991 and 1994 the cost of the average state-university education climbed at least 10 percent a year. Since 1980 the cost in most states has tripled or quadrupled. So much so that today the nine million students in public higher education pay an average of $9,285 a year— far from nominal. Costs at the prestigious "flagship" state universities are catching up with those at private universities. The University of California at Berkeley, for instance, is now nearly $14,000 and the University of Virginia over $10,500.

On top of this, as tuition and fees have risen, so has the cost of getting a student loan to cover them. While the main student-loan program created in 1965 is interest free so long as the student is in college, a second charges interest even during the school years.

Says writer Nicholas Lemann, "Even if a state-university education pays off richly in the long run, allowing it to go from practically free to expensive changes the bargain between the citizen and the state. For most Americans public education is the most important government service—important economically, important socially because it binds us together as a people, and important psychically because it represents opportunity, the central American value.

"It gives a distinctive feeling to this country if, unlike the rest of the world, we offer education at all levels in an open and unrestricted way to everyone who qualifies. This unique and precious national commitment is now diminishing."

In an election year "battle of the tax breaks," Clinton proposed a $7.9 billion tax credit for college tuition.

Called "Hope Scholarships," it is based on a successful program that has tripled college attendance in parts of Georgia, where it is financed by state lottery revenue. The incentive is designed to give millions of middle-class and working-class Americans, currently priced off the nation's campuses, the opportunity for further education.

The initiative suggested a $1,500-a-year tax credit for two years. No strings attached for a college freshman, but to get the tax credit the second year the student would have to achieve at least a B average the first year.

In a commencement address at Princeton University, Clinton said, "Today, more than ever before in the history of the United States, education is the fault line . . . between those who will prosper and those who will not in the new economy."

He said it is "clear that because of cost and other factors, not all

Americans have access to higher education." And, recalling the post–World War II decision to make twelve years of education the norm, he repeatedly called for "nothing less than to make the thirteenth and fourteenth years of education as universal to Americans as the first twelve are today."

14. Consumer Choice

The biggest catalyst for fundamental change is choice. Choice produces diversity of supply, and efficiency.

State schools are essentially monopolies. They generally earn the same (allocation per pupil) whether they produce superior results or inferior results, and they are not sensitive to the individual demands of their "consumers" (the students and their parents).

Here's a radical proposal. We're indebted to Dr. James Tooley, writing in a challenging book entitled *Education Without the State,* published by the Institute of Economic Affairs in London, for the basic idea.

The state should take the money it currently spends per student and pay it into a Lifelong Individual Fund for Education—LIFE. The fund is then spent by the parent/student, but only on approved outlets both public and private, including home study courses, night classes, CD-ROMs, and flexi-schooling. In other words, the consumer pays and seeks the best service for his or her circumstances.

We think this kind of program could be started on a wide scale at secondary-school entrance age. Anyone could contribute extra money to LIFE accounts—parents, grandparents, students themselves, and perhaps local employers or trusts. LIFE accounts would be interest-bearing at banks or as mutual funds. We envisage they would be on electronic smart cards that would include the student's up-to-date record of achievement.

> **Lifelong learning is now a central concern of governments at all levels, industries of all sizes, and all sections of the education community as we move rapidly toward a knowledge-based economy.**
>
> **GRANT THOMAS, ONE OF THE ORGANIZERS OF THE SECOND GLOBAL CONFERENCE ON LIFELONG LEARNING**

The intention is that the "consumer" would then be able to buy the education that suits her needs and the supplier (including but not exclusively schools) would have the incentive to provide the best quality choice and price.

This would lead many schools to consider contracting out services and looking for innovative ways to satisfy demand (e.g., better use of new technology). We think infrastructures would also improve as private capital would undoubtedly be invested in creating the most attractive school possible.

Student motivation would be kept high by arranging for LIFE funds to be released progressively but only once the student reached an agreed-upon level of competence in each subject.

If children leave school early, there would still be money in their LIFE accounts. If they discover later that they need better qualifications, they could go back to further their education. At the moment the savings to the state from people who leave school early helps pay for the extra years of education of people who stay on. (The result, as someone has memorably put it, is that "bus drivers subsidize lawyers.")

LIFE accounts could be the mechanism to bring economic reality to the concept of a lifelong learning society. Moreover, the fact that some early dropouts might go back to school at an older age might well be a dramatic lesson of the value of education to the young people who are still in school.

The idea of an Individual Learning Account is not new. The Commission on Social Justice set up by the UK's Labour party commended the idea because it would "allow individuals to learn how and when it was appropriate to them."

The result of such choice would be that successful schools would bid up the salary of outstanding teachers. The incentive for innovation and improvement, which isn't urgently felt in the existing system, would produce a steady improvement in the quality of teaching, facilities, and the relevance and breadth of curricula that are offered.

Schools offering a poor curriculum, substandard teaching, and inadequate results would simply not survive or, as happens in the real world, would get "taken over" by successful enterprises.

As "choice" schools evolve better ideas and concepts to deliver a better service to their customers, they would be in a position to license others to use their ideas.

We see such schools evolving into Community Learning Centers.

As successful schools attracted more students, they would develop the funds to create, for example, high-quality library facilities and multimedia centers and a parenting center where advice and materials would be made available to parents.

The multimedia centers will put students on-line to worldwide knowledge networks, and information and ideas on their one-year Community Project could be swapped and debated. And the same facilities could be offered at extended hours to the community for a fee—becoming a local University of the Third Age, for example. School would become a mental fitness center for the whole community.

We think the LIFE concept and Community Learning Centers start to make a reality of lifelong learning.

To the critics who will say that parents don't have the information to make the right educational choices, we say we trust them to choose their children's food! We don't provide state food shops. Why not apply choice to education if you can apply it to something as basic as food?

15. Make Every Organization a M•A•S•T•E•R Organization

When organizations act upon the fact that their own survival and prosperity depend on developing the all-around potential of their workforce, they are beginning to create an organization of personal mastery.

And when companies set up programs to teach creativity and analytical thinking and communication skills and teamwork to their employees, they are not only filling in the gaps left by our current educational system, they are directly helping prevent the growth of the low-wage/low-skill/low-employment section of our society.

16. Make Education Everyone's Business

Every child needs a whole village to complete its education.

American First Lady Hillary Rodham Clinton took up the message of this African proverb in her book *It Takes a Village*. There is wide agreement that education is **everyone's** concern. And business is anxious to play its part.

Some industrial giants have taken a commendable leading role. Motorola is a good example.

It circulates booklets to the homes of all its employees to encourage them to take an active role in the growth and development of their children. Says Gary Tooker, vice chairman and chief executive officer of the giant corporation, "This will help Motorola in its quest to stimulate improvement in the educational system in America. It will also help ensure the availability of a premier workforce of lifelong learners as we move into the next century."

We'd like to see companies help directly in the following practical ways:

- Sponsor a school. Primary schools in particular struggle for resources.
- Open up personal development programs—like thinking-skills programs—to the children of the workforce.
- Donate time. Work shadowing—where students spend several days a year working alongside adults at their workplace—is having a beneficial impact in Sweden. "It must be good for the children," remarked John Abbott to one such adult who was being work-shadowed, "Yes, but it's even better for us," replied the businessperson. "The students sometimes ask us such searching questions as 'Why do we do this, why do you do that?' Sometimes we can't answer—because there is no logical reason. We've done it that way so long, it needed a fresh mind to question the purpose."
- Make distance-learning materials available to parents at a discount. One huge UK retail group with a staff of forty thousand is offering its employees CD-ROMs, books, our *FUNdamentals* program, and lunch-time classes on parenting skills.

We see local communities becoming much more active with their schools—not just the parents of existing students, but the whole community.

This should be the real dividend from the productivity revolution. As long as companies share the economic benefits of increased productivity with their workers—so they can earn the same income in fewer hours—then those workers will have the extra time that can be donated back to the community.

These contributions can include the labor to improve buildings and provide maintenance. (A recent U.S. survey highlighted the

fact that the majority of students considered their physical surroundings substandard. What kind of message does that send
about the value our society places on education?) Other contributions can be in the form of auxiliary teaching of computer skills,
art, foreign languages, basic business studies, citizenship skills, the
emotional education curriculum, communication skills, etc.

Company involvement can ensure that there is a pool of mentors
so each child can turn to skilled adults to develop proficiency in a
visual or performing art. If we are to have a new "golden age" of
leisure, we need a basis for using and enjoying it in ways that extend us.

And because the new generation will have had specific experience of community projects, involving care of their elderly, for
example, they in turn will grow up with a much deeper sense of
community themselves.

It could be the start of a virtuous circle of higher and higher
quality education for every single citizen, of education focusing on
enabling each child to become the very best she can be. We might
visualize it as follows:

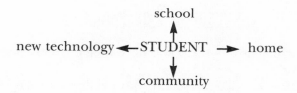

The theme of this book is that we need a revolution. A revolution in what we learn and how we learn it. In what is taught and
how it is taught. Revolutions always start from the bottom up, never
from the top down. They start when ordinary people become angry with the status quo and demand urgent action. It happens
when they network together to create a critical mass.

The time is now.

The ordinary people are people like us—and you.

Our aim is to change the culture. To persuade people that they should care about their personal learning in the same way that we are all gradually learning to care about the environment and our own health. To help them to understand that learning pays—and nothing much else does so today.

To spread the good news that everyone is capable of further useful learning and that it is never too late to begin.

A learning society would be able to offer everybody the opportunity of a better life.

Sir Christopher Ball, director of learning at the Royal Society for the Encouragement of the Arts, Manufactures, and Commerce (RSA), chancellor of the University of Derby, launching the 1996 National Campaign for Learning in the UK.

THE VISION——A SUMMARY

1. Make learning-how-to-learn and becoming a creative-analyst top priorities

There needs to be a commitment to providing everyone with access to courses on the most important and fundamental skills: learning how to learn and how to become a creative-analyst.

2. Get serious about preschool education

The early years are the critical learning years. More attention needs to be devoted to helping parents create a rich, stimulating home environment as well as providing more opportunities for children to attend nursery schools.

3. Work toward smaller primary classes

Classes at primary school level should have no more than fifteen children so each child can receive more personal attention.

4. Promote parent power at primary level

Schools and parents need to work more closely together so

that parents can complement (and extend) in the home what the child is doing at school.

5. Encourage secondary students to take responsibility
At secondary school level, students should be empowered to take more responsibility for the manner in which they are learning.

6. Exploit the new technology
There must be a dramatic expansion of the use of computer technology, which gives students ready access to especially gifted teachers as well as multimedia information and the ability to learn at one's own pace.

7. Pay teachers more—and expect more
Teaching is one of the most vital jobs anyone can have in today's society. We should be more demanding of our teachers while acknowledging that quality teachers deserve greater financial rewards—teachers performing at lower levels should be paid less.

8. Put brain-based schooling to work
Cooperative learning needs to be widely introduced in schools, and students encouraged to work on "real world" problems while establishing their own rules of acceptable behavior.

9. Extend the school year
Students need to spend more time in school—six weeks more is recommended. The long summer vacation goes back to the days of the agrarian society, when children were needed to help work in the fields!

10. Involve members of the community
Hire retired people or others interested in working flexible hours to work as classroom assistants. People with expertise in particular subjects could become mentors to students.

11. Modernize the curriculum
Secondary-school students should receive an "emotional education" to become socially responsible. They should learn "citizenship skills" for the real world—how to set up a business,

read a balance sheet, manage time and money, etc. And they should give one year of community service to experience working in the real world.

12. Modify the exam system

Assessment needs to be built into the school curriculum, in the classroom on an ongoing basis. Students should be judged on their performance in building a portfolio of work and given meaningful face-to-face feedback rather than one-time, remote scoring, on a "make or break" basis.

13. Reduce the time it takes to get a degree

Students could obtain a B.A. or B.S. in just two years with improved efficiency and greater use of technology—and with meaningful cost savings.

14. Initiate consumer choice

Establish individual education funds, or a voucher program on an electronic smart card, whereby the student can spend his personal allocation on the kind of teaching and educational materials he selects. Schools would have an incentive to provide the best quality, choice, and price. Free market competition.

15. Make every organization a M•A•S•T•E•R Organization

For continued prosperity, companies and employees need to follow the obligations outlined at the end of Chapter 19 in which responsibility is shared for adding value to the company and the employee, providing quality service, maintaining continuous improvement, and embracing change.

16. Make education everyone's business

Local communities, schools, and businesses all need to work together so that individuals appreciate the benefits of becoming lifelong learners.

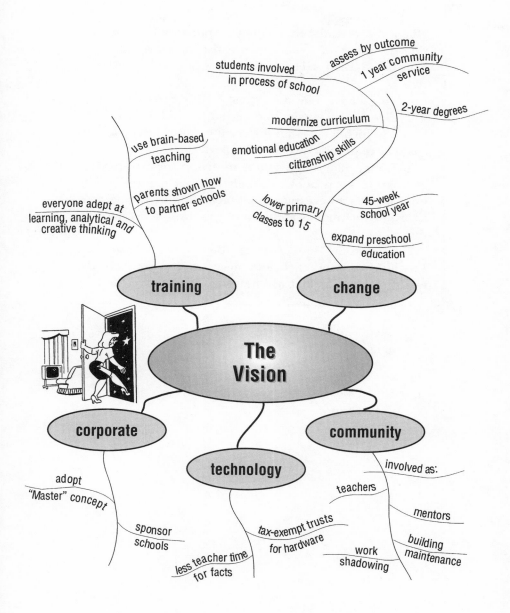

WHAT NOW?

When you've finished reading it, put this book to one side for a few days—and then revisit it. Browse through it again. Reread sections that appear particularly relevant.

Having had a few days "rest," your refreshed mind will digest previously undigested material. Don't be afraid to highlight—with different colored pens—key areas that require action on your part.

This may be a tough course of action for avid readers who try to keep books in their original pristine condition. But it's a necessary implementation of Accelerated Learning techniques and ensure you turn advice into action.

Get started: Don't just sit there. Put Accelerated Learning into practice and discover for yourself the world of benefits that will be yours.

For Further Study

As you've discovered, the broad principles of Accelerated Learning can be applied throughout life—from the earliest years through to one's golden years.

Accelerated Learning Systems has, therefore, with the aid of a panel of international consultants, developed age-related programs as well as targeting specific subjects using the concepts described in this book. Our goal has been to make it as easy as possible for the committed learner to put theory into practice.

EARLY LEARNING

The fact that 50 percent of a child's brain capacity is developed in the first five or six years of life means that it's **essential** that your child—or grandchild—grow up in a rich, thought-provoking environment.

We have developed a program for eighteen-month-to-six-year-olds called *FUNdamentals* that aims for a happy, **well-rounded** child. There are games and activities to ensure your child will read early, will be able to write, and will understand the concepts behind addition, subtraction, and division.

The reading games include over six hundred word cards and many original board games. The math games include Montessori-style number rods, dot cards with numerals on the back, and an idea called the "Magic L game," which can make multiplication understandable—even to a five-year-old.

The program, however, goes beyond being a flying start in the 3R's. There are games to build vocabulary, physical skills, creativity, concentration, musical ability, logical thinking, memory, values, and self-esteem. Parents, grandparents, or other caregivers will certainly never be stuck for something worthwhile to do, because *FUNdamentals* contains over a thousand ideas for "purposeful play."

The program is designed to make the utmost of the time parents are able to spend with their children, turning even everyday activities like unpacking the shopping bag or car journeys into worthwhile learning opportunities.

There's a video, guidebook, a take-anywhere book of activities and games, plus word cards, math games, and writing templates. The program has already been recommended by child-development experts.

There's also a version for parents of newborns through to the age of eighteen months, when gentle stimulation can make an important difference.

HIGHER GRADES FOR STUDENTS

A program called *Accelerate Your Learning* has been produced with the aim of helping secondary school students improve their exam results (and motivation).

A video, an audiotape, and action handbooks teach them how to read and absorb information faster, improve memory and writing skills, and generally study more effectively.

The program enables each student to uncover his or her preferred way of learning and acquire the learning techniques that best match that learning style.

Documented results from various educational authorities showed significant improvements in exam results when this program was introduced, and in the UK it has been recommended by the National Confederation of Parent-Teachers Associations.

It's not enough simply to urge teenagers to get better results; you need to give them the practical techniques to make that success possible. We have tried to ensure that *Accelerate Your Learning* contains all of those techniques.

NEW JOB SKILLS

Learning faster than the competition is a core skill for both individuals and organizations. This is the aim of the *Accelerated Learning Techniques* program, published by Nightingale Conant.

It teaches people in business how to learn any subject or skill in the way that best suits their individual learning styles. The purpose is working smarter, not harder—learning more in less time.

Designed as a fundamental component for any company intending to become a learning organization.

A FOREIGN LANGUAGE IN WEEKS

You can buy in any language—but you can sell only in your customer's language! Mastering a foreign language really is a major career and school advantage and definitely enhances the pleasure of travel.

Accelerated Learning foreign language courses have been proven to accomplish in weeks what might have taken years through conventional methods. They use a multisensory immersion approach with lots of games and activities to cater to a wide variety of learning styles.

The basic language is learned from a series of entertaining radio plays with real-life situations on twelve audiocassettes. Unique "Memory Maps" illustrate the main phrases very vividly. When you recall the images, you recall the words. A video gets you physically acting out key words and phrases, and another unique feature, the Name Game, builds vocabulary in a surprisingly short time. There are parts you can practice in the car, and some sequences are even repeated to music. The intention is to make the words as easy to remember as the words of a song.

The combination of auditory, visual, and physical learning really does accelerate the learning process. The record so far was just thirty-one hours of study to qualify for the Institute of Linguists

Preliminary certificate. BBC news recently featured a school where ten times more students using Accelerated Learning got top marks compared with conventional courses. Other schools have compressed two years' work into as little as three months, and the programs are widely used by banks, airlines, and many *Fortune* 500 multinationals.

ARTISTIC ABILITY

Master art tutor Nancy Margulies has taught thousands to draw. Most started out doubting their ability, yet after just a few hours using her unique, simple, step-by-step instruction they were able to produce portraits and drawings they were proud to show. Because everyone has the basic ability to draw—when they are shown how.

Now her method has been captured on video and in a fully illustrated guidebook. The program is called *Yes, You Can Draw!* It covers everything you need to know to bring out your own artistic ability.

CORPORATE TRAINING

A *Training and Development Program* enables managers and trainers to apply the principles of Accelerated Learning to their existing and future training sessions—whatever the duration or training content.

It lays out a carefully researched sequence of activities for the trainer to follow. Different activities are designed to engage different forms of intelligence.

The result is that each trainee is able to learn with his or her strongest form of intelligence—and the subject is also presented, explored, and reviewed in several different ways during the training day. So there is a depth of understanding as well as breadth of appeal across all learning styles. It is, to use Dr. Howard Gardner's phrase, "Multiple Chance Learning."

The program contains four manuals, three videotapes, and three audiocassettes. The manuals explain the sequence of activities that produce Accelerated Learning in trainees. The videotapes demonstrate the program in action.

The program includes over eighty tested activities and there is a validated test to enable trainees to identify their own learning preferences.

The program is completed by attending a full ready-to-deliver sample training day on Customer Satisfaction in the Accelerated Learning format. This includes a trainer's manual with all the necessary charts, scripts, handouts, and activities, plus a demonstration video.

With this comprehensive package of "mixed-media" materials, an organization is fully equipped to convert any existing training course to the Accelerated Learning format, or produce one from scratch. The process is applicable to all types of organizations and has been successfully used to train all types of employees.

Resources

For further information about Accelerated Learning

United Kingdom

Colin Rose
Accelerated Learning Systems
Ltd.
50 Aylesbury Road
Aston Clinton, Aylesbury
Bucks. HP22 9AH
United Kingdom
Phone: 011-44-1296-631177
Fax: 011-44-1296-631074
e-mail:
colinrose@globalnet.co.uk

United States

Malcolm J. Nicholl
Accelerated Learning Systems,
Inc.
1945 Camino Vida Roble,
Suite A.,
Carlsbad, CA 92008
Phone: 1-619-931-7618
Fax: 1-619-931-0603
e-mail: als@u-s.com

Australia

Katrina Spencer
Rose Research International
P.O. Box 618
Mount Ommaney
Queensland 4077
Australia
Phone: 011-61-7-3278-8011
Fax: 011-61-7-3278-8330

New Zealand

Judy Green
A. L. Associates
P.O. Box 24-123
144 Marine Parade
New Brighton
Christchurch 7
New Zealand
Phone: 011-64-3-382-2400
Fax: 011-64-3-382-2401

South Africa

David Morris
Accelerated Learning Systems
Pty Ltd.
14 Milner Road
Tamboerskloof
Cape Town
South Africa
Phone: 011-27-21-221738
Fax: 011-27-21-261827
e-mail: als-sa@iafrica.com

National Committee for
Citizens in Education
10840 Little Patuxent Parkway,
Suite 301
Columbia, MD 21044

SuperCamp
Learning Forum Foundation
1725 South Coast Highway
Oceanside, CA 92054-5319
Phone 1-619-722-0072
Fax: 1-619-722-3507

HOME SCHOOL RESOURCES

Advisory Centre for Education
1b Aberdeen Studios
22–24 Highbury Grove
London N5 2EA
United Kingdom

Education Otherwise
P.O. Box 120
Leamington Spa
Warwickshire CV32 7ER
United Kingdom

Educational Heretics Press
113 Arundel Drive
Bramcote Hills
Nottingham NG9 3FQ
United Kingdom

TEACHING AND EDUCATIONAL RESEARCH RESOURCES

American Federation of
Teachers
555 New Jersey Avenue N.W.
Washington DC 20001
Phone: 1-202-879-4400
Fax: 1-202-879-4556

Association for Supervision
and Curriculum Development
1250 N. Pitt Street
Alexandria, VA 22314
Phone: 1-703-549-911
Fax: 1-703-299-8631

Center for Critical Thinking
Sonoma State University
1801 E. Cotati Avenue
Rohnert Park, CA 94928
Phone: 1-707-664-2940

Center on Learning,
Assessment and School
Structure (CLASS)
39 Main Street
Geneseo, NY 14454
Phone: 1-716-264-9895

The Coalition of Essential
Schools
Brown University
1 Davol Square
Providence, RI 02903
Phone: 1-401-863-3384
Fax: 1-401-863-2045

The Cooperative Learning
Center
University of Minnesota
60 Pike Hall
159 Pillsbury Drive SE.
Minneapolis, MN 55455
Phone: 1-612-624-7031
Fax: 1-612-626-1395

Educational Resources
Information Center (ERIC)
U.S. Department of Education
Office of Educational
Research and Improvement
Washington DC 20208-1235

International Alliance for
Learning (IAL)
10040 First Street
Encinitas, CA 92024-5059

Phone: 1-619-634-5146
Fax: 1-619-632-1305

National Association of
Secondary School Principals
1904 Association Drive
Reston, VA 20191
Phone: 1-703-860-0200
Fax: 1-703-476-5432

Phi Delta Kappan
P.O. Box 789
The Education Honorary
Society
Bloomington, IN 47402-0789
Phone: 1-812-339-1156
Fax: 1-812-339-0018

Worldwide Education service
35 Belgrave Square
London SW1X 8QB
United Kingdom

CORPORATE TRAINING RESOURCES

Enhance Training
908 Crest Drive
Encinitas, CA 92024
Phone: 1-619-942-7009
Fax: 1-619-942-7009
e-mail:
103105.3076@compuserve.com

Bibliography

Books

Abbott, John. *Learning Makes Sense.* Herts., UK: Education 2000 Trust, Letchworth Garden City, 1994.

Allman, W. F. *Apprentices of Wonder: Inside the Neural Network Revolution.* New York: Bantam, 1989.

Armstrong, Thomas. *Awakening Your Child's Natural Genius.* Los Angeles: Jeremy P. Tarcher, Inc., 1991.

Armstrong, Thomas. *In Their Own Way: Discovering and Encouraging Your Child's Personal Learning Style.* Los Angeles: Jeremy P. Tarcher, Inc., 1987.

Armstrong, Thomas. *7 Kinds of Smart.* New York: Plume Books, 1993.

Baddeley, A. D. *Your Memory: A User's Guide.* Garden City Park, NY: Avery, 1993.

Ball, Sir Christopher. *Learning Pays: The Role of Post-Compulsory Education and Training.* London: R.S.A., 1991.

Ball, Sir Christopher. *Profitable Learning: Summary Report, Findings, and Action Plan.* London: R.S.A., 1992.

Baron, Joan B., and Robert J. Sternberg. *Teaching Thinking Skills: Theory and Practice.* New York: W. H. Freeman & Co., 1987.

Beck, Joan. *How to Raise a Brighter Child.* New York: Pocket Books, 1986.

Beyer, Barry K. *Developing a Thinking Skills Program.* Boston: Allyn and Bacon, 1988.

Bills, Robert E. *Education for Intelligence? Or Failure?* Washington, D.C.: Acropolis Books, 1982.

Bloom, Benjamin S., ed. *Developing Talent in Young People.* New York: Ballantine, 1985.

Borysenko, J. *Minding the Body, Mending the Mind.* London: Bantam Press, 1988.

Boyd, William Lowe, and Herbert J. Walberg, eds. *Choice in Education: Potential and Problems.* Berkeley: McCutchan Publishing Corp., 1990.

Boyer, Ernest L. *Ready to Learn: A Mandate for the Nations.* Lawrenceville, NJ: The Carnegie Foundation for the Advancement of Teaching, 1991.

Brewer, Chris, and Don G. Campbell. *Rhythms of Learning.* Tucson: Zephyr Press, 1991.

Briggs, John. *Fire in the Crucible: The Self-Creation of Creativity and Genius.* Los Angeles: Jeremy P. Tarcher, Inc., 1990.

Buzan, Tony. *Make the Most of your Mind.* New York: Linden Press, 1984.

Buzan, Tony. *Use Your Perfect Memory.* New York: NAL-Dutton, 1984.

Buzan, Tony, and Barry Buzan. *How to Use The Mind Map Book: Radiant Think-*

ing to Maximize Your Brain's Untapped Potential. New York: NAL-Dutton, 1994.

Caine, Geoffrey, Renate N. Caine, and San Crowell. *MindShifts.* Tucson: Zephyr Press, 1994.

Cameron-Bandler, Leslie, David Gordon, and Michael Lebeaue. *Know-How-Guided Programs for Inventing Your Own Best Future.* San Rafael, CA: FuturePace Inc., 1985.

Canfield, Jack, and Harold C. Wells. *One Hundred Ways to Enhance Self-Concept in the Classroom: A Handbook for Teachers and Parents.* Englewood Cliffs, NJ: Prentice-Hall, 1976.

Churchill, Winston. *My Early Life: A Roving Commission.* New York: Scribner's, 1987.

Clark, Ronald W. *Einstein: The Life and Times.* New York: Avon Books, 1994.

Coles, M. J., and W. D. Robinson, eds. *Teaching Thinking: A Survey of Programmes in Education.* Bristol, Avon, UK: Bristol Press, 1989.

Collins, Marva. *Ordinary Children, Extraordinary Teachers.* Norfolk, VA: Hampton Roads, 1992.

Commission on the Skills of the American Workforce. *America's Choice: High Skills or Low Wages.* Rochester, NY: National Center on Education and the Economy, 1990.

Costa, Arthur, James Bellanca, and Robin Fogarty, eds. *If Minds Matter: A Foreword to the Future,* Vol. 2. Palatine, IL: IRI/Skylight Publishing, 1992.

Costa, Arthur L. *Developing Minds: A Resource Book for Teaching Thinking,* Revised Edition, Vol. 1. Alexandria, VA: ASCD, 1991.

Csikszentmihalyi, Mihaly. *Flow: The Psychology of Optimal Experience.* New York: Harper & Row, 1990.

Davidow, William H., and Michael S. Malone. *The Virtual Corporation.* New York: HarperBusiness, 1992.

Davis, Stan, and Jim Botkin. *The Monster under the Bed.* New York: Simon & Schuster, 1994.

De Bono, Edward. *Lateral Thinking: Creativity Step-by-Step.* New York: Harper & Row, 1970.

DePorter, Bobbi. *Quantum Learning.* New York: Dell, 1992.

Diamond, Marian C. *Enriching Heredity: The Impact of the Environment on the Anatomy of the Brain.* New York: The Free Press, 1988.

Dickinson, Dee, ed. *Creating the Future.* Aston Clinton, Bucks., UK: Accelerated Learning Systems, 1991.

Dryden, Gordon, and Colin Rose. *FUNdamentals: The Building Blocks to Raise a Brighter, Happier Child.* Aston Clinton, Bucks., UK: Accelerated Learning Systems, 1996.

Dryden, Gordon, and Jeannette Vos. *The Learning Revolution.* Torrance, CA: Jalmar Press, 1994.

Edelman, Gerald M. *Bright Air, Brilliant Fire: On the Matter of the Mind.* New York: BasicBooks, 1992.

Elias, Maurice J., and John F. Clabby. *Building Social Problem-Solving Skills: Guidelines From a School-Based Program*. San Francisco: Jossey-Bass, 1992.

Ellis, David B. *Becoming a Master Student*. Rapid City, MD: College Survival, Inc., 1985.

Evans, Peter, and Geoff Deehan. *The Descent of Mind: The Nature and Purpose of Intelligence*. London: Grafton Books, 1990.

Evans, Peter, and Geoff Deehan. *The Keys to Creativity: Unlocking the Secrets of the Creative Mind*. London: Grafton Books, 1988.

Eyre, Linda and Richard. *Teaching Your Children Values*. New York: Simon & Schuster, 1993.

Feuerstein, Reuven. *Instrumental Enrichment: An Intervention Program for Cognitive Modifiability*. Baltimore: University Park Press, 1980.

Fisher, Robert. *Teaching Children to Think*. Chelterham, UK: Stanley Thorves, 1990.

Fiske, Edward B. *Smart Schools, Smart Kids: Why Do Some Schools Work?* New York: Simon & Schuster, 1991.

Fogarty, Robin, and James Bellanca. *Multiple Intelligences: A Collection*. Palatine, IL: IRI/Skylight Publishing, 1995.

Frankl, Viktor E. *Man's Search for Meaning*. New York: Washington Square, 1963.

Gardner, Howard. *Frames of Mind: The Theory of Multiple Intelligences*. New York: BasicBooks, 1985.

Gardner, Howard. *Multiple Intelligences: The Theory in Practice*. New York: BasicBooks, 1993.

Gardner, Howard. *The Unschooled Mind: How Children Think and How Schools Should Teach*. New York: BasicBooks, 1991.

Gardner, Howard, Mindy L. Kornhaber, and Warren K. Wake. *Intelligence: Multiple Perspectives*. New York: Harcourt Brace College Publishers, 1996.

Gates, Bill. *The Road Ahead*. New York: Viking, 1995.

Gawain, Shakti. *Creative Visualization*. Mill Valley, CA: Whatever Publishing, 1979.

Gazzaniga, Michael S. *Mind Matters: How Mind and Brain Interact to Create Our Conscious Lives*. New York: Houghton Mifflin, 1988.

Gazzaniga, Michael S. *The Social Brain: Discovering the Networks of the Mind*. New York: BasicBooks, 1985.

Glasser, William. *Control Theory in the Classroom*. New York: Harper & Row, 1986.

Glasser, William. *The Quality School: Managing Students without Coercion*. New York: Harper & Row, 1990.

Goldberg, Philip. *The Intuitive Edge*. New York: A Jeremy P. Tarcher/Putnam Book, 1983.

Goleman, Daniel. *Emotional Intelligence*. New York: Bantam Books, 1995.

Handy, Charles. *The Age of Unreason*. London: Century Hutchinson, 1989.

Harman, Willis, and Howard Rheingold. *Higher Creativity: Liberating the Unconscious for Breakthrough Insights*. Los Angeles: Jeremy P. Tarcher, 1984.

Hart, Leslie A. *Human Brain and Human Learning*. New York: Longman, 1983.

Harth, E. *The Creative Loop: How the Brain Makes a Mind*. Reading, MA: Addison-Wesley, 1993.

Hawkins, David, et al. *Communities That Care*. San Francisco: Jossey-Bass, 1992.

Healy, Jane M. *Endangered Minds: Why Children Don't Think and What We Can Do about It*. New York: Simon & Schuster, 1990.

Holt, John. *How Children Fail*. New York: Dell, 1964.

Houston, Jean. *The Possible Human: A Course in Enhancing Your Physical, Mental, and Creative Abilities*. Los Angeles: Jeremy P. Tarcher, 1982.

Hughes, Felicity. *Reading and Writing before School*. London: Jonathan Cape, 1971.

Hunt, David E. *Beginning with Ourselves: in Practice, Theory, and Human Affairs*. Cambridge, MA: Brookline Books, 1987.

Hutchison, Michael. *Megabrain*. New York: Ballantine Books, 1987.

Jackendorf, Ray. *Patterns in the Mind: Language and Human Nature*. New York: BasicBooks, 1994.

Jensen, Eric P. *Super-Teaching*. Del Mar, CA: Turning Point, 1988.

Johnson, David W. *Reaching Out: Interpersonal Effectiveness and Self-Actualization*. Englewood Cliffs, NJ: Prentice-Hall, 1990.

Johnson, David W., and R. Johnson. *Circles of Learning: Cooperation in the Classroom*. Edina, MN: Interaction, 1990.

Johnson, David W., and R. Johnson. *Learning Together And Alone*. Englewood Cliffs, NJ: Prentice Hall, 1990.

Johnson, David W., and R. Johnson. *Structuring Cooperative Learning: Lesson Plans for Teachers*. Edina, MN: Interaction, 1987.

Johnson, Virginia. *Hands-On Math*. Cypress, CA: Creative Teaching Press, 1994.

Kammeraad-Campbell, Susan. *Doc. The Story of Dennis Littky and His Fight for a Better School*. Chicago: Contemporary Books, 1989.

Kaye, Peggy. *Games for Learning*. New York: Noonday Books, 1991.

Kaye, Peggy. *Games for Reading*. New York: Pantheon Books, 1984.

Kearns, David T., and Denis P. Doyle. *Winning the Brain Race: A Bold Plan to Make Our Schools Competitive*. San Francisco: ICS Press, 1991.

Kline, Peter. *The Everyday Genius*. Arlington, VA: Great Ocean Publishers, 1988.

Kline, Peter, and Bernard Saunders. *Ten Steps to a Learning Organization*. Arlington, VA: Great Ocean Publishers, 1993.

Lazear, David. *Seven Pathways of Learning: Teaching Students and Parents about Multiple Intelligences*. Tucson: Zephyr Press, 1994.

Lazear, David. *Seven Ways of Knowing: Teaching for Multiple Intelligences*. Palatine, IL: IRI/Skylight Publishing, 1991.

Lazear, David. *Seven Ways of Teaching: The Artistry of Teaching with Multiple Intelligences*. Palatine, IL: IRI/Skylight Publishing, 1991.

LeBoeuf, Michael. *Imagineering: How to Profit from Your Creative Powers*. New York: McGraw-Hill, 1982.

Le Poncin, Monique, with Michael Levine. *Brain Fitness: A Proven Program to Im-*

prove Your Memory, Logic, Attention Span, Organizational Ability, and More. New York: Fawcett Columbine, 1990.

Lipman, Matthew. *Harry Stottlemeier's Discovery.* Upper Montclair, NJ: Institute for the Advancement of Philosophy for Children, 1982.

Lipman, Matthew, and Ann M. Sharp. *Philosophy in the Classroom,* 2nd ed. Philadelphia: Temple University Press, 1980.

Lorayne, Harry, and Jerry Lucas. *The Memory Book.* London: Wyndham Publications, 1974.

Lozanov, Georgi. *Suggestology and Outlines of Suggestopedy.* New York: Gordon & Breach, 1978.

Luria, Aleksandr R. *The Mind of a Mnemonomist.* New York: Basic Books, 1968.

Machado, Luiz. *The Brain of the Brain: The Key to the Mysteries of Man.* Rio de Janeiro: Cidada do Cérebro, 1990.

Maddox, Harry. *How to Study.* London: Pan Books, 1963.

Margulies, Nancy. *Mapping Inner Space.* Tucson: Zephyr Press, 1991.

Margulies, Nancy. *Yes, You Can Draw.* Aston Clinton, Bucks. UK: Accelerated Learning Systems, 1991.

Markova, Dawna, Ph.D. *The Art of the Possible: A Compassionate Approach to Understanding the Way People Think, Learn, and Communicate.* Emeryville, CA: Conari Press, 1991.

Marquardt, Michael J. *Building the Learning Organization.* New York: McGraw Hill, 1996.

May, Rollo. *The Courage to Create.* New York: W. W. Norton, 1975.

McCord, Joan and Richard Tremblay, eds. *The Prevention of Antisocial Behavior in Children.* New York: Guilford, 1992.

McNally, David. *Even Eagles Need a Push: Learning to Soar in a Changing World.* Eden Prairie, MN: TransForm Press, 1990.

Michalko, Michael. *Thinkertoys: A Handbook of Business Creativity for the Nineties.* Berkeley: Ten Speed Press, 1991.

Minsky, Marvin. *The Society of Mind.* New York: Simon & Schuster, 1986.

Missimer, Connie. *Good Arguments: An Introduction to Critical Thinking,* 2nd ed. Englewood Cliffs, NJ: Prentice-Hall, 1986.

Nadler, Gerald, and Shozo Hibino. *Breakthrough Thinking: Why We Must Change the Way We Solve Problems and the Seven Principles to Achieve This.* Rocklin, CA: Primo Publishing & Communications, 1990.

Naisbitt, John. *Megatrends.* New York: Warner Books, 1982.

Naisbitt, John, and Patricia Auburdene. *Megatrends 2000.* New York: Morrow, 1990.

Nickerson, Raymond S., David N. Perkins, and Edward E. Smith. *The Teaching of Thinking.* Hillsdale, NJ: Lawrence Erlbaum Associates, 1985.

Olsen, Robert W. *The Art of Creative Thinking.* New York: Harper & Row, 1980.

Ornstein, Robert. *The Evolution of Consciousness: The Origins of the Way We Think.* New York: Touchstone, 1991.

Ornstein, Robert, and Paul Ehrlich. *New World, New Mind: Moving Toward Conscious Evolution.* New York: Doubleday, 1989.

Ornstein, Robert, and D. Sobel. *The Healing Brain: Breakthrough Discoveries about How the Brain Keeps Us Healthy.* New York: Simon & Schuster, 1987.

Ornstein, Robert, and Charles Swencionis, eds. *The Healing Brain: A Scientific Reader.* New York: The Guilford Press, 1990.

Osborne, A. F. *Applied Imagination.* New York: Scribner's, 1963.

Ostrander, Sheila, and Lynn Schroeder, with Nancy Ostrander. *Super-Learning.* New York: Delacorte Press, 1979.

Ostrander, Sheila, and Lynn Schroeder, with Nancy Ostrander. *Super-Learning 2000.* New York: Delacorte Press, 1994.

Palmer, Lyelle. *Kindergarten Maximum Stimulation: Results over Four Years at Westwood School, Irving.* Winona State University, MN, 1993.

Parnes, Sidney J. *The Magic of Your Mind.* Buffalo, NY: Bearly, Ltd., 1981.

Paul, Richard W. *Critical Thinking: What Every Person Needs to Survive in a Rapidly Changing World.* Santa Rosa, CA: Foundation for Critical Thinking, 1990.

Paul, Richard W., A.J.A. Ginker, et al. *Critical Thinking Handbook: K–3rd Grade. A Guide for Remodeling Lesson Plans in Language Arts, Social Studies, and Science,* 2nd ed. Santa Rosa, CA: Foundation for Critical Thinking, 1990.

Pedler, Mike, John Burgoyne and Tom Boydell. *The Learning Company: A Strategy for Sustainable Development.* Maidenhead, Berks., UK: McGraw Hill, 1991.

Perkins, David. *The Mind's Best Work.* Cambridge, MA: Harvard University Press, 1981.

Perkins, David. *Outsmarting IQ: The Emerging Science of Learnable Intelligence.* New York: The Free Press, 1995.

Pike, Robert W. *Creative Training Techniques Handbook.* Minneapolis, MN: Lakewood Books, 1990.

Popcorn, Faith. *The Popcorn Report.* New York: Doubleday, 1991.

Postman, Neil, and Charles Weingartner. *Teaching as a Subversive Activity.* New York: Delacorte, 1979.

Rae, John. *Too Little, Too Late: The Challenges That Still Face British Education.* Glasgow: William Collins, 1989.

Reinsmith, William. *Archetypal Forms in Teaching: A Continuum.* Westport, CT: Greenwood Press, 1992.

Restak, Richard. *The Modular Brain.* New York: Scribner's, 1994.

Rich, Dorothy. *MegaSkills.* Boston: Houghton Mifflin, 1988.

Rico, Gabriele L., *Writing the Natural Way: Using Right-Brain Techniques to Release Your Expressive Power.* Los Angeles: Jeremy P. Tarcher, 1983.

Rifkin, Jeremy. *The End of Work: the Decline of the Global Labor Force and the Dawn of the Post-Market Era.* New York: A Jeremy P. Tarcher/Putnam Book, 1995.

Robbins, Anthony. *Awaken the Giant Within.* New York: Summit Books, 1991.

Robinson, Ken. *The Arts in Schools: Principles, Practice, and Provision.* London: BPCC Oyez Press, 1982.

Rogers, Carl R. *Freedom to Learn for the Eighties*. New York: Macmillan, 1983.

Rogers, Carl R. *On Becoming a Person*. Boston: Houghton Mifflin, 1961.

Rosenfield, Israel. *The Invention of Memory: A New View of the Brain*. New York: BasicBooks, 1988.

Rowntree, Derek. *Learn How to Study: A Guide for Students of All Ages*. London: Macdonald Illustrated, 1990.

Rylatt, Alastair. *Learning Unlimited*. Sydney, Australia: Business & Professional Publishing, 1995.

Samples, Bob. *Open Mind/Whole Mind: Parenting and Teaching Tomorrow's Children Today*. Rolling Hills, CA: Jalmar Press, 1987.

Sarason, Seymour B. *The Predictable Failure of Education Reform: Can We Change Course Before It's Too Late?* San Francisco: Jossey-Bass, 1990.

Scriven, Michael. *Reasoning*. New York: McGraw-Hill, 1976.

Senge, Peter M. *The Fifth Discipline: The Art and Practice of the Learning Organization*. New York: Doubleday, 1990.

Siegel, Bernie S. *Love, Medicine, and Miracles*. New York: Harper & Row, 1986.

Sizer, Theodore R. *Horace's Compromise: The Dilemma of the American High School*. Boston: Houghton Mifflin, 1984.

Sizer, Theodore R. *Horace's School: Redesigning the American High School*. New York: Houghton Mifflin, 1992.

Slavin, Robert E. *Cooperative Learning*. New York: Longman, 1983.

Smith, Anthony. *The Mind*. London: Hodder and Staughton, 1984.

Springer, Sally P., and Georg Deutsch. *Left Brain, Right Brain*. W. H. Freeman, New York, 1989.

Staff of the New City School. *Celebrating Multiple Intelligences: Teaching for Success*. St. Louis, MO: The New City School, 1994.

Sternberg, Robert J. *Intelligence Applied: Understanding and Increasing Your Intellectual Skills*. New York: Harcourt Brace Jovanovich, 1986.

Sternberg, Robert J. *The Nature of Creativity: Contemporary Pyschological Perspectives*. New York: Cambridge University Press, 1988.

Sternberg, Robert J. *The Triarchic Mind: A New Theory of Human Intelligence*. New York: Viking, 1988.

Stone, Karen F., and Harold Q. Dillehunt. *Self Science: The Subject Is Me*. Santa Monica: Goodyear Publishing Co., 1978.

Sylwester, Robert. *A Celebration of Neurons: An Educator's Guide to the Human Brain*. Alexandria, VA: ASCD, 1995.

Tavris, Carol. *Anger: The Misunderstood Emotion*. New York: Touchstone, 1989.

Tobin, Daniel R. *Re-Educating the Corporation: Foundations for the Learning Organization*. Essex Junction, VT: Oliver Wright Publications, 1993.

Tooley, James. *Education without the State*. London: The Institute of Economic Affairs, 1996.

Tracy, Brian. *Maximum Achievement*. New York: Simon & Schuster, 1993.

Tribus, Myron. *Selected Papers on Quality and Productivity Improvements*. Washington, DC: National Society of Professional Engineers, 1991.

Vygotsky, Lev S. *Mind in Society: the Development of Higher Psychological Processes.* Cambridge, MA: Harvard University Press, 1978.

Walton, Mary. *The Deming Management Method.* New York: Perigee Books, 1986.

Weinstein, Claire E., Ernest T. Goetz, and Patricia A. Alexander, eds. *Learning and Study Strategies.* San Diego: Academic Press, 1988.

West, Thomas G. *In the Mind's Eye.* Buffalo, NY: Prometheus Books, 1991.

Whimbey, Arthur, and Jack Lackhead. *Problem Solving and Comprehension.* 3rd ed. Philadelphia: Franklin Institute Press, 1982.

White, Burton L. *The First Three Years of Life.* New York: Prentice Hall, 1986.

Wick, Calhoun W., and Lu Stanton Leon. *The Learning Edge; How Smart Managers and Smart Companies Stay Ahead.* New York: McGraw Hill, 1993.

Wlodkowski, Raymond J., and Judith H. Jaynes. *Eager to Learn: Helping Children Become Motivated and Love Learning.* San Francisco: Jossey-Bass Inc., 1990.

Wujec, Tom. *The Complete Mental Fitness Book.* London: Aurum Press, 1989.

Wurman, Richard Saul. *Information Anxiety.* New York: Doubleday, 1989.

Zdenek, Marilee. *The Right-Brain Experience.* London: Corgi Books, 1985.

Articles

"Accelerate Their Learning." *Northside Chronicle* (Australia) (December 18, 1993).

Barasch, Marc. "Welcome to the Mind-Body Revolution." *Psychology Today* (July–August 1993).

Barinaga, Marcia. "To Sleep, Perchance to . . . Learn? New Studies Say Yes." *Science* (July 29, 1994).

Beentjes, J., and T. Van der Voort. "Television's Impact on Children's Reading Skills: A Review of Research." *Reading Research Quarterly* 23, no. 4, pp. 389–413 (1988).

Begley, Sharon. "Your Child's Brain: How Kids Are Wired for Music, Math, and Emotions." *Newsweek* (February 19, 1996).

Berg, Deanna. "It's Time to Redefine What We Mean by Success." *The Atlanta Journal-Constitution* (November 28, 1993).

Best, Fred, and Ray Eberhard. "Education for the 'Era of the Adult.' " *The Futurist* (May–June 1990).

Blythe, Tina, and Howard Gardner. "A School for All Intelligences." *Educational Leadership* (April 1990).

Bolanos, Patricia J. "From Theory to Practice: Indianapolis' Key School Applies Howard Gardner's Multiple Intelligences Theory to the Classroom." *The School Administrator* (January 1994).

Brink, Susan. "Smart Moves: New Research Suggests That Folks from Eight to Eighty Can Shape Up Their Brains with Aerobic Exercise." *U.S. News & World Report,* "1995 Health Guide" (May 15, 1995).

Campbell, Bruce. "Multiple Intelligences in Action." *Childhood Education* (Summer 1992).

Caplan, M., R. P. Weissberg, J. S. Grober, P. J. Sivo, K. Grady, and C. Jacoby. "Social Competence Promotion with Inner-City and Suburban Young Adolescents: Effects of Social Adjustment and Alcohol Use." *Journal of Consulting and Clinical Psychology* 60, no. 1 (1992).

Cetron, Marvin J., and Margaret Evans Gayle. "Educational Renaissance: Forty-three Trends for U.S. Schools." *The Futurist* (September–October 1990).

Church, George J. "Jobs in an Age of Insecurity." *Time* (November 22, 1993).

Condon, George E., Jr. "Clinton Proposes $1,500-a-Year Tax Credit for Two College Years." *The San Diego Union-Tribune* (June 5, 1996).

Crick, F., and T. Mitchison. "The Function of Dream Sleep." *Nature* 304, pp. 111–114 (1983).

Cummings, Jeffrey L. "Dementia: the Failing Brain." *The Lancet* (June 10, 1995).

Davidson, Idelle. "What's Your Child's Learning Style?" *First* (September 20, 1993).

"A Degree of Dismay." *The Sunday Times* (UK) (May 28, 1995).

Dentzer, Susan. "How to Train Workers for the 21st Century." *U.S. News & World Report* (September 21, 1992).

DeVries, D., and K. Edward. "Learning Games and Student Teams: Their Effects on Classroom Process." *American Journal of Educational Research* 10, pp. 307–318 (1973).

Editorial, *Internet World* (January 1996).

Elias, M. J., and R. P. Weissberg. "School-Based Social Competence Promotion as a Primary Prevention Strategy: A Tale of Two Projects." *Prevention in Human Services* 7, no. 1 (1990).

Elias, M. J., M. A. Gara, T. F. Schuyler, L. R. Branden-Muller, and M. A. Sayette. "The Promotion of Social Competence: Longitudinal Study of a Preventive School-Based Program." *American Journal of Orthopsychiatry* 61 (1991).

Ennis, Robert H. "Critical Thinking and the Curriculum." *National Forum* 65, no. 1, pp. 28–31 (Winter 1985).

"Eyes Closed, It's Time for a Lesson." *Daily Mail* (UK) (March 10, 1993).

Fernie, David E. "Profile: Howard Gardner." *Language Arts* (March 1992).

Finn, Chester C., Jr. "The Biggest Reform of All." *Phi Delta Kappan* 71, pp. 584–92 (April 1990).

Fishman, Katherine Davis. "Get Smart about Your Child's IQ." *Child* (February 1996).

Fiske, Edward B. "Impending U.S. Jobs 'Disaster': Work Force Unqualified to Work." *The New York Times* (September 25, 1989).

"French the Fast Way." Sydney Sunday *Herald* (June 17, 1990).

Gardner, Howard. "Reflections on Multiple Intelligences—Myths and Messages." *Phi Delta Kappan* (November 1995).

Gardner, Howard, and Thomas Hatch. "Multiple Intelligences Go to School: Educational Implications of the Theory of Multiple Intelligences." *Educational Researcher* (November 1989).

Garner, Richard. "Save Our Schools Campaign." *Daily Mirror* (UK) (December 15, 1995).

Gill, Mary Jayne, and David Meier. "Accelerated Learning Takes Off." *Training & Development Journal* (January 1989).

Golden, Daniel, and Alexander Tsiaras. "Building a Better Brain." *Life* (July 1994).

Green, J. Howard, and Stacy Perman. "Doing Well by Doing Good." *Newsweek* (May 29, 1996).

Greenberg, M. T., C. A. Kusche, E. T. Cook, and J. P. Quamma. "Promoting Emotional Competence in School-Aged Children: The Effects of the PATHS Curriculum." *Development and Psychopathology* 7 (1995).

Halal, William E., and Jay Liebowitz. "Telelearning: the Multimedia Revolution in Education." *The Futurist* (November–December 1994).

Hales, Dianne. "How to Remember When You're Always Forgetting." *Ladies' Home Journal* (August 1995).

Handy, Charles. "To the Head of the IQ." *The Sunday Times* (UK) (February 27, 1994).

Haney, W. and G. Madaus. "Searching for Alternatives to Standardized Tests: Whys, Whats, and Whithers." *Phi Delta Kappan* (1989).

Hawkins, J. D., E. Von Cleve, and R. F. Catalano. "Reducing Early Childhood Aggression: Results of a Primary Prevention Program." *Journal of the American Academy of Child and Adolescent Psychiatry* 30 (1991).

Henkoff, Ronald. "Companies That Train Best." *Fortune* (March 22, 1993).

Hornblower, Margot. "It Takes a School." *Time* (June 3, 1996).

"How to Learn Uni-level German in Ten Days." *Armidale Express* (Australia) (January 19, 1994).

John, Liz. "The Learning Game." *Managing Schools Today* 4, no. 3. (1993).

Kelly, Dennis. "Poll Finds Mix of Good, Bad and Mediocre." *USA Today* (May 13, 1996).

Kelly, Dennis and Henry Tamara. "Governors Vow to Reach Academic Goal." *USA Today* (March 28, 1996).

Kennedy, Marge. "Finding the Smart Part in Every Child." *Good Housekeeping* (October 1994).

Kinni, Theodore B. "Guerrilla Learning: Continuous Education on a Tight Budget." *Industry Week* (November 21, 1994).

Kirschenbaum, Robert J. "An Interview with Howard Gardner." *Gifted Children Today* (November–December 1990).

"The Learning Revolution." *Business Week* (U.S.) (February 28, 1994).

Lemann, Nicholas. "With College for All." *Time* (June 10, 1996).

Lemonick, Michael D. "In Search of the Mind." *Time* (July 17, 1995).

Lemonick, Michael D. "Tomorrow's Lesson: Learn or Perish." *Time* (Fall 1992).

Levy, Steven. "Dr. Edelman's Brain." *The New Yorker* (May 2, 1994).

MacLean, P. "A Mind of Three Minds: Educating the Triune Brain." In *Education and the Brain,* 77th National Society for the Study of Education Yearbook, ed. J. Chall and S. Mirsky. Chicago: University of Chicago Press, 1982.

Miller, G. A. "The Magical Number Seven, Plus or Minus Two: Some Limits on Our Capacity to Process Information." *Psychological Review* 63, pp. 81–97 (1956).

"Mind and Brain: A Special Issue Devoted to Brain Theory and Research." *Scientific American* (September 1992).

Mishkin, Mortimer, and Mortimer Appenzeller. "The Anatomy of Memory." *Scientific American* (February 1987).

Neimark, Jill. "It's Magical. It's Malleable. It's . . . Memory." *Psychology Today* (January–February 1995).

Nelson, Kristen. "Seven Ways of Being Smart." *Instructor* (July–August 1995).

Oddleifson, Eric. "What Do We Want Our Schools to Do?" *Phi Delta Kappan* (February 1994).

O'Donnell, J. A., J. D. Hawkins, R. F. Catalano, R. D. Abbott, and L. E. Day. "Preventing School Failure, Drug Use, and Delinquency Among Low-Income Children: Effects of a Long-Term Prevention Project in Elementary Schools." *American Journal of Orthopsychiatry* (1994).

Page, Susan. "Wanted: 100,000 Tech-Wise Teachers to Be Mentors." *USA Today* (June 4, 1996).

Paul, Richard W. "Critical Thinking: Fundamental Education for a Free Society." *Educational Leadership* 42, pp. 18–25 (September 1984).

Perkins, David N. "Thinking Frames: An Integrative Perspective on Teaching Cognitive Skills." Unpublished paper delivered at ASCD Conference on Approaches to Teaching Thinking, Alexandria, VA (August 1985).

Perry, Nancy J. "The Workers of the Future." *Fortune* (Spring 1991).

"Preventing Alzheimer's Disease." *Health News & Review* (Spring 1995).

"Pulling in the Family." *The Sunday Times* (UK) (July 23, 1995).

"Reach Every Student." *Learning* (January–February 1995).

Schrof, Joannie M. "Brain Power." *U.S. News & World Report* (November 28, 1994).

Scott-Clark, Cathy. "A-Level Football Goes on School Curriculum." *The Sunday Times* (UK).

Scott-Clark, Cathy. "Schools Have Largest Classes since 1979." *The Sunday Times* (UK) (May 26, 1996).

Scott-Clark, Cathy, and Charles Hymas. "Former Pupils Sue over Their Bad Education." *Sunday Times* (UK) (February 25, 1996).

Simon, Bonnie Ward. "Will Studying Increase My Child's IQ?" *Washington Parent* (July–August 1995).

Skolnick, Andrew A. "Brain Researchers Bullish on Prospects for Preserving Functioning in the Elderly." *Journal of the American Medical Association* (April 22, 1992).

Smith, Lee. "Memory: Why You're Losing It, How to Save It." *Fortune* (April 17, 1995).

Stewart, Thomas A. "Your Company's Most Valuable Asset: Intellectual Capital." *Fortune* (October 3, 1994).

Sylwester, Robert. "Expanding the Range, Dividing the Task: Educating the Human Brain in an Electronic Society." *Educational Leadership* 48, no. 2, pp. 71–78 (October 1990).

Sylwester, Robert. "Research on Memory: Major Discoveries, Major Educational Challenges." *Educational Leadership* 42, no. 7, pp. 69–75 (April 1995).

Sylwester, Robert. "What the Biology of the Brain Tells Us About Learning." *Educational Leadership* (December 1993–January 1994).

Szabo, Joan C. "Training Workers for Tomorrow: Business, Labor, and Government Must Work Together to Plug the Skills Gap and Keep America Competitive." *Nation's Business* (March 1993).

Toch, Thomas, with Robin M. Bennefield, Dana Hawkins, and Loeb. "Why Teachers Don't Teach." *U.S. News & World Report* (February 26, 1996).

"Update on Alzheimer's Disease." *Harvard Mental Health Letter* (February 1995).

Valentine, Elizabeth. "Accelerated Learning: The New Competitive Weapon?" *New Zealand Banker* 5, no. 3 (February 1993).

Weiner, Myron F. "Alzheimer's Disease: What We Now Know—and What You Can Now Do." *Consultant* (March 1995).

White, Kristin. "How the Mind Ages." *Psychology Today* (November–December 1993).

Wild, Russell. "It's Not What You've Got; It's How You Use It. Here's a Guide to Clear Thinking." *Men's Health* (April 1992).

Williams, Gurney, III. "Memory Myths." *Longevity* (July 1992).

Woo, Elaine. "Governors Agree to Set Higher Goals for Nation's Schools." *Los Angeles Times* (March 28, 1995).

Wright, Charles. "Put the Ball in Students' Court to Boost Faculty Productivity." *The Oregonian* (February 3, 1994).

Transcripts

From the Beginning. Prime Time Live. ABC (January 25, 1995).

The Man Who Made Up His Mind. Horizon. BBC (January 24, 1994).

Index